Philip Matyszak has a doctorate in Roman history from St John's College, Oxford. He is the author of numerous bestselling books on the ancient world, including *The Greek and Roman Myths*, *Ancient Magic*, *Forgotten Peoples of the Ancient World* and *The Gods and Goddesses of Greece and Rome*, all published by Thames & Hudson.

Joanne Berry is a Roman historian and archaeologist, and an Associate Professor of Classics at Swansea University. Much of her research has focused on the ancient site of Pompeii and she is the author of *The Complete Pompeii*, also published by Thames & Hudson.

Philip Matyszak & Joanne Berry

A
HISTORY OF
ANCIENT ROME
IN 100 LIVES

with 20 illustrations

First published in the United Kingdom in 2008 under
the title *Lives of the Romans* by Thames & Hudson Ltd,
181A High Holborn, London WCIV 7QX

First published in the United States of America in 2008
in hardcover under the title *Lives of the Romans* by
Thames & Hudson Inc., 500 Fifth Avenue, New York,
New York 10110

This compact paperback edition first published in 2023

Lives of the Romans © 2008 Thames & Hudson Ltd, London

A History of Ancient Rome in 100 Lives © 2023
Thames & Hudson Ltd, London

British Library Cataloguing-in-Publication Data
A catalogue record for this book is available from the
British Library

Library of Congress Control Number 2022945674

ISBN 978-0-500-29705-6

Printed and bound in the UK by CPI (UK) Ltd

MIX
Paper | Supporting
responsible forestry
FSC
www.fsc.org   FSC® C171272

Be the first to know about our new releases,
exclusive content and author events by visiting
thamesandhudson.com
thamesandhudsonusa.com
thamesandhudson.com.au

Contents

Part 3
Life in Troubled Times 88 BC–AD 14   80

Part 4

Romans and Caesars AD 14–75

Part 5

Citizens of the Empire AD 75–200

Part 6

Decline and Fall   AD 200–476   203

Introduction

Portrait of a People

A state is at least as much about people as about geography. Who rules the state and how, how the people live their lives, and how the different parts of society interact – these are the things that give the state its identity. This book sketches out a picture of a particular nation through the individual lives of its citizens. Many of the people who shared in the 2,000-year history of ancient Rome have left traces of their lives for us to discover in inscriptions, discarded letters, biographies and myth. Often this is sufficient to form a portrait of these people, their circumstances and character. Each life, while complete in itself, also forms part of a larger picture, a mosaic that gives us a glimpse of what Rome meant to those who lived under its rule.

By selecting 100 lives from the different eras of Rome's existence we can form a chain across time and space which encompasses the entire story of the ancient city. The lives in this book run from the mythical foundation of Rome, when Romulus and Remus were found abandoned on the banks of the Tiber, to the western empire's final days when its last emperor, Romulus Augustulus, was deposed by barbarian overlords.

And just as Rome's empire grew, so does the geographical scope of this book. In the early period almost all those we describe walked the Roman Forum, and were familiar with the city's seven hills. But to later generations, as Rome expanded, the city became a place for occasional visits, for elections or the games. To later generations still, Rome was a legendary presence over the seas, home to an emperor whom most of his subjects would never see, yet the influence of the city still pervaded the daily lives of those subjects, be they in London or Damascus. The lives of these citizens of the later empire illustrate the huge diversity of existence under the rule of Rome, with examples including a soldier in Asia Minor, a mother in Egypt, an architect in Rome and a Christian saint in Britain.

The lives in this book have been selected by several criteria. First, they must have been Roman citizens, although some interesting cases have been given the benefit of the doubt. They must have left some kind of testimony of their lives – in monuments, history or myth – sufficient to build at least a partial picture of who they were. Their lives should have been either highly exceptional (and so of interest in themselves) or absolutely average (thus giving us a glimpse into the day-to-day lives of ordinary Romans). The result is a canvas on which are painted five score lives and stretching across the Roman empire, taking in different times and a wide range of geographical locations. Some of the lives described here were happy and uneventful, others desperate, tragic and dramatic. The selection includes emperors, slaves, mistresses, entertainers, workmen, soldiers and poets, men and women of every age and social class. Particular attention has been given to those whom one might call the 'supporting cast' – the people who make fleeting appearances in the biographies of the mighty and fade from the scene as the focus moves on.

Most Romans were not concerned with palace politics or the mechanics of how to conquer barbarian states. More often they worried about the rent, about absent family members, and about their social standing. They struggled with government bureaucracy, complained about their taxes, and enjoyed their festivals and family celebrations. For understanding Rome and its empire, the lives of such people are just as important as the captains and kings who dominate the classical texts. Here, with the help of modern tools such as epigraphy, archaeology and prosopography, we tell their stories.

The six sections of the book are organized in chronological order. Particular attention has been given to when Rome was going through one of its many transitions – from kingdom to Republic, from Republic to empire, or from conquering invader to beleaguered colossus. Therefore, while some sections stretch across centuries, other sections have time spans measured in decades. Likewise, the sheer extent and diversity of the later empire demands a greater number of people to properly tell its story.

From the beginnings of Rome to the empire's fall in the west, these 100 lives have been chosen to reflect what it meant to be Roman. From shepherds to emperors, they reflect in a microcosm the tens of generations whose lives and experiences in their totality created the drama that was ancient Rome.

Part 1

Royal Subjects to Republican Citizens

753–300 BC

Pre-Roman Italy was not an empty land awaiting the blessing of civilization from the seven hills. Civilization was already present, thanks to the influence – both direct and indirect – of the already ancient cultures of Greece, Egypt and Mesopotamia. The Greeks had colonies in southern Italy, many of which, from Naples to Croton, are still thriving today. The Etruscan culture dominated the north; the Romans were to learn much of their skill in building, law and religion from the Etruscans. Italy, like Greece to which it owed so much, had no nation-states. Rather, the peninsula was a mosaic of cities, each with its own territory, feuds and petty wars with its neighbours. Nor was the situation static – the Etruscans were steadily losing ground to the Gauls pressing in from the north, and the Greeks were always looking to expand their territory along the coasts.

Between the Greeks and the Etruscans lay the plain of Latium. The people living here had their own cities, language and culture which they defended against both the Etruscan armies and predatory hill tribes such as the Aequi and Volscians. Indeed, they were strong enough not only to hold their own but also to expand, and some time in the mid-8th century they founded a new city on the very border of Etruscan territory, at the point where the river Tiber was first bridgeable. Legend (with some support from modern archaeology) tells us that the first act of the new settlers was to build a wall – the inevitable tradition due to the hostility of their neighbours. The new settlement was planted squarely across the Via Salaria, the ancient trade route that carried salt from the coast to the interior. While we have a detailed account of the founding of Rome, we know that this is the version that the Romans more or less agreed on over 500 years after the foundation. We know from writers like Plutarch that other versions existed, and the accuracy or otherwise of the Roman foundation myth is a topic of much heated debate.

It is clear that as a foundation in archaic Italy, the proto-city of Rome had to grow or die, and it chose to grow aggressively. Roman tradition admits that the criterion for early Roman citizenship was possession of two legs and a pulse; ex-bandits, escaped slaves and retired mercenaries were all welcome. The legend unabashedly tells that when the settlement ran short of women, these were kidnapped from the neighbours. Thus, far from being a beacon of Mediterranean culture, early Rome was regarded as a blot on the landscape by those who noticed the place at all. Yet Rome's precarious existence gave its citizens a strong respect for the gods, and, given that its early population came from a variety of social and ethnic backgrounds, the Romans both needed and enforced firm, clear laws laying out the limits of what was permissible in this new society. A militaristic culture added organization, and its citizens the energy and enterprise they had demonstrated in coming to Rome in the first place. Thus all the ingredients for a successful city were in place almost from the foundation – and the foundation was at an excellent location.

It is uncertain how Rome fell under Etruscan domination. According to legend, a wealthy Etruscan émigré established himself in the city, and eventually became king. There is plenty of precedent, both in the literary and archaeological record, for the Mediterranean aristocracy possessing such mobility, but it cannot be ruled out that Roman tradition has deleted an Etruscan military conquest from its history. In any case Rome retained its independence under the Etruscan monarchs, and its own foreign policy. During a century of almost unrelenting warfare Rome had established itself as first among equals within the group of Latin states, though by the end of the monarchical period Rome's empire was not much larger than the municipal boundaries of the present-day city.

In 510 BC, at a time when legend and fact are still almost impossible to separate, Rome's aristocracy were forced to share power with the citizen army. This army had been essential not only in deposing the tyrannical king Tarquin, but also in ensuring that he stayed deposed, since Tarquin had used his considerable diplomatic skill to raise a coalition of allies against the rebel state. Rome became a possession of its people – a Republic (*res publicae*) – and the ferocity with which it was defended caused its attackers to draw back. The common people of Rome fought not only against foreign enemies, but also against repeated attempts by the aristocrats to reassert their dominance. From the tension between plebeian and patrician arose the Roman constitution, admired and imitated both in antiquity and early modern times.

Yet Rome was still a tiny state, almost inconsequential in the geopolitics of the Mediterranean. For generations the Romans fought a war with the neighbouring city of Veii, which was so close by that its remains now lie in the northern suburbs of the modern city. The state was so small that most Romans who did not live in the city were still close enough to get there after a short walk. The Romans of the day did not think in imperial terms but from the perspective of a typical Italian city-state that had grown only slowly in the past centuries. The catalyst for the city's explosive growth was the conquest of Veii, but this was followed almost immediately by the sack of Rome by the Gauls in about 390 BC. Rome quickly recovered from the attack, which marked the high tide of Gallic expansion into Italy. However, defeat by the Gauls made an already militaristic society even more so, at a time when Rome's immediate neighbours had suffered as much or more from the Gallic rampage. The weakened and disorganized states around Rome were in no shape to resist their well-organized and highly motivated neighbour, not least because Rome did not so much conquer peoples as incorporate them wholesale into the citizen body. Within a generation, the expansion of Rome had gained an irresistible momentum that made it the dominant power in Italy.

1 | FAUSTULUS

The shepherd who adopted Romulus and Remus

The story of Rome's origins is a tangled skein of fact and nonsense over which scholars have endlessly squabbled. Even Livy, writing 2,000 years ago, remarked, 'the old tales appear more attractive as ballads than solid historical record'. Like Livy, we can neither confirm nor refute the legends, but if Faustulus did not exist, then we can be certain that people much like him lived on the seven hills just before Rome was founded.

Faustulus was a shepherd, allegedly the royal herdsman for the nearby city of Alba Longa. He was an Arcadian, Greeks who had settled in the area and merged with the indigenous Latin peoples. We know from archaeological research into the beginnings of Rome that there were communities living in crude huts on the hills; probably shepherds who descended to the valleys in daytime to tend to their flocks. At this time the valley of the Roman Forum was a marshy bog, frequently filled by flooding from the river Tiber.

After one such inundation of the valley, some time in the early 8th century BC, Faustulus came upon an amazing sight. As he made his way down the Palatine Hill, he saw a she-wolf licking the mud-spattered bodies of twin baby boys, who had been spilled from a richly decorated basket that had been left tangled in the branches of a fig tree by the receding floodwaters. The she-wolf had recently whelped, and she had relieved the pressure on her dugs by feeding the children with her milk. In some versions of the tale, Faustulus was alone when he found the twins, in others he was with a group of fellow shepherds. He had a reputation as a solid citizen, and after discussion the other shepherds agreed to allow him to take the twins for his wife to rear, since one of her own children had recently died. Legend claims that the twins were the children of a princess and Mars, the god of war (to whom, incidentally, wolves were sacred). They had been jettisoned into the Tiber through political scheming by an evil king. The sad reality is that what one historian has rather brutally called 'post-natal contraception' was commonplace in the ancient world, and unwanted children were frequently abandoned to the mercy of passing strangers, or indeed, wild animals.

Faustulus' wife was Acca Laurentina (*akka* is 'mother' in Sanskrit, an ancestral relative of Latin). According to one ancient writer, Aulus Gellius, she was worthy of that accolade as she had 11 other sons. Another writer, Dio of Halicarnassus, comments that Acca Laurentina might have been the she-wolf of the legend. 'Having formerly prostituted her beauty, she had been nicknamed *lupa*, the she-wolf.' Romans of later generations told both versions of the story, and proudly pointed out the fig tree where the twins were found, and an ancient hut of the type in which the twins were reared. With Romulus and Remus (as the boys were named) the other children of Laurentina formed a band of brothers that was frequently claimed throughout history as the origin of an elite priesthood called the Arval Brethren.

When Faustulus told Romulus and Remus of their royal origins, they lived up to their hero status and deposed the evil king, restoring truth and justice in Alba Longa, the city of their birth. Then they returned to the Palatine with a host of followers and the intention of founding a city. However, the brothers fell out, with supporters of one brother wanting to found the city of Reme on the Aventine Hill, and the others wanting Rome on the Palatine. The dispute became ugly, and as fighting broke out, Faustulus threw himself between the warring factions, distraught at the thought that one of his adopted sons might die. He was killed in the fighting, and his sacrifice was in vain. Remus was killed – by some accounts slain personally by his brother. Romulus went on to found his city, but Faustulus was not forgotten. Later generations believed that a stone lion in the Forum marked his tomb. The Faustulus name lived on in a branch of the Pompeia clan in Rome, one of whom honoured his alleged ancestor on a handsome silver coin, depicting him with the twins and the she-wolf.

2 | TITUS TATIUS
Outraged Sabine father

Titus Tatius, like Romulus, was a figure of legend, but the Romans used his story to explain a historical fact: the growth of Rome through a fusion of two different peoples, the Romans and the Sabines.

By offering asylum to any man who would make Rome his home, Romulus peopled his new city with criminals and outcasts in the 8th century BC. Rome grew rapidly in both size and influence, much to the alarm of its neighbours. But they consoled themselves with the belief that this upstart power would last only a single generation – for there were no women in the new city, and thus no threat of future generations of Romans. Despite Romulus' entreaties the nearby cities refused to grant the right of intermarriage, and so the Romans were forced to desperate measures. Romulus organized a festival and games in honour of Neptune, and his neighbours were enthusiastic in their attendance, curious about the new city. Among them were the Sabines with their wives and families. As the Sabines were distracted by the games, the Roman youth abducted their womenfolk and forced them into marriage.

What were the Sabine fathers to do? How could they wage war on their sons-in-law, particularly since their daughters had swiftly grown to like their new husbands and their new honoured status in Rome? How could they accept the insult paid to them by the Romans? The desire for revenge triumphed over newly established ties of kinship. The outraged fathers appealed to Titus Tatius, the powerful king of the Sabine city of Cures, to lead them against Rome, and he was appointed general of the combined Sabine forces.

Yet Tatius did not move against Rome as quickly as some of the fathers had expected, and a few of them rashly attacked Roman territory without him. Romulus promptly defeated them; but, listening to the pleas of the stolen women, granted them Roman citizenship. Many of the fathers moved to Rome to be near their daughters.

Finally Tatius was ready to act against Rome, and Romulus met a worthy opponent. Tatius did not act hastily, but with purpose and deceit. Romans would later tell different versions of the story, but all with the same outcome: Tarpeia, the daughter of the commander of the Roman citadel, opened the gates of Rome to the Sabines. She may have been in love with Tatius and allowed herself to believe that he would marry her, or she may have intended to betray the Sabines to Romulus. The least flattering version claims that she wanted the bracelets and rings worn by the Sabine warriors, and demanded from them 'what they had on their shield-arms' in payment for her treachery. Her comeuppance was swift: once inside the citadel the Sabines crushed her beneath their shields, Tatius giving 'no honour to crime'.

Inside the city, the Sabines squared off against the Romans and the ensuing battle was brutal. It was halted only by the Sabine women, who flung themselves between their fathers and their new husbands. As Livy records; 'Silence fell and not a man moved. A moment later the rival captains stepped forward to conclude a peace. Indeed, they went further: the two states were united under a single government, with Rome as the seat of power.'

Romulus and Tatius became joint kings of Rome, and while individual citizens of Rome were still called 'Romans', collectively the people of Rome became known as the 'Quirites', in honour of the Sabine city of Cures. The end result was that Rome doubled in size. Three 'centuries' of knights were created. They were named the Ramnenses after Romulus, the Titienses after Tatius, and the Luceres, possibly after Lucumo (an Etruscan warrior who aided Romulus). One of Tatius' acts was also to divide the land they had conquered between Rome's citizens. Recognizing the warlike spirit of the Romans, he hoped that farming would promote a love of peace among them.

King Tatius ruled in apparent harmony with Romulus for five years before becoming involved in a dispute with the people of the nearby city of Lavinium, caused by a group of Sabines raiding that territory. When an embassy arrived at Rome and demanded compensation, Tatius refused to surrender the guilty parties. The ambassadors were then attacked and killed by a group of Sabines. Not long afterwards, Tatius and Romulus went to Lavinium to perform a sacrifice. Tatius was murdered before the altar by a group of angry Lavinians.

Romulus is said to have felt less distress at his death than was strictly proper: possibly the joint reign was not, in fact, entirely harmonious; possibly he felt that Tatius deserved what he got. Tatius was buried on the Aventine Hill, his grave possibly marked by a laurel grove known as the 'Lauretum', named for the 'Laurentes' (Lavinians) who had killed him.

3 | TANAQUIL
King-maker

Tanaquil was a king-maker. Proud and aristocratic, she had no doubts about her role in life and worked tirelessly to achieve her ends, aiming to ensure that she, her husband and her family received the status and respect that she thought they deserved.

According to legend, this formidable young woman came from the Etruscan city of Tarquinia, where she married Lucumo, the wealthy son of an immigrant, in *c.* 620 BC. Her fellow Etruscans, however, despised her husband as an outsider, the son of a foreign refugee, and Tanaquil, who was, in the words of Livy, 'not the sort to put up with humbler circumstances in her married life than those she had been previously accustomed to', found the social situation intolerable. She persuaded Lucumo that they should move to Rome, where there would be plenty of opportunities for an able man (with an ambitious wife) to improve his situation. In that rapidly expanding community, advancement need not depend on family background.

Tanaquil and Lucumo set off for Rome in their carriage. They had gone as far as the Janiculum Hill when an eagle suddenly swooped down and snatched Lucumo's hat from his head. A minute later it returned, 'as if it had been sent by heaven for that very purpose' and neatly replaced the hat on Lucumo's head. Tanaquil was thrilled. As an Etruscan, she had knowledge of portents – even though as a woman she was not permitted to divine or to prophesy – and she knew that Lucumo's future was secure. No dream was impossible, no fortune too high to hope for.

They drove on to Rome, where Lucumo took the name Lucius Tarquinius Priscus (known to us as Tarquin) and soon came to the attention of the king, Ancus Marcius. He became indispensable to Ancus, and, when the king died, he was named guardian of his sons. This he used to good effect, sending the children off on a hunt while he himself campaigned successfully in Rome to be made king in their place.

Tanaquil reigned supreme within the royal palace, and is described by Plutarch as 'a sensible and queenly woman'. Then one night a little boy in the household named Servius Tullius (no. 4) was lying asleep when his head burst into flames. The king and queen rushed to the scene of the commotion, and Tanaquil swiftly stepped in to prevent the boy's head from being doused in water, commanding silence and declaring that he should be left to wake of his own accord. When he opened his eyes a few minutes later the fire went out by itself. It was clear to Tanaquil that this event was another sign from the gods, and Livy has her declare to her husband: 'Believe me, he will one day prove a light in our darkness, a prop to our house in the day of its affliction.' Thanks to Tanaquil's intervention, Servius Tullius was brought up as a prince in the palace, and eventually was betrothed to Tarquin and Tanaquil's daughter.

Indeed, with Tanaquil's help, Servius was designed for greatness. The day came that assassins attacked and mortally wounded Tarquin. Tanaquil acted swiftly, closing the palace gates to prying eyes and summoning Servius to Tarquin's deathbed. Livy describes how she goaded him to action: 'Rise to your true stature; follow the gods who long ago by the circlet of heavenly fire declared that your head should wear the crown. Let the memory of those flames, assuredly divine, rouse you to act.' She then went to an upper room of the palace and addressed the crowds from a window. The king, she claimed, was alive and being tended. He would recover; but in the meantime the people should obey Servius who would deputize for the king. Her speech was matter-of-fact, designed to inspire confidence. Tarquin's death was thus concealed for several days, until Servius' position was secure.

Tanaquil twice conferred the crown on her chosen candidate. She was decisive and manipulative, a scheming woman in the mould of the Greek enchantress Medea – and, like Medea, probably was a literary creation. Her story helps to explain the arrival of the Etruscans at Rome and their period of power within the city. But her actions were never those of a proper Roman matron, epitomized by Lucretia (no. 6). This foreign interloper was the first woman to wield political power at Rome, and many others would follow her example.

4 | SERVIUS TULLIUS
From captive to king

Servius Tullius single-handedly transformed the city of Rome; indeed, he is often considered to be its second founder. Yet his origins remain obscure. The miracle of his flaming head brought him to the attention of Tanaquil (no. 3), but what was his status in the palace before this event? Most ancient sources believed the embarrassing story that he and his mother were slaves in the household. Livy attempted to explain this away by instead claiming that Servius' father had in fact been prince of Corniculum. He was killed when the Romans took over the town, and his wife (who was pregnant) was taken prisoner. She was later recognized by Tanaquil, who invited her to live in the palace and permitted her to raise her son there.

Despite his humble origins, Servius grew up as a prince of Rome. He married the king's daughter, held military commands and other positions of responsibility, and rose to prominence in the Senate. It was jealousy of his influence and position that spurred the assassination of Tarquin, and it was the swift action of Tanaquil that ensured his succession to the throne. Then, to neutralize opposition to his hold on the throne, Servius married his daughters to Tarquin's sons – a tactic destined ultimately to fail.

Servius set about reorganizing the Roman army according to a fixed scale of wealth and rank. He carried out a census, dividing up Rome's population into 'centuries' according to a property qualification. Those with property to the value of 100,000 asses or more formed the 'First Class'. Beneath them were another four classes, all obliged to equip themselves with weapons and/or armour. The First Class wore helmets, round shields, greaves and breast-plate, sword and spear, much like Greek hoplite soldiers; the Fifth Class carried only slings and stones. Those people who were found to have less than 11,000 asses in the census were exempt from military service. Thus, as in many Greek city-states of the period, the wealth, military responsibility and political privilege of Rome's citizens were tightly interrelated. Equal rights for all were abolished, and replaced with a sliding scale – needless to say, the votes of the First Class carried the most weight.

Servius then turned his attention to the city itself, which was becoming overcrowded. He extended the city boundaries to take in two more hills (the Quirinal and Viminal) and more of the Esquiline Hill, and constructed a wall at the same time. He also saw to it that the Temple of Diana was built jointly by the Romans and their neighbouring Latin communities, an act symbolizing the end of conflict between them and establishing Rome's position as leader of the Latins.

Despite these achievements, one of Tarquin's sons (known as Tarquin Superbus – 'the Proud') was fomenting trouble in Rome, proclaiming to all who would listen that Servius had taken the kingship illegally. At this point Servius slipped up. Going against the Senate, he distributed land captured in Rome's wars amongst the people, then held an election for the kingship. He was, of course, the common favourite. But the Senate was left seething and open to Tarquin's malicious machinations, in which he was aided by his wife, Tullia – Servius' own daughter. She was determined to emulate Tanaquil, and spurred Tarquin to canvass among Rome's upper classes. His support grew until one day he felt confident enough to enter the Senate House and seat himself on the king's chair. He summoned the senators and vilified Servius, claiming that he was a slave, and the son of a slave, and had usurped the throne from its rightful heir – Tarquin.

Servius rushed to the Senate House and confronted Tarquin. Livy describes how 'Tarquin had gone too far to turn back, and it was now all or nothing for him. Young and vigorous as he was, he seized the aged Servius, carried him bodily from the House and flung him down the steps into the street.' Worse was to follow. As the stunned Servius made his way back, unattended, to the palace, he was caught and murdered, possibly at his own daughter's command. Livy relates how she had driven to the Senate House in her carriage in order to be the first to congratulate Tarquin. In fear of the crowds he sent her home, and on the way she came across her father's mutilated body. In an act of 'bestial inhumanity', she drove over it.

Thus ended the 44-year reign of Servius, and the ancient sources agree that it had been a good one. Livy even claims that 'one of its most notable marks was the fact that with Servius true kingship came to an end; never again was a Roman king to rule in accordance with humanity and justice'.

5 | BRUTUS
Liberator of Rome

The history of the Roman Republic both begins and ends with a Brutus. Marcus Brutus assassinated Julius Caesar 500 years after Lucius Brutus expelled Rome's last king and established the Republic which Caesar overthrew. Both Marcus and Lucius Brutus were known and trusted by the autocrats they destroyed.

Lucius Iunius Brutus was part of the royal family. His maternal grandfather was Tarquin Superbus, Tarquin the Proud, who came to power through a palace coup and ruled through awe and fear (no. 4). Brutus' father was Marcus, one of the richest men in Rome. Unfortunately for Marcus, Tarquin needed money for a building programme which included a massive temple to Capitoline Jupiter. Consequently Marcus met an untimely, if not unexpected, death and soon afterwards his older son was murdered. Tarquin became the guardian of the family estate and the surviving son, Lucius.

Although still a boy, Lucius realized that, as a ward of the Tarquin family, survival lay in seeming as unthreatening as possible. He pretended to be simple-minded, so successfully that he received the *cognomen* (nickname) 'Brutus' for his doltish behaviour. His status was little better than a *delicatus*, a slave-child household pet who entertains the other children. The 'other children' were Tarquin's sons Titus, Arruns and Sextus, who made Brutus the butt of their jokes and games.

Brutus was taken with the Tarquin brothers to Delphi to ask the enigmatic oracle about the significance of an omen. But while they were there, the brothers could not resist an additional question, 'who among us will rule next in Rome?' The oracle replied: 'Whosoever is the next to kiss his mother.' As the brothers left, Brutus, who had tagged along, fell flat on his face. This was consistent with his character and the brothers did not notice that when he fell, Brutus had taken care to kiss the Earth, Gaia, the mother of all.

In Rome the political situation was deteriorating. The plebs seethed beneath Tarquin's oppression, and every supposed treachery that the king brutally punished among the aristocrats further alienated the rest. Tarquin, like many a politician in trouble, tried to distract his people with a foreign adventure, in this case against the nearby Rutulians, who not coincidentally had the fabulously wealthy Ardea as their principal city. Brutus was made *tribunus celerum*, Tarquin's second-in-command. This reflected less Tarquin's faith in Brutus than his distrust of anyone he considered more competent. During the Rutulian war, the young Sextus met Lucretia (no. 6), wife of Tarquinius Collatinus, a cousin of the royal clan. This lady so impressed the youngest Tarquin with her modesty and beauty that he returned to her a few days later and raped her.

Unable to live with the dishonour, Lucretia killed herself, but not before telling of her ravishment. To everyone's surprise it was Brutus who turned the crime of the king's son into a campaign against the king himself. Livy tells how 'Brutus, while the others were absorbed in grief, drew out the knife from Lucretia's wound. Holding it up, dripping with her blood, he shouted, "By this blood, so innocent until a prince befouled it, I swear before the gods, that I will hunt down Lucius Tarquinius Superbus, his accursed wife, and all his children, with sword, with fire, yes, using as much force as it takes; and I will not permit them – nor anyone else – to be kings in Rome!"'

Using the authority that Tarquin himself had given him, Brutus summoned an assembly. He reminded the common people of Tarquin's tyranny, and described the rape of Lucretia as the last act of a wicked regime which had begun when Tarquin's wife had killed the previous king, her own father (no. 4). Now this lady fled the city one step ahead of the mob. Lucretia's father was the prefect of the city, so Brutus left him in charge while he and a body of chosen men rushed to the army at Ardea, neatly sidestepping Tarquin who was hurrying back to Rome along the same road. The army enthusiastically welcomed Brutus, and threw out Tarquin's sons. The two oldest rejoined their father who had found Rome barred against him. Sextus, perhaps doubting his father's welcome, went to the town of Gabii where he was quickly killed by the many enemies he had made there.

Brutus forced Collatinus into exile. Although one of the leaders of the revolution and the husband of the victim of Sextus' rape, Collatinus was a member of the Tarquin family, and the people of the city did not trust him completely. Nor was their suspicion of Tarquinian plots unjustified. The Tarquins still had friends in Rome, and to these they sent ambassadors, who pretended to discuss the return of Tarquin's personal property while secretly fomenting insurrection. Among those who became involved were Brutus' own sons, Titus and Tiberius. Consequently, as one of the two praetors governing Rome, Brutus had to order the death of his own children. 'During the whole time, the father's countenance betrayed his feelings, but the father's stern resolution was still more apparent as he superintended the public execution.'

Next Tarquin tried military force instead of subversion, allying with the Etruscans and marching on Rome. Two men with a grudge, Brutus and Tarquin's son Arruns, sought out and killed each other in the subsequent conflict. Although Tarquin was defeated, Rome's liberator died while the Republic he founded was less than a year old.

Was Brutus man or myth? Although descendants of a family known as the Iunian Bruti are a historical fact, the Lucius Brutus they claimed as an ancestor was of royal blood, undoubtedly a patrician, whereas his 'descendants' were plebeian. And as Brutus died within months, if not weeks, of killing his sons, where did that later line come from? Also, the sources are sure that Tarquin reigned for 25 years, in the course of which our Brutus went from a boy to the father of almost adult children – a tight but not impossible chronology. Lucius Brutus stands at that juncture when the myths of the origins of Rome begin to solidify into history, but in his day the process was certainly very far from complete.

6 | LUCRETIA
Perfect Roman matron

Lucretia was the wife of Tarquinius Collatinus, a kinsman of Tarquin the Proud. One night, during the long siege of Ardea in 509 BC, her husband and his friends were drinking, and they began to boast about the various virtues of their wives. After heated argument, Collatinus proposed that they ride the 20 miles back to Rome and then on to his home town of Collatia, surprising each wife on the way, to see what they were up to. Thus began a tragic chain of events that would eventually lead to the expulsion of the king and establishment of the Roman Republic.

The other wives were found at banquets, in the greatest luxury, but Collatinus' boasts about Lucretia held true. According to Livy, Lucretia was at work: 'it was already late at night, but there, in the hall of her house, surrounded by her busy maid-servants, she was still hard at work by lamplight upon her spinning.' Always the good hostess, Lucretia promptly served her new guests supper, too.

Livy reports how Sextus Tarquinius, son of the king, became inflamed with desire, on account of both her beauty and her proven virtue; Cassius Dio instead claims that he desired to ruin her reputation. Either way, he found the opportunity to return to Collatia, was received warmly by Lucretia without question as the friend of her husband, and was invited to stay in the guest-room. Later that night Sextus went to her chamber, armed with a sword. Unsurprisingly she resisted his attempts at seduction, and was unmoved even by the threat of death. So Sextus tried another tactic – he threatened her reputation. 'If death will not move you,' cried Sextus (according to Livy), 'dishonour will. I shall kill you first, then cut the throat of a slave and lay his naked body by your side. Will they not believe that you have been caught in adultery with a servant – and paid the price?' Lucretia submitted, and Sextus had his way with her.

The next morning, Lucretia summoned her father, Lucretius, and her husband Collatinus to tell them what had happened. They tried to comfort her, but she was determined. Livy has her declare: 'I am innocent of fault, but I will take my punishment. Never shall Lucretia provide a precedent for unchaste women to escape what they deserve.' With this, she drove a knife into her heart.

The political fall-out of these events was dramatic, but Lucretia's final words have a moral significance, too. Lucretia killed herself rather than bring shame to her husband and to her family. Her story – embellished and elaborated on many times, and possibly even a fiction from the outset – is that of the perfect Roman matron. Lucretia tends house, works wool and supervises her slaves carefully. She possesses all the virtues that Romans thought good Roman women should have. These are the virtues, along with obedience and fertility, that in later years were celebrated in funerary inscriptions and eulogies, representing the ideal, but not the norm. Lucretia's behaviour was something to aspire to. Hundreds of years later – when, for example, the emperor Augustus claimed to wear only the clothes made by the women of his own family (except on special occasions!) – it still resonated with the Roman public.

7 | CLOELIA
The girl who defied Lars Porsenna

When expelled from Rome in 509 BC, the tyrant king Tarquin made common cause against his former city with an Etruscan king, Lars Porsenna of Clusium. The nascent Roman Republic was hard-pressed to resist the combination of Roman royalists and Etruscans, but tradition says they fought heroically. Most famous of these heroic early Republicans is Horatius Cocles, who, with two companions, held the bridge over the Tiber until it was destroyed behind him, thus preventing the Etruscans from storming into the city.

Nevertheless, Porsenna still threatened Rome with siege. A young man called Mucius slipped across the river, and attempted to assassinate the Etruscan king. Mucius was captured, and in order to intimidate him, Porsenna threatened to have Mucius burned alive. In reply, Mucius voluntarily thrust his right hand into the flames, and informed Porsenna that his threats carried no weight. Impressed, Porsenna released Mucius and offered to negotiate with the Romans.

As one of the terms of the negotiations, Porsenna demanded 20 hostages, exacted from noble Roman families. Twenty hostages was a usual sum from what we know of hostage-taking in the archaic era, but Porsenna's demand was unusual in that he required ten of the hostages to be female. This was not a contemporary or later Roman practice, but may have been Etruscan. One hostage was a girl called Cloelia, of the Cloelian family, wealthy nobles from the Alban Hills near Rome. Cloelia was inspired by the feats of Horatius and Mucius, and when she saw an opportunity to escape, she jumped at it.

> They chanced to be held in a part of the Etruscan lines not far from the river Tiber. Several other girls agreed to follow her, so one day the group suddenly slipped away from their guards, and Cloelia led them across the Tiber, with hostile missiles raining into the water around them.

This account of the escape is from Livy's *History of Rome*. It was written half a millennium after the event, by which time the story had become confused (or had been invented, according to more sceptical historians). Other Roman writers, such as Plutarch and Dio, have their own versions, including one where Cloelia escapes on horseback.

All agree that Cloelia shepherded her little band safely home, but their gallant escape was in vain. Lars Porsenna was furious and threatened to break off negotiations if the hostages were not returned. He was particularly keen to regain Cloelia, who he knew was the ringleader of the escapees. Although her life was forfeit for having fled the Etruscan camp, Cloelia agreed that it was in Rome's interest that she should return. Her honourable behaviour, and that of her city, had a calming effect on Porsenna. He began to consider that the new Republic might be better friends than the Tarquins. Consequently, Cloelia's welcome on her return to captivity was warmer than she had been expecting. Instead of execution, Cloelia's bravery received praise from the king himself. Porsenna presented her with various gifts, including a warhorse in full caparison, and invited her to return again to Rome with half the hostages, this time with his blessing.

Not unexpectedly, this distressed the Tarquins, who saw their chances of repossessing Rome fast slipping away. They conspired to kidnap the returning hostages to gain leverage in the negotiations, and in the process perhaps destroy the new-found trust between Romans and Etruscans. However, like the Etruscans before them, the Tarquins underestimated the girls they were dealing with. A hostage called Valeria broke free, and swiftly summoned help. The nefarious attempt by the Tarquins gave Porsenna further justification for breaking his former alliance. He lifted the siege soon afterwards, leaving his supplies behind as a gift to the Romans, and as a demonstration that shortage of supplies had not caused his departure.

The Romans celebrated the bravery of the hostages with a statue of a girl on horseback. This stood on the *Via Sacra*, or 'Sacred Way', one of the major streets of Rome. It may have represented Cloelia with her warhorse, or Valeria riding to seek rescue, or both. What became of Cloelia thereafter is unknown, but a C. Quintus Cloelius Siculus was consul soon afterward, as were other Cloelians in succeeding generations.

Juvenal writes: 'Who should strike a blow for freedom like Horatius the Hero, and Mucius? Or Cloelia, the hostage, the heroine who swam the Tiber, back when that river was Rome's frontier.'

8 | VINDICIUS
The slave who betrayed a conspiracy

Escaped slaves were among Rome's founders, but Romans still enslaved others. By some estimates, it is believed that at the time of Rome's Republican revolution in 509 BC slaves perhaps constituted between a third and a fifth of the population. Few did more to improve the lot of these slaves than a young man called Vindicius.

Vindicius was himself a slave in the household of the aristocratic Aquillian family. He found himself in the room when a group of young nobles met with ambassadors of the exiled king Tarquin. Something about the group made Vindicius uneasy. With a slave's instinct for avoiding trouble, he hid himself behind a large chest. Horrified, he listened to a conspiracy to kill the consuls and restore Tarquin's tyrannical rule. Worse still, two of the conspirators were the sons of Brutus (no. 5), one of those consuls.

A slave's life hung at his master's whim, and if his eavesdropping was discovered, Vindicius would die. And who would believe a slave? Vindicius decided to consult Valerius Poplicola, the most approachable and morally upright aristocrat in Rome. Valerius listened with horror, and locked Vindicius in the room to keep him safe, putting his own wife on guard at the door whilst he started an investigation. A raid on the Aquillian household produced letters revealing the treasonous plot, and the guilty aristocrats were arraigned for trial.

Vindicius was still in grave peril. The state trembled on the verge of civil war, and the Aquillians and their supporters demanded the return of their slave. Collatinus, one of the consuls, was disposed to allow this for the sake of peace, but Valerius stood firm, even battling to rescue Vindicius when he was seized. The Roman people threw their support behind Valerius, and partly through Vindicius' testimony, the conspirators were executed.

As a reward for the considerable danger he had undergone for the Republic, Vindicius was granted his freedom and a large sum of money. His freeing also set a precedent, as the historian Livy explains. 'After him it was observed as a rule, that all who were set free in this manner were considered to have the rights of Roman citizens.' This did much to maintain social harmony for future generations, as Roman slaves thereafter had the incentive of freedom and citizenship for good behaviour. And the name Vindicius lives on, for when our assertions are proven true despite difficult circumstances, we are said to be vindicated.

9 | CINCINNATUS
From ploughman to dictator

Lucius Quinctius Cincinnatus was the model of simple Roman virtue. He was one of the noble leaders of Rome who, in the words of Dio of Halicarnassus, 'worked with their own hands, led frugal lives, did not chafe under honourable poverty, and, far from aiming at a position of royal power, actually refused it when offered'.

Cincinnatus had three sons, all of whom matched him in austerity and haughtiness. It is due to the actions of one of his sons, Caeso Quinctius, that Cincinnatus first appears in the ancient sources. Caeso was a physically impressive young man who had distinguished himself both on the battlefield and in the courts. He vigorously led senatorial opposition to the plebeian cause, and was not above a bit of violence to make his point. The ordinary citizens of Rome detested him, and were overjoyed when one of the tribunes brought a case against him in 461 BC. Cincinnatus and others pleaded his case, blaming youthful excess and extravagance, but to no effect. Caeso was imprisoned to await trial, and was only released when his father and other leading senators stood bail for him (the first ever example of this). Caeso promptly absconded, leaving Cincinnatus to pay up: he had to sell all he owned, moving to live in a deserted hovel across the Tiber.

But in a period of intense political turmoil at Rome, Cincinnatus was soon back in the public eye. In 460 BC an army of slaves and exiles seized the Capitol; only with the help of the neighbouring Tusculans did Rome recover from this outrage, and one of her consuls was killed in the process. Cincinnatus was elected consul in his place, much to the surprise and horror of the people. According to Livy, his first act was to castigate the Senate for allowing the tribunes to incite the people and cause political strife. He then attempted to raise troops to fight the Volscians and Aequi, who were threatening Roman territory, but was thwarted by the tribunes. The Senate failed to support him, and so Cincinnatus and his fellow consul refused to stand for re-election.

Cincinnatus retired to his small farm, to the west of the Tiber, preferring honest labour to politics. And working his land was where he was found two years later by a delegation from Rome. During that time, Rome had been at war with the Volscians and Aequi, and had been ravaged by internal conflicts incited by the tribunes. Then the Sabines had raided Roman territory, and the Aequi had besieged one of the consuls and his army. The Romans turned to the one man they felt could save the day – Cincinnatus – and they offered him the dictatorship (see pl. VI). Dio of Halicarnassus reports how 'Quinctius, when he learned that he had been appointed dictator, far from being pleased at receiving so great an honour, was actually vexed, and said: "This year's crop too will be ruined, then, because of my official duties, and we shall all go dreadfully hungry."' Nevertheless, he donned his toga, and returned to Rome. There he suspended legal business, closed the shops and forbade the transaction of any private business. Rome was to concentrate on assembling an army, which Cincinnatus himself then led, with resounding success, against the Aequi mountain tribe. He returned to Rome in triumph, gave an account of his achievements to the people and resigned his dictatorship. He refused to accept land, slaves or booty from the campaign. Instead, once more according to Dio of Halicarnassus, 'he retired again to that small farm of his and resumed his life of a farmer working his own land in preference to the life of a king, glorying more in his poverty than others in their riches'.

His retirement lasted until 439 BC, when his city called upon him yet again. The conflict between the patricians and plebeians had continued unabated during this 20-year interval, and Rome had suffered the depredations of the decemvirate too (see no. 10). Now certain plebeians threatened to overthrow the established order and were stockpiling arms. The Senate turned once more to Cincinnatus for leadership. His initial protests on account of his age – by now over 80 – were brushed aside and he was named dictator once more. The main conspirator was summoned to his presence, but killed as he attempted to flee.

The legend of Cincinnatus has inspired generations. What better accolade for George Washington – who resigned his command upon the defeat of the British – than to be called an American Cincinnatus? And Cincinnati itself was named by a member of the Society of the Cincinnati, set up after the war to honour Washington.

10 | VERGINIUS
Centurion and revolutionary

After the establishment of the Roman Republic in 509 BC Rome's influence expanded through a series of wars with her neighbours. But at home there was political and social unrest, and in many respects the story of Verginius encapsulates the essence of this period.

The Roman people were divided into patricians and plebeians. The patricians were members of Rome's oldest families, wealthy landowners who held a monopoly of all high office and controlled the legal system. All other citizens were plebeians, excluded from public offices except the tribunate. They did, however, play an important part in the army, and they used this to agitate for equality with the patricians. Among other things, they demanded a written code of laws. Finally after years of strife, the patricians gave in in 452 BC. A 'Board of Ten', known as the decemvirs, was set up to establish this code, and all the normal offices of government were abolished for one year. The result was the ten 'Tables of Law', which would remain the foundation of public and private law for centuries to come. So grateful were the people that they decided to elect another Board of Ten for the next year to add a further two tables.

At this point one of the original decemvirs, Appius Claudius, secured re-election, and under his influence the decemvirs began to exploit their position, effectively turning themselves into ten kings, using gangs of thugs to bully and rob the people and executing those who opposed them. And when their second year of office came to a close, they refused to step down. There are many examples of their tyranny, but the one that eventually led to their downfall involved a Roman girl, who, like Lucretia (no. 6), became a catalyst for action.

Verginia was a beautiful young girl of humble origins. Her father was Lucius Verginius, an upright centurion of good reputation who was serving in Rome's army against the Aequi. He had betrothed his daughter to Lucius Icilius, an ex-tribune. Appius Claudius, however, was smitten with Verginia; he tried to seduce her with money and promises, but when these failed he resorted to underhand tactics. Taking advantage of Verginius' absence from Rome, he instructed one of his freedmen, also named Claudius, to claim Verginia as his slave. He attempted to do this one morning in the Forum, but was prevented by the crowds, who leapt to Verginia's defence. Instead Verginia was brought before the court, presided over by Appius himself. The freedman Claudius claimed that Verginia had been stolen from his house, where she had been born, and brought up as Verginius' daughter. Verginia's advocates argued that the case should be postponed until Verginius could be summoned back to Rome. Appius agreed, but attempted to take custody of Verginia in the meantime. The arrival of Icilius prevented this – at the threat of mob violence, Appius agreed to allow Verginia home until the following day.

Verginius was summoned, and reached Rome in time despite Appius' attempts to delay him. The events are narrated by Livy: 'Verginius entered the Forum leading his daughter by the hand – he in mourning, she in rags'; they were followed by women weeping silently. Appius mounted the tribunal and declared that Verginia was Claudius' slave. He had brought an armed escort to ensure his judgment. None could help Verginia, and her father was spurred to drastic action. Leading Verginia to one side, he stabbed her through the heart, crying: 'There is only one way, my child, to make you free.'

Verginius fled back to the army. 'His arrival was immensely impressive: long before he reached the camp he could be seen because of the crowd of some 400 citizens who accompanied him out of sympathy for his lacerated feelings; his naked weapon was still in his hand, and his clothes were covered with blood.' His daughter was better dead than dishonoured, he claimed, and he appealed to the troops to march on Rome. First they occupied the Aventine, then moved on to the Sacred Mount, followed by the people of Rome. The streets were deserted; only the Senate remained. Already hostile to the decemvirs, the Senate persuaded them to resign and re-established the tribunate. Elections followed, and Verginius, Icilius and Publius Numitorius (Verginia's great-uncle) were among those chosen by the people. Appius Claudius was brought to trial and prosecuted by Verginius himself for attempting to enslave a free woman. Appius was thrown into prison; Claudius, his henchman, was exiled. Verginia's ghost, according to Livy, found rest at last.

11 | MARCUS MANLIUS
Defender of the Capitol

The early years of the 4th century BC were among the darkest in Roman history. The Senones, Gauls led by the warlord Brennus, rampaged south through Italy, and smashed a combined army of

Romans and their allies at the Battle of the Allia on 18 July 390 BC. Rome was left defenceless, and the Gauls pillaged the city and killed those senators who refused to flee. Only one part of the city held out against the invaders, the Capitoline Hill, Rome's citadel of last resort.

Among the Capitoline's defenders was Marcus Manlius, of an already distinguished patrician family which boasted among its members the great Cincinnatus (no. 9). Marcus himself had been consul in 392 BC, and his military prowess against the Aequi had earned him a minor triumph. However, Manlius had been forced to resign his office when he came down with illness.

The Gallic sack had left Marcus' house intact, for he lived on the Capitoline Hill near the Temple of Juno. One night he was roused by the hissing and cackling of the sacred geese, and discovered that the Gauls had found a way up the hill. The Roman guards, who had falsely believed that the steep slopes would keep them secure, had been killed. The invaders were now clambering up a narrow path, and Marcus and his household were able to hold them at bay until the rest of the garrison joined in throwing back the invaders.

The Gauls had been forced to this desperate night attack because their numbers were reduced by illness (through a failure to bury those they had massacred, suggests Plutarch), and because an army raised by the Roman general Furius Camillus was preventing them from foraging for fresh supplies. On being thrown back from the Capitoline, the Gauls attempted to negotiate but were driven from Rome by force.

As a hero of Rome, further prestigious offices and glory awaited Manlius. He turned his back on these, however, and threw himself behind the cause of the plebeians. Many had lost their livelihood in the recent turmoil and were desperately in debt. Manlius agitated so effectively on their behalf that the aristocracy had to appoint a dictator to maintain order. But like most Roman magistrates, dictators were also military leaders. While Cossus, as this dictator was called, was away on campaign, Manlius led a near-revolution in Rome in which the poor rioted in protest against their creditors. Unsurprisingly, when Cossus returned, Manlius was flung into prison. The plebeians were awarded fresh grants of land to compensate for the loss of their champion, but the move was unsuccessful. Popular pressure forced the release of Manlius.

His incarceration had, if anything, increased Manlius' zeal, and his enemies fomented a growing suspicion that Manlius' true goal was not the betterment of the poor, but to use their plight as the vehicle for becoming king. As Manlius' demagoguery grew more extreme he began to lose his moderate support, until finally his political opponents were strong enough to charge him with attempted treason.

Treason trials were conducted in the Campus Martius by the *comitia centuriata*, the whole of the Roman people voting in their centuries, as happened in the annual elections for magistrates. However, those trying Manlius realized that this meant the trial happened almost in the shadow of the Capitoline Hill that Manlius had defended so bravely. Proceedings were hastily reconvened in a less evocative location, where Manlius was duly condemned. He was thrown to his doom, a fate reserved for criminals and traitors, from the Tarpeian rock, ironically, yet again on the heights of the Capitoline.

To atone for the deeds of Marcus Manlius, his clan resolved that none of their members would ever again bear the name of Marcus. This promise was kept through the centuries of distinguished service which the family gave the city.

There is much about the story of Manlius which is uncertain and many historians contend that the Capitoline Hill fell with the rest of Rome, and the legend of Marcus and the geese is a face-saving fiction. However, the Romans certainly believed it, and Juno's temple was named Juno Moneta ('Juno Gives Warning'), with an honoured place for the geese which had saved the city from total defeat.

12 | TITUS MANLIUS
A soldier killed on his father's orders

In 340 BC Rome was at war with her former allies, the Latins. The Latins had supplied Rome with troops during the city's early wars of conquest, and now they demanded full equality with Rome. They were scornfully dismissed by the consul of that year, Titus Manlius Torquatus, who claimed he would kill the first Latin to enter the Senate.

Torquatus was the most prominent Roman of his day, consul for the third time in 340 BC and previously dictator. He had come to the fore as a young man, first by defending his father from prosecution by a tribune and then for defeating a Gaul in single combat and removing a gold torque from his body (hence the 'torquatus' part of his name). He was renowned for his patriotic devotion and Roman pride, and with his fellow consul, Publius Decius Mus (no. 13), decided to reintroduce strict military discipline to the Roman army in their fight against the Latins. The reason for this was simple. The Latins spoke the same language, had the same customs, weapons and military organization – the potential for confusion and error was great. In particular, they declared that no man should engage the enemy without specific orders.

One man, however, ignored these orders. Titus Manlius was Torquatus' son, and no doubt he strove to emulate his famous father's deeds. While reconnoitring the enemy camp he was challenged to single combat by Geminus Maecius, a Latin champion. 'And so', says Livy, 'forgetting his father's supreme authority and the consuls' order, he threw himself headlong into a fight where it mattered little whether he won or lost.' Victorious, he stripped his enemy of his armour and weapons and returned to his father, accompanied by the cheers of his fellow soldiers.

Impressed as he was by his son's valour, Torquatus did not shy from punishing him. Duty to the state overcame personal feelings,

and there was only one possible punishment for direct disobedience of a consular command. Manlius was bound to a stake and,
according to Valerius Maximus, 'slaughtered like a sacrificial victim',
to the horror of onlookers. Unsurprisingly, no other soldier was
tempted to break ranks; Livy even claims that Torquatus' stern
action did the soldiers good. And from that time the imposition of
the strictest military discipline has been known as 'Manlian orders'
or the 'Manlian rule'.

13 | DECIUS MUS
Self-sacrifice to the gods

Although plebeian, the inappropriately named Mus family (*mus*
means mouse) had given Rome faithful and brave military leaders
for generations. Publius Decius Mus, who became consul in 312 BC,
was of this tradition. Mus' fellow consul was Marcus Valerius
Maximus of Rome's great Valerian family, and when Mus was
consul again in 308 BC, he shared office with Quintus Fabius
Maximus (an ancestor of the great general who fought Hannibal
in the Punic Wars). Another highly aristocratic Roman, Cornelius
Scipio Barbartus, made Mus his second-in-command when he was
dictator in 306 BC.

Mus was a successful general, fighting campaigns against the
Samnite and Etruscan peoples, but he also took a keen interest
in legislation. As censor in 304 BC he was back in harness with
Q. Fabius Maximus, and the pair passed important legislation on
the status of freed Roman slaves (see no. 8). Later still, in 300 BC,
he took on the reactionary elite, and helped to push through the
Ogulnian law, which opened up certain priestly offices to the plebeians. In Rome top priesthoods were electoral posts, and for his
efforts Mus was elected as the first plebeian priest in the college
of pontiffs.

Fabius Maximus and Decius Mus evidently enjoyed campaigning together, both militarily and politically, as they did so again successfully for the consulship of 297 BC, and continued Rome's war with the Samnites. The year 295 BC saw the pair again in office, elected as safe hands at a time when Etruscans, Gauls, Samnites and others were united in war against Rome. However, when the armies met, the Romans began to buckle under the Gallic assault. But Mus had a terrible precedent to call upon. His father had been consul in 340 BC when Rome was locked in war with the Latins. An omen announced that, to bring the war to an end, on one side a general and on the other a whole army would be dedicated to the gods of the underworld. Mus' father had sacrificed himself to ensure the annihilation of the enemy army. One tradition has him standing, as the rite ordained, on a spear and shrouded in his toga while he submitted to the dread ritual performed by a priest; in another he made a suicidal charge at the enemy. In either case the outcome was secure: Rome won victory against the odds.

Now, in his army's hour of need, the son did the same. The superstitious Gauls, believing that if Rome's general died their whole army was doomed, lost first their morale and then the battle, and so Mus' sacrifice brought victory. Such was the power of this precedent that when the Macedonian general Pyrrhus was campaigning against the Romans a generation later, he gave orders that at all costs the son of Decius Mus must not be allowed to die in battle against him.

Part 2

From Italians to Romans

300–88 BC

When Rome first clashed with Carthage in 264 BC, the Hellenistic empires to the east had no reason to think that they were under any threat. True, Rome had expanded to occupy all of southern and central Italy, but few, even in Rome, believed that they would expand much further than this. Indeed, there is no evidence that the Romans consciously set out to build themselves an empire. However, circumstances had given them a society where wealth and power were directly linked to military success, and generations of almost constant warfare had made the army very good at achieving that success. Carthage was defeated in 241 BC after a titanic struggle (the First Punic War), which was resumed in 218 BC with the war against Hannibal (the Second Punic War). Roman victory in 202 BC led the Romans to campaign against Hannibal's ally Philip of Macedon, and from there to a series of campaigns which led to Rome's dominance of the eastern Mediterranean.

A factor that made Rome uniquely suited to empire was the extraordinary openness of its society. Those conquered by Rome became citizens, not subjects. Such were the benefits of citizenship that the grandchildren of some of Rome's bitterest enemies ended up fully subscribing to the Roman project. For example Arpinum, the hill town that the Romans captured from the Samnites in 303 BC, was later to give Rome two of her greatest citizens in Caius Marius and Marcus Tullius Cicero (no. 29). Even for those brought to Rome as slaves, the situation was not hopeless. Some were freed by their compatriots (for example Judaism obliged its followers to buy the freedom of their co-religionists), and others earned freedom for themselves. Freed slaves became citizens, some of whom became very rich, and the children of others went on to hold high political office in their home towns. The fact that these strengths were built into the fabric of society meant that the rapid growth of the Roman state did not so much stretch its resources as add to them.

At the same time, expansion into the Hellenistic world opened Roman eyes to hitherto unregarded aspects of civilization. After their initial bemusement at the first Greek philosophers to arrive in their city, the Romans, such as Cornelia mother of the Gracchi (no. 23), found themselves developing a taste for fine art, theatre and literary pursuits. Greeks were soon in demand as doctors, secretaries and schoolteachers, and their sculpture was adapted to Roman taste by men such as Pasiteles (no. 27). Despite this, the Romans never fully trusted these new citizens of their empire, considering them to be too clever, and somehow fallen from their former glory. Nevertheless, the Greek contribution was significant to a culture which had highly developed engineering and utilitarian skills, and an appreciation of the finer things in life.

With the growth of the empire, Roman citizenship came to be highly valued. As this progressed, however, it also became something to be guarded and given only grudgingly. Towards the end of this period, Rome's allies in Italy observed that they were doing much of the paying and fighting for Rome's new empire, but receiving fewer of the benefits. By 140 BC, it was evident to many intelligent Romans that the system needed comprehensive reform. Yet reform hurts those with an interest in the status quo, and Rome's senators were doing very well as things were.

The short-sighted and greedy Senate of the later Republic was directly responsible for the crisis into which Rome was about to plunge. Not only did the elite refuse to share the benefits of empire, they actively persecuted those, such as the Gracchus brothers, who tried to make them do so. During this period, the pressures of political life in Rome had vastly increased the cost of a political career. Aspiring politicians often began their campaigns by going deeply into debt to bribe the electorate, and later attempted to repay those debts with money extracted from the unfortunate provincials they came to govern. At the start of the 1st century BC senatorial misgovernment left Rome facing rebellion abroad and civil war at home. For a while in 90 BC the rebel armies threatened the very existence of Rome, and the state only saved itself by giving ground, and allowing citizenship to most Italians. However, absorbing citizens town by town was different from taking in entire peoples at a time. Consequently, Rome's citizen legions became populated with professional soldiers, many of whom knew little of the Roman democratic tradition, and who had personal experience of fighting the Senate and people of Rome. These men looked not to Rome, but to their generals, men like Cornelius Sulla (no. 25), for reward for their personal loyalty. Rome's senate was about to find that it had exchanged one form of crisis for another.

14 | REGULUS
Crucified general

By the middle of the 3rd century BC, Rome controlled the whole of mainland Italy and was recognized as a major power by her neighbours. At this point the Romans became embroiled in a conflict with the Carthaginian empire over Sicily that would eventually make them the master of the Mediterranean world. The war was initially fought on land, but, as it dragged on, the Romans were inspired to take to the seas for the first time.

Marcus Atilius Regulus was the greatest of Roman patriots. Consul for the second time in 256 BC, the ninth year of what is known as the First Punic War, he was placed in command of the new Roman fleet. While anchored off Tyndaris in Sicily, the Romans surprised the Carthaginian fleet and defeated it. The next summer, Regulus again defeated the Carthaginians at Ecnomus, and succeeded in landing on the coast of Libya. The Romans took the city of Aspis, garrisoned it, and reported back to Rome. While awaiting a reply they plundered the countryside.

Messengers soon arrived from Rome – the Senate was ecstatic. Regulus was to remain with his troops; the other consul (Marcus Manlius Vulso Longus) was to return with the fleet to Rome. Regulus was left with 40 ships, 1,500 infantry and 500 cavalry, which he used to repel Carthaginian attempts to dislodge him. Enemy towns were captured as Regulus advanced along the coast, and it looked for a while as if he would take Carthage itself. But, according to Polybius, he was 'afraid that his successor as consul might arrive from Rome before Carthage fell and thus deprive him of the glory of its capture'. He attempted to negotiate terms with the Carthaginians, but his conditions were too severe; they were offended and refused to submit.

At this point, Regulus' luck changed. Fresh mercenary troops from Sparta arrived to fight for the Carthaginians. Their commander,

Xanthippus, took command of the Carthaginian effort. The Romans met the Carthaginians in pitched battle and lost. Many were trampled by elephants, others cut down by cavalry. Around 500 escaped – including Regulus – only to be captured shortly afterwards. 'Here we see the very man, who only a little while before had refused any pity or mercy to the vanquished, himself led captive and pleading before his victims for his own life,' writes Polybius.

The Carthaginians sent Regulus back to Rome. He was to negotiate peace, or, at the very least, an exchange of prisoners, and he was made to swear a solemn oath that he would return to Carthage if he failed in this task. Despite this, he convinced the Senate against both courses of action. Horace put these rousing words in his mouth:

> I have seen our standards nailed up in Punic temples, and weapons that were stripped from our soldiers with their arms twisted behind their free-born backs, and the fields once ravaged by our armies again under cultivation. If a soldier is ransomed with gold, I suppose he will be all the fiercer when he comes home. You are adding financial loss to moral disgrace.

Then, unmoved by the pleas of his wife and children, and of the crowds who had gathered, he honoured his oath and returned to Carthage where he was tortured and executed. There are different versions of his fate, probably fictitious, that have become the stuff of legend. Florus claims that he was crucified; others report that he was shut into some kind of contraption that deprived him of sleep. Valerius Maximus, for example, reports that 'the Carthaginians cut off Regulus' eyelids, shut him in a machine in which sharp points stood out from all angles and killed him from lack of sleep and extension of pain, a torture undeserved by the sufferer but richly deserved by its authors.'

Regulus' story was undoubtedly embellished, but in the eyes of later generations he was the kind of Roman who had made

Rome great. Rather than see his city humiliated and weakened, he sacrificed himself – the supreme example of traditional Roman virtue and valour.

15 | FABIUS PICTOR
Rome's first historian

The Fabians were one of Rome's oldest families. A Fabius was among the decemvirs exiled from Rome after the overthrow of the tyrannical Appius Claudius, and the family were nearly wiped out when they single-handedly waged war on Rome's neighbour and rival, the Etruscan city of Veii. The surviving Fabians established themselves as Rome's foremost military dynasty; a position they held until the end of the Carthaginian wars.

Pictor (meaning painter) was a cognomen, a type of nickname. This was necessary to distinguish individual male Fabians, who very frequently shared the praenomen of Quintus. The appellation of Pictor dates to the end of the 4th century BC when Gaius Fabius, grandfather of Fabius Pictor, commissioned a battle tableau in the Temple of Salus, the Roman goddess of health. It was the first painting of that type seen in Rome.

Quintus Fabius Pictor, the grandson, was born about 50 years later in *c.* 254 BC. The exact date may be earlier as by 225 BC he was campaigning against Gauls in northern Italy. Polybius, a Greek historian who was held in Rome as a hostage a few decades later, tells us that Fabius became a Roman senator. While the order of Roman magistracies had not yet fully settled into the strict ladder of offices known as the *cursus honorum*, it is nevertheless probable that Fabius achieved at least the rank of quaestor.

Fabius took up arms again when Hannibal invaded Italy in the Second Punic War of 218 BC, and in 216 BC he was one of the few Roman senators to survive taking part in the Roman defeat at Cannae. (As might be expected of a warrior aristocracy, Roman generals led from the front, and suffered appalling casualties.) But Cannae nevertheless marked the end of Fabius' military career. He was sent to Greece by the Senate, to consult the oracle at Delphi about Rome's misfortunes.

Whilst in Greece, Fabius discovered that the Romans were losing the propaganda war by default. The Macedonians, the dominant power in Greece, strongly favoured the Carthaginians, and many of the contemporary histories took the Carthaginian viewpoint – as no Roman histories existed. Until Fabius set about remedying this, Rome had no historiographical tradition, but there was plenty of raw material for the aspiring historian. The great dynasties had their own family records, and the city authorities had conscientiously listed the city's annual magistrates and kept copies of treaties.

Fabius compiled these into a history of Rome from the foundation, which he held to have been in 747 BC – the 'first year of the eighth olympiad', until his own times. (We know, for example, that he gave a description of Hannibal's victory at the Battle of Trasimene.) Early historiographers believed that Fabius, as the first Roman to try writing history, was necessarily an annalist, a crude historian who reported events in diary form with little attempt at synthesis or following threads of events. However, Fabius was writing history as argument, and was undoubtedly familiar with the sophisticated techniques of the great Greek historian Thucydides, and he may have tried to emulate him. Fabius wrote in Greek – not just because he was writing partly for a Greek audience, but because it probably did not occur to him not to. Greek was the language of education in the 3rd century BC, just as Latin was in early modern Europe. A Latin translation was made later, though some surviving 'extracts' might be from Q. Fabius Maximus Servilianus (the consul in 142 BC), who also tried his hand at writing history.

Sadly Fabius' entire work is now lost. However, his history was used extensively by Greek historians, including Polybius (who took issue with Fabius' pro-Roman bias) and Dio of Halicarnassus.

Later scholars have combed through surviving ancient texts to find traces of Rome's first historian. The first results of these searches appeared during the Renaissance as *De Fabio Pictore ceterisque Fabiis Historicis*. From the surviving fragments, it seems that Fabius wrote not only military history, but also of constitutional and legal changes in Rome.

Fabius Pictor took Roman history from the shadows of myth and placed it solidly on a factual basis. His contemporary, Cato the Elder, followed this with a work in Latin, a tradition followed by the later great Roman historians Livy and Tacitus, whose works have largely survived.

We know little of Fabius' later life. He may have held an honorary position in one of Rome's many priestly colleges. He was married, although details about his wife are unknown. His son (inevitably called Quintus Fabius Pictor) became praetor in 189 BC. As with his birth, it is not known exactly when Fabius died. That he held no major public office might indicate an early death, but ill-health or the concerns of writing history may also account for this.

16 | PLAUTUS
Roman playwright

Titus Maccius Plautus was the master of Roman comedy. Not only was he the most popular and successful playwright of his era, but his works (which are the earliest surviving complete examples of Latin literature) have also been enjoyed and imitated by later generations. Yet frustratingly little is known of Plautus the man.

It is thought that he was born *c.* 254 BC in Sarsina, a small town in the Umbrian hills to the north of Rome. In good Italian tradition, the name 'Plautus' probably reflects a physical trait, meaning 'broad-footed'. Much later, when he achieved Roman citizenship, the name Maccius (or Maccus) was added, probably a reference to the stock comic character Maccus (the buffoon). At an early age he moved to Rome, was taken on as a stage assistant to a company of players, and eventually began acting comic parts himself.

Somehow Plautus managed to save enough money to go into business as a merchant-shipper. But Aulus Gellius tells us that 'after losing in trade all the money which he had earned in employments connected with the stage, he had returned penniless to Rome, and to earn a livelihood had hired himself out to a baker, to turn a mill'. In his spare time he may have gone back to performing, but this is uncertain. He did, however, study Greek drama, and he began adapting Greek comedies for the Roman stage. By his early forties his plays were being performed in Rome. Later detractors such as Horace might have been sniffy at what they considered to be poor literature ('he is eager to drop a coin into his pocket and, that done, he cares not whether his play falls or stands square on its feet'), but there is no doubt about the plays' popularity with Roman theatre-goers. His name became enough to ensure a hit. Nothing else is known of his life, except that he was incredibly successful. After his death, in 184 BC according to Cicero, his name was appended to many plays that he had not himself written. Aulus Gellius remarks that in his day (2nd century AD) there were about 130 plays under Plautus' name and that one learned man (Lucius Aelius) considered only 25 to have been written by Plautus.

Plautus' comedies may have been direct translations of Greek originals, but it is most commonly held that he used Greek plays as models, adapting or diverging from the original as the muse took him. His characters have Greek names and live in Greek cities, but they are Romans. Stock characters include the clever slave, the arrogant soldier, the lecherous old man, the formidable matron, the seductive prostitute and the lovesick young man – all familiar figures in Greek comedy transferred to the Roman stage. Of them all, the most vivid are the slaves, leading to speculation that Plautus himself had originally been of slave origin (as indeed was the case with many actors). Slaves are the prime agents of Plautine comedy.

They are lazy and insolent, cunning and sophisticated, uncouth and aggressive, and occasionally loyal and helpful. Many enjoy playing tricks, demonstrating in the process that they are cleverer than their masters.

> PALAESTRIO: Listen, and I will conduct you into the purlieus of my ingenuity; you shall be privy to my purposes.

> PERIPLECTOMENUS: I shall not betray a word of them.

> PALAESTRIO: My master, let me tell you, is a man wrapped up in an elephant's hide; he has no more intelligence than a stone.

Roman theatre in this period was a part-time affair, connected to particular religious festivals. Plays were commissioned for a festival and performed over a single day or series of days in temporary wooden theatres. This was the period of the Punic Wars, a time of hardship for the Roman people who were repeatedly asked to make sacrifices for the state, and reminded – by Cato the Elder (no. 17) among others – of the traditional Roman virtues of frugality and hard work. Plautus' comedy provided a release for the ordinary Roman. Within the safety of the theatre traditional values could be mocked and rules flouted. Old men are belittled, husbands steal from their wives, wives are adulterous and young men wish their fathers dead. Cato's dictates are completely ignored.

> CALIDORUS: Will you give me 2,000 drachmas today?

> PSEUDOLUS: I will. Now don't say another word. One thing I warn you though – so don't say I didn't tell you – if all else fails, I shall have to touch your father for it.

> CALIDORUS: Heaven bless you and keep you mine forever! But… as a dutiful son… I feel bound to say – why not try my mother too?

17 | CATO THE ELDER
A pillar of virtue

In his lifetime, Marcus Porcius Cato saw Rome transformed from the most important city-state in Italy to the dominant power of the Mediterranean world. Conquest and the spoils of war led to profound changes to Roman society and culture. But not all these changes were seen as desirable by traditionally minded Romans such as Cato.

He was born in 234 BC in Tusculum, a Latin town 15 miles to the southeast of Rome that enjoyed the privileges of Roman citizenship. His family were probably members of the local aristocracy, and some may have been enrolled in the equestrian order. Certainly they were wealthy, though Cato himself stressed the austerity and industry of his youth, which was spent largely in a villa in Sabine territory that he had inherited from his father.

In 218 BC the Second Punic War against Carthage broke out and Hannibal invaded Italy. A year later, at the age of 17, Cato enlisted in the Roman army. For the next 13 years he campaigned in Campania and Sicily, first in the ranks, later as military tribune. By 204 BC he had a political career. Although a *novus homo* ('new man'), he had the support of the influential patrician Lucius Valerius Flaccus, and was elected to the office of quaestor. He was plebeian aedile in 199 and in 198 BC was sent as praetor to govern Sardinia, where he distinguished himself from his more avaricious predecessors by cutting his expenses (provinces were obliged to pay for the upkeep of their governors).

In 195 BC Cato held the consulship with his patron, Flaccus, and was immediately involved in a vehement dispute over the repeal of the Oppian Law. This law had been passed 20 years earlier at the height of the Punic Wars and forbade Roman women to possess more than a half-ounce of gold, to wear varicoloured dresses or ride in carriages except on special occasions. Now in more prosperous times women wanted their finery back, and they took to the streets to argue their case. Cato was outraged by such immodest behaviour, and later Livy would put these words in his mouth: 'If each of us, citizens, had determined to assert his rights and dignity as a husband with respect to his own spouse, we should have less trouble with the sex as a whole; as it is, our liberty, destroyed at home by female violence, even here in the Forum is crushed and trodden underfoot....' He believed that if the law were repealed, and the women of Rome were freed from constraints that conservatives such as Cato believed were fundamental to maintaining traditional Roman morality, there would be no limit to the demands of women.

Cato then set out for Spain, where he took over command of Rome's armies. Here he enjoyed great military successes, collecting large revenues from Spanish mines and celebrating a triumph upon his return to Rome the following year. The next few years are obscure, but his marriage to Licina, a woman of noble family, and the birth of his first son probably took place now. According to Plutarch he educated his own son in the traditional Roman manner rather than allow him to be taught by a Greek slave, as had become common practice at Rome. He taught his son about ancient Roman traditions, and to ride, to hurl the javelin, to box, to endure heat and cold, seeking to mould him into a sturdy Roman soldier. He also attempted to prejudice his son against the prevailing love of Greek culture, by telling him that Rome would lose her empire when she had become infected with Greek letters.

In 191 BC Rome went to war against Antiochus III in Greece. Cato travelled east as military tribune and Roman envoy to Greek cities, taking the opportunity to stay in Athens to learn more about Greek culture and society. He then played a distinguished role in defeating Antiochus – and was swift to make sure that everyone knew it, arriving back in Rome first with news of the victory. There he became embroiled in various disputes over the next few years, often concerning misconduct in public life. There is good reason to suppose that one of the underlying reasons for this was the upcoming election for the censorship – Cato was campaigning, and setting forth his political agenda – to uphold traditional Roman values and fight against luxury and the corruption of Roman morals. His first candidature in 189 BC failed, but in 184 BC he was elected censor, with Flaccus once more his partner.

To be censor was to hold the most dignified and sacred of Roman magistracies. Two censors were elected every five years to compose a register of Roman citizens and their property, to safeguard Roman morals and to administer state finances and public works. Cato took his duty very seriously indeed, expelling from the senate seven men he considered to be unworthy. One was a former consul, whom Cato accused of carrying out an execution at a banquet to gratify the whim of a boy lover. Another was accused of kissing his wife in public in front of their daughter. The censors also took measures to restrict luxury goods at Rome by taxing them severely. Cato believed that it was a citizen's duty to maintain and increase his property, not to waste it. Another action was to tear down private buildings built on public land and shut off public water that had been diverted into private houses. Finally, the censors undertook the cleaning and extension of the sewer system, and the construction of buildings and roads. Fragments of Cato's speeches from this time demonstrate that his actions were controversial and bitterly opposed. Livy comments that the quarrels generated now occupied Cato for the rest of his life.

Cato remained an outspoken and influential politician for the next 34 years, and he was prosecuted 44 times in politically motivated lawsuits. Many of his speeches were later published; Cicero knew over 150 of them and the remnants of around 80 are still extant today. Cato railed against the luxuries and excesses that were becoming common among Rome's nobility and fought against the influence of Greek culture on traditional Roman morality. In 155 BC a delegation of Athenian philosophers came to Rome and the city's youth flocked to hear them. Plutarch comments that Cato was 'distressed, fearing lest the young men, by giving this direction to their ambition, should come to love a reputation based on mere words more than one achieved by martial deeds'. He used his influence in the senate to secure the swift departure of these dangerous ambassadors. He agitated, too, for the final destruction of Carthage, believing that Rome would never be safe until her greatest enemy was destroyed. All his speeches in the Senate were concluded with the famous statement, 'Carthage must be destroyed'. Eventually he prevailed.

In addition to his political involvements, he found time to write a history of Rome, entitled the *Origines*, the first in Latin. He composed a collection of didactic statements, and wrote on military matters, the education of young Romans and the profitable management of farms. One famous piece of advice was to 'sell worn-out oxen, hides, an old wagon, old tools, an old slave, a sickly slave, and whatever else is superfluous'. He married again when he was almost 80 years old; his second wife appears to have been the daughter of a freedman, and she bore him another son. He died at the age of 85, in autumn 149 BC.

18 | FABIUS MAXIMUS
The general who delayed Hannibal

Quintus Fabius Maximus Verrucosus was known as 'the Delayer' (*cunctator*). Initially intended as an insult, this epithet later became a compliment of the highest order, since his defensive strategy of avoiding direct battle with Hannibal's army ultimately led to the salvation of Rome.

Fabius Maximus was born in *c.* 275 BC into one of the most distinguished patrician families of Rome, the Fabii. His career was thus assured: he would hold the consulship five times, be appointed dictator and achieve the office of censor. He was given the cognomen 'Verrucosus' because he had a small wart on his upper lip. According to Plutarch he was also called *ovicula* ('lambkin') as a child, due to his gentle nature and because he showed extreme caution even when playing.

Fabius probably served in the army during the First Punic War, but his role is unknown. He held the consulship in 233 BC, winning a triumph for his victory over the Ligurians. He went on to be censor in 230 BC and consul again in 228 BC. When Hannibal captured the Spanish city of Saguntum (which was under Roman protection), it was Fabius who declared war on Carthage. He then advised the Romans to caution, noting the small size of Hannibal's army and believing that its strength would burn out on its own. His advice was ignored, and the Romans suffered a crushing defeat at Lake Trasimene in 217 BC. In the aftermath of this disaster Fabius was named dictator by the Senate. As dictator he had command of the Roman armies, and he kept them close to Hannibal, without directly engaging him, and adopted a scorched earth policy, so that Hannibal was prevented from gathering supplies. This strategy was highly effective yet extremely unpopular at Rome and even among Fabius' officers. His second-in-command openly called him a coward, disobeyed him and attacked Hannibal, but Hannibal had anticipated the assault. Fabius was forced to march to the rescue of his irresponsible officer.

When Fabius' term as dictator ended, the consuls resumed military command; after the elections of the following year, the new consuls chose to meet Hannibal in pitched battle at Cannae. Their losses were enormous, and almost brought the Roman state to its knees. Once more the people turned to Fabius for salvation, as Plutarch informs us: 'For when the people had felt secure, it was Fabius who had appeared to be cautious and timid, but now, when all others were giving way to boundless grief and helpless bewilderment, he was the only man to walk the streets with a resolute step, a serene expression, and a kindly voice.' Calm was restored at Rome. The people sent two contrasting generals into the field: Fabius, who was known as the 'Shield of Rome', and Marcellus, the 'Sword of Rome'. The first harried Hannibal without engaging him, the second exhausted him with frequent battles. Together they proved Rome's salvation.

The people of Rome elected Fabius' son (of the same name) consul in 213 BC. To see if he was worthy of that honour, Fabius mounted his horse and rode towards the young man, a direct affront. The new consul ordered Fabius to dismount and approach on foot. The crowd were outraged at this insult to the elder Fabius, but Fabius himself leaped from the horse and embraced his son for understanding the dignity of his new office.

Fabius' only other military intervention came in 209 BC when, as consul once more, he retook the city of Tarentum. In the meantime, another general had been sent to Spain. Scipio Africanus drove the Carthaginians from that country and on his return to Rome proposed that the fight should be taken to Carthage itself. Only Fabius opposed him, accusing Scipio of hot-headedness. His opposition was to no avail, however. Scipio crushed Carthage.

Fabius Maximus did not live to hear of the triumph of his rival. He sickened and died in 203 BC, at about the same time that Hannibal finally sailed from Italy. Every Roman citizen contributed towards the cost of his funeral 'because they felt that they were burying the father of the people'.

Fabius Maximus was one of Rome's greatest heroes, immortalized by Virgil in the *Aeneid*: 'you are Fabius the greatest of them, Maximus, the only Roman who can give us back success by inactivity.' His legacy can be seen today. The 'Fabian Strategy' is the military strategy by which pitched battles are avoided in favour of wearing down an opponent by attrition. 'The Fabian Society' in Britain is so named because it seeks to use this technique to create a socialist society through gradual change.

19 | CLAUDIUS MARCELLUS
Besieger of Syracuse

The birth of Marcellus was contemporary with the outbreak of the first great war with Carthage in 264 BC. So long was this struggle that Marcellus came of age before the war ended (in 241 BC). He fought as a soldier in the Sicilian campaign, and there saved the life of his brother Otacilius with a particularly bloody demonstration of his skill in hand-to-hand combat. Plutarch says his warlike ability gave him the name Marcellus (from Mars, the god of battles), but in fact the Marcelli in Rome date back to at least 350 BC. The family were a branch of Rome's great Claudian line which had arrived in Rome at the start of the Republic, and which later contributed two of Rome's first four emperors, Tiberius and Claudius.

Marcellus was poorly educated, and ill-suited to times of peace. His career languished until 225 BC, when he became *curule aedile*. He was also an augur, responsible for taking the omens. He had a son with exceptionally good looks which allegedly aroused the lust of Marcellus' fellow aedile. The indignant Marcellus confronted his colleague with lewd conduct before the entire Senate. Accuser and accused were known by reputation, which decided the case. The aedile received a large fine which Marcellus dedicated to the gods.

Shortly afterwards in 222 BC, Rome entered a major war with the Insubrian Gauls in north Italy. When a demagogic firebrand was elected consul, the senate used the pretext of unfavourable omens to depose him. As a plebeian and a soldier of note Marcellus was acceptable to people and senate alike, and became the replacement consul. The deposed consul's colleague also lost his job as collateral political damage, so Marcellus had a Cornelius Scipio as his fellow in office. The pair were highly successful, though Polybius maintains that Scipio was the brains of the partnership, and Marcellus the inspiration to the men. Marcellus defeated the Gallic king in single combat, becoming only the third Roman to win Rome's highest commendation, the *spolia opima,* an accolade achieved by personally killing the enemy king while commanding a victorious army in battle. The war ended with the Romans capturing Milan.

Marcellus lapsed once more into obscurity. But when Hannibal led his forces into Italy and destroyed a Roman army at Lake Trasimene, Marcellus' reputation led to his selection as praetor in 216 BC. He was raising troops in Rome when news came of another victory by Hannibal at Cannae. Rome had lost a consul, the largest army the city had ever raised, and her reputation as an invincible military power. Capua in Campania immediately defected to Hannibal. Marcellus left a small garrison to keep order in Rome, and hurried southward to stabilize the situation, en route rounding up the shattered remnants of the army, and preventing the defection of the city of Nola.

Marcellus unexpectedly became consul the following year. His predecessor had died in north Italy, victim of the war's ferocious attrition rate among Rome's leaders. Marcellus' election gave Rome two plebeian consuls, something the patrician aristocrats refused to countenance. As a compromise Marcellus' consulship was annulled on religious grounds, but he was 'properly' elected in 214 BC. That year Marcellus' colleague was Fabius Maximus, 'the Delayer', one of Rome's greatest generals (no. 18). After Marcellus had beaten back yet another Carthaginian assault on Nola (allegedly killing some of Hannibal's elephants in the process), he joined Fabius in capturing the strategic stronghold of Casilinum. The garrison surrendered to Fabius, but Marcellus massacred most of them nevertheless. This led to a rupture between the two generals, and Marcellus was sent to command in Sicily. There Marcellus championed those survivors of Cannae who had been exiled to Sicily as punishment for being defeated. These men were allowed back into the legions, but Marcellus decreed 2,000 to be deserters and executed them.

Marcellus' brutal style alienated the Sicilians, and pro-Carthaginian politicians effortlessly outmanoeuvered him to gain control of Syracuse, the most important city in Sicily. Abandoning diplomacy, Marcellus marched on the city to resolve matters in the way that he did best. The siege of Syracuse was memorable for the infernal engines of Archimedes, the city's resident genius. Dart-firing catapults bombarded the soldiers, while on the seaward side counter-balanced cranes lifted Marcellus' ships from the water and dunked them back stern-first. Eventually just the sight of a rope-end appearing over the battlements was enough to send the Romans fleeing. Marcellus resigned himself to starving out his opponents, grimly enduring Carthaginian attacks and the diseases which inevitably afflicted armies encamped in one place for too long. The city finally fell through a tower left undefended, either thanks to treachery or because the Syracusans indulged themselves too well in a religious festival. Although her citizens were spared massacre, Syracuse was plundered into destitution and Archimedes killed by the vindictive legionaries (see pl. ix).

The severity of the sack meant that when Marcellus left for Rome to celebrate a minor triumph (called an ovation), he was followed by a delegation of indignant Sicilians intent on protesting to the senate. Intense diplomacy resulted in the Syracusans agreeing to honour Marcellus as patron and protector, while in return Marcellus agreed to resume his command anywhere but Sicily. This brought him up against Hannibal in Apulia. In the subsequent years of campaigning Marcellus avoided abject defeat, and even claimed a victory, though this left his army cut to shreds and left Hannibal largely undamaged. This forced Marcellus to hasten to Rome to defend his generalship, which he did so successfully that he was elected consul for the fifth time.

Marcellus' return to his army was delayed by unrest in Etruria and bad omens. Eventually, joined by his fellow consul Crispinus, he hastened to resume the war. Sadly, the pair chose to reconnoitre a hill just when the Carthaginians were doing the same. The considerably smaller Roman force was ambushed, and both consuls killed. The son of Marcellus escaped; Hannibal sent him his father's corpse with full military honours. Hannibal once reportedly said: 'I look on Fabius as a schoolteacher, because he punishes my mistakes. But Marcellus is a rival, for he tries to hurt me whenever he can.'

20 | QUINCTIUS CRISPINUS
Duel to the death with an old friend

In Rome's many wars, it was not uncommon for friends to end up in opposing battlelines. Sometimes friendships survived such military disagreements. That of Titus Quinctius Crispinus did not. The Quinctians were one of the few families which, like the Manlians, had their residence on the Capitoline. As an established Roman family, they had ties with many of the aristocratic families of Italy. Crispinus enjoyed such a relationship with Badius, a Campanian from the rich farmlands south of Rome dominated by the city of Capua. When Badius was visiting Rome he had fallen ill, and was nursed back to health at Crispinus' house. Thereafter the two were 'on terms of the greatest intimacy'. The pair had formed a relationship known as *hospitium*, sometimes translated as 'guest-friendship'. A *hospes* provided hospitality and friendship to his guest-friend when he visited the city. The connection was also maintained by correspondence and often by diplomatic and business relations.

Hannibal's invasion of Italy in 218 BC severed the ties between Roman and Campanian. Capua declared for the Carthaginians, resulting in Crispinus and Badius being on opposing sides of a bitter divide. The Capuan cavalrymen were famous for their skill, but even they, combined with the Carthaginian army, were no match for the Roman manpower, which slowly ground down the Carthaginian forces. In 212 BC Roman forces, including Crispinus, advanced on Capua. After the initial skirmishes, Badius came to the city gates and asked for Quinctius Crispinus. This was not uncommon, for friends often sought each other out during a break in hostilities to catch up on old times, and for a bit of informal diplomacy.

Instead of the friendly chat that he was probably expecting, Crispinus received a storm of abuse. His old friend and guest formally renounced his *hospitium*, and challenged Crispinus to fight to the death. The Romans were not enthusiastic about single combats (called monomachy), though inured to them after years of fighting the Gauls. Roman military tradition decreed that, although Romans should not issue such challenges (there were exceptions), they could respond if their commander agreed. The indignant Crispinus promptly sought and received such permission.

This duel was a cavalry engagement. Riding horses at one another was a difficult manoeuvre, as horses at that time had no stirrups, and the combatants wielded both shield and spear. Crispinus struck first, planting his spear firmly in Badius' left shoulder. Having unhorsed his opponent, Crispinus dismounted and drew his sword to finish the job. Badius abandoned his idea of mortal combat, and fled. Crispinus helped himself to his opponent's horse and shield and returned in triumph to the Roman lines.

For publicly besting a Campanian in that nation's favoured form of combat Crispinus achieved great fame. The historians Livy and Valerius Maximus used variations of his story to tell how personal ties were ruptured by the war, and how even Roman society, which favoured collective military force, still recognized and rewarded individual feats of valour.

21 | LAELIUS
Friend of Scipio Africanus

Gaius Laelius was among those who strongly influenced Roman history whilst remaining in the background. Though possessing neither distinguished ancestors nor a great fortune, he succeeded in gaining access to the charmed circle of Rome's political elite. He began, as did his contemporary Cato, by hitching his star to that of a major political figure – in this case, Cornelius Scipio the younger (later to be known as Scipio Africanus). Scipio and Laelius were much of an age, being born in about 235 BC.

We hear of Scipio early in the Hannibalic war, when Livy tells us he saved his father's life at the Battle of Ticinus in 218 BC, and rallied the Roman remnants after Cannae in 216 BC. However, Laelius only appears as Rome gathered enough strength to fight back against the Carthaginians in Spain in 210 BC. Laelius was a competent admiral, and in command of the Roman fleet. He worked closely with Scipio in planning the ultimately successful assault on Carthago Novo, Carthage's capital in Spain, and was entrusted with bearing the spoils from the captured city back to Rome. Returning to Spain, Laelius became Scipio's trusted confidant and right-hand man. He took part in the many battles and sieges of the war in Spain, and took to the water again to foil the Carthaginian admiral Adherbal's attempt to bring support to Carthaginian loyalists in Gades (modern Cadiz).

Despite this military success, Laelius' major contribution to the war was diplomatic. He was Rome's favoured envoy to Syphax, a king who held a pivotal role in the power politics of North Africa. Syphax threw off the Carthaginian yoke in 214 BC and thereafter tried to remain neutral between Rome and Carthage, whilst simultaneously fending off his powerful and predatory neighbour Massinissa. Laelius tried hard to keep Syphax at least neutral, but Carthage presented an irresistible offer of marriage to the incredibly beautiful Sophonisba, daughter of the Carthaginian general Hasdrubal. Syphax married her in 206 BC and thereafter became a zealous supporter of Carthage.

Laelius turned to Massinissa, a Numidian king and rival to Syphax who commanded a host of light cavalry and whose allegiance was crucial in defeating Carthage. Laelius led the fleet which worked with Massinissa's land forces to capture the town of Hippo Regius on the African coast. Thereafter he led the campaign against Syphax, and finally in 204 BC he captured the king in the city of

Cirta after an arduous desert campaign. Massinissa now rewarded himself with Syphax's lands – and Syphax's wife. The appalled Laelius immediately ordered Massinissa to give Sophonisba into Roman power before she succeeded in undermining his allegiance. Massinissa had already weakened to the point where he offered Sophonisba the choice of surrendering or taking poison. Sophonisba drank the poison without hesitation. Laelius and Massinissa both took part in the Battle of Zama in 202 BC, fighting in the cavalry which led the decisive charge into Hannibal's reserves. Zama was the last battle of the war, and it was Laelius who brought to Rome news of final victory in the city's long struggle with Hannibal.

Later, Laelius' memories and anecdotes of these years were immortalized by his friend Polybius who mined the old general's experiences for inclusion in his history. But after the war Laelius' influence waned, as did the star of his patron Scipio. From early in his career Scipio and his circle led the adoption of Hellenistic ways which was eventually to create the fused Greco-Roman civilization. However, in this and many political issues, Scipio was opposed by the stubborn and spiteful opposition of Cato the Elder and his adherents. It was probably their influence which saw Laelius fail at his first bid for the consulship (although he succeeded in 190 BC). It was also his political weakness which prevented him gaining a lucrative command in the wars in Asia Minor against Antiochus III, though he did travel east, both as a companion to Scipio's brother and later as an ambassador to King Perseus of Macedon. His last official posts were in Gaul. He served in Cisalpine Gaul as governor for two years, and as a delegate investigating gubernatorial wrongdoing in 171 BC. It is uncertain when he died.

Laelius had a son (also called Laelius) who in many ways followed in his father's footsteps. Like Laelius senior, he was close friends with a Scipio, and an enthusiast of Hellenism. The younger Laelius gained the nickname Laelius the Wise, perhaps because of his philosophical studies, but more probably because he drew back from forcing controversial land legislation through the Senate.

(Later Gaius Gracchus was to reintroduce very similar laws, and die for it.) Cicero's reflection *On Old Age* is sometimes called the *Laelius*, as Laelius (junior) is one of the major characters, though he probably would have refuted Cicero's assertion that his father was a close friend of Cato.

22 | SPURIUS LIGUSTINUS
Soldier who worked his way up the ranks

Citizens of Rome. I am Spurius Ligustinus, of the Tribe
Crustumina, and I come of Sabine stock. My father left
me half an acre of land and the little hut in which I was
born and brought up. I am still living there today …
I have completed 22 years of service in the army, and
I am now over 50 years old.

Livy claims that the centurion Spurius Ligustinus was born *c.* 220 BC. In actual fact he was probably a fictional character, a composite figure created by Livy to personify changes that took place in the recruitment and structure of the Roman army in the period after the Second Punic War, when Roman power spread beyond Italy to east and west.

Service in the Republican Roman army was a part-time obligation for citizens, particularly the modest peasant farmers who owned enough land to equip themselves as heavy infantry, the core of the army. Rome's early wars were fought against neighbouring Italian peoples, and short terms of annual service were possible. However, the Second Punic War saw extended campaigns in Spain and Africa, and subsequent Roman intervention in the Hellenistic world led armies to Greece and beyond, where they served year-round. It was no longer possible for Roman soldiers to fight a brief summer campaign and then return to their farms for the harvest.

In 171 BC four legions were levied, two of which were to serve against the Macedonian king Perseus. But too many centurions (lower-ranking officers) responded to the call to arms – spurred on by the prospect of war-spoils – and they protested when they were placed in the ordinary ranks in the army. In a departure from normal procedure, one respected centurion, Spurius Ligustinus, was permitted to address the People's Assembly. He described how, from humble peasant origins, he was first recruited to serve in Macedonia in 200 BC. After two years' service he was promoted to junior centurion. He volunteered to serve again almost immediately, this time in Spain, and took another step up in the hierarchy of centurions. He details other campaigns in which he fought, in Greece against the Aetolians and the Seleucid king Antiochus III and, again, in Spain. As he gained in experience, he continued to receive promotion until he reached *primus pilus* (the highest ranking centurion in a legion). He was decorated for bravery 34 times (although he gives no details of his acts), and he received the Civic Crown six times, an oak leaf wreath awarded for saving the lives of fellow soldiers. Despite his advanced age in 171 BC, he declared his willingness to serve again in whatever capacity the people deemed fit, for the honour of defending the Republic and not for his own personal glory. After such a noble-minded speech, Spurius Ligustinus was of course given the position of chief centurion, and the other centurions accepted their demotion to the rank and file.

Spurius Ligustinus had served in all of Rome's most lucrative wars, had risen through the ranks and achieved renown, and had reaped the benefits of the spoils of war. His military career typifies (in exaggeratedly patriotic terms) the lives of many Roman men of the middle and late Republic who had become *de facto* career soldiers, and it illustrates the extent to which centurions were drawn from the ranks of experienced soldiers to become the backbone of the army.

23 | CORNELIA
Mother of the Gracchi

Cornelia was the epitome of a perfect Roman *materfamilias*. Noble by birth and character, she was respected by senators and kings, and adored by the common people of Rome. Her father was Scipio Africanus, the national hero who defeated Hannibal in the Second Punic War. For this reason alone she could expect to marry well, but the Cornelians were also one of the oldest clans in Rome, and currently in a period of political ascendancy. As a child of the Roman aristocracy, her marriage reflected her father's political needs more than her personal inclinations. Her older sister married a fellow Scipio called Nasica, a rigid conservative, so Cornelia's marriage embraced a different constituency in the person of Tiberius Sempronius Gracchus, a *populares*, or, as his enemies would have it, a demagogue. It is said that Scipio made the betrothal without consulting his wife, who was furious until she heard that Cornelia's spouse was to be Gracchus, the son-in-law she had been hoping for. Although Scipio and Gracchus collaborated politically, some historians relate that personal relations between the two were frosty. Gracchus, however, was a dutiful and loving husband. He and Cornelia had 13 children, and legend said that Gracchus died by sacrificing himself for Cornelia. The story was that two snakes were discovered in the children's room. A soothsayer told Gracchus that killing both snakes would destroy the whole family, as would allowing both snakes to escape. If the female snake were killed, Cornelia would die, but Gracchus himself would perish if the male snake was killed. Gracchus killed the male snake, and died soon afterwards.

Roman aristocratic girls often married as soon as they were *viripotens* (capable of intercourse). So a girl in her early teens could wed a man 25 or more years her senior, making widowhood highly probable even without an ophidian curse. Roman demographics were as lethal with young children as with elderly husbands – all but three of Cornelia's children died, leaving her with Tiberius, her eldest son, his brother Gaius, and a daughter, Sempronia. Rejecting offers of remarriage, including one from the ruler of Egypt, Ptolemy, Cornelia threw herself into her children's education. Herself the daughter of a philhellene, she spoke fluent Greek, and her Latin diction was superb. Her letters survived until the time of Cicero, who comments favourably on them. To the mother's formidable abilities were added the oratorical tuition of Diophorus of Mytilene and the philosophical talents of Blossius of Cumae, whom Cornelia engaged as tutors. None doubted that Cornelia's offspring were destined for greatness, least of all Cornelia, who repeatedly reminded her children that she should be remembered not as Cornelia, daughter of Scipio, but as Cornelia, mother of the Gracchi.

Tiberius Gracchus started promisingly. Under the command of his relative, Publius Cornelius Scipio Aemilianus, Tiberius was the first man over the walls of Carthage when the Punic wars resumed in 149 BC. Aemilianus himself married Sempronia, and was to give invaluable help to the family. Tiberius was fighting in Spain, a place where his father had campaigned with great distinction. At this point, however, the Roman army was trapped and facing extinction until Tiberius negotiated a truce. Instead of praising him for saving the army, however, the Senate arrogantly rejected the treaty, and if Scipio Aemilianus had not lent his support Tiberius would have been impeached as well. In 133 BC, an avenging army under Scipio wiped out the Spanish. In Rome, a politically wounded and bitter Tiberius was elected Tribune of the Plebs.

As the official champions of the common people, tribunes could both propose laws and stop them being passed. Tiberius proposed to reinvigorate Rome's army and peasant stock by giving them land – land which, perhaps not coincidentally, many Roman aristocrats had illegally seized for themselves and which would instead end in the hands of Tiberius' supporters among the common people. The aristocrats, hardened political in-fighters, at once got another tribune to block the proposal. With typical Roman stubbornness Tiberius refused to back down and if one tribune was blocking his proposal, he in turn would block all other business of the Roman state. He finally broke the deadlock by controversially having the obstructing tribune deposed from office. His furious opponents claimed that Tiberius planned to become king of Rome. On the news that Tiberius planned to serve another year as tribune, his uncle Scipio Nasica led a lynch mob that fell on Tiberius' supporters and slew Tiberius himself. Aemilianus refused to condemn outright the murder of his brother-in-law, and when he died soon afterwards Cornelia's enemies alleged that she and Sempronia had conspired to poison him. How Cornelia felt about her son's tribunate is unknown, but she encouraged, or at least failed to prevent, Gaius from following in his brother's footsteps.

When Gaius became tribune in 124 BC, Cornelia persuaded him not to persecute the tribune who had opposed Tiberius, although other enemies were prosecuted or exiled. Mother and son remained close whilst Gaius passed a frenzy of legislation that helped change Roman governance from that of an Italian city-state to suzerain of a Mediterranean empire. Like Tiberius, Gaius rapidly alienated the Roman conservatives with his abrasive style, his support for the non-Roman people of Italy and his passing of powers from the Senate to the equestrians of Rome. Like his brother, Gaius refused to compromise with his aristocratic opponents, and was killed by the Senate amid scenes of civic chaos. Ultimately much of the Gracchan legacy survived, but the short-sighted selfishness of Rome's elite successfully blocked reforms that might have averted the Italian rebellion of 90 BC, and the senate's own eventual subjugation to the Caesars.

Having outlived both her sons, the grieving Cornelia withdrew from Rome. Her household in Misenum became a centre of learning and a beacon of Hellenic culture. She continued to be idolized by ordinary Romans, and in her old age was honoured by a statue commemorating her as she had wished – as mother of the Gracchi.

24 | RUTILIUS RUFUS
The perils of virtue

Rutilius Rufus was a rarity in his day, a virtuous man at a time when Roman moral standards were in virtual freefall. Born around 160 BC, Rufus learned his unflinching approach to public duty from the Stoic philosopher Panetius. Like most young Roman aristocrats he served in the army, seeing action with Scipio Aemilianus in the Spanish wars. Soon afterwards he married Livia, a daughter of the same aristocratic house that later gave a wife to the emperor Augustus. He was beaten in elections to the consulship of 115 BC despite his impeccable record and connections (his sister had married into the Cotta clan, another politically powerful family), probably because he was unable to match the underhand tactics of his opponent, the rascally and devious Aemilius Scaurus (who later managed to get himself elected as head of a committee investigating his own misconduct).

The final decade of the 2nd century BC saw Rufus back on campaign, this time in Africa. A fellow officer was the ambitious and demagogic Marius. Unsurprisingly, given their very different ethics and personalities, the two men developed a deep loathing for each other. Rufus' sentiments were strengthened when Marius succeeded in undermining his superior officer and took command of the war for himself (see pl. x). Rufus left Africa, and later stood again for consul, being elected in 106 BC. His year in office was spent undoing the damage of Rome's massive defeat by Germanic tribesmen at Arausio, a defeat which threatened the survival of Rome itself. Rufus realized that the army needed to be more flexible and more mobile to cope with fast-moving irregular troops such as the Numidians and Germans. Rufus made major changes to adapt the army to the new circumstances, improving its drill and reducing the baggage train, and had the dubious pleasure of seeing these changes built upon by his successor, and dubbed 'the Marian military reform'.

Rufus' next office was as legate in the Roman province of Asia. Officially subordinate to Mucius Scaevola, an old family friend, Rufus was left in sole charge after Scaevola had to return to Rome. Appalled by the greed and corruption of the Roman tax-gatherers in the province, Rufus firmly put a stop to their extortionate activities. However, these same tax-gatherers had powerful friends in Rome, and on his return Rufus was prosecuted – for extortion and corruption. A kangaroo court unhesitatingly found him guilty, and Rufus was exiled. He went to live in Smyrna (in modern-day Turkey), among the grateful people he was accused of exploiting, and whilst there he wrote a personal and highly influential history of his times.

Although an exile, Rufus was deeply respected, and was visited by every Roman of note who came to Asia. The blatant injustice of his condemnation thoroughly discredited the court system as it then stood, and also tarnished the reputation of Marius, who had gleefully backed the prosecution.

25 | SULLA
The Roman who conquered Rome

According to Plutarch, the Romans had equal contempt for those who lost inherited wealth and those who rose to wealth from poverty. Thus they doubly despised Lucius Cornelius Sulla, born of modest means but of an aristocratic family who became richer (said a contemporary) than was possible for an honest man. Sulla was certainly a renegade, a vindictive and violent conqueror, possibly a murderer, but also not a man who cared greatly what others thought of him. Both friends and foes could agree on the accuracy of the epitaph he left for himself, that no man was a better friend or worse enemy.

As a youth, Sulla lacked the means even to begin the *cursus honorum*, the ladder of offices leading to the pinnacle of power in

Rome. Instead he kept company with theatre folk and other riff-raff, a taste he retained throughout his life. However, his stepmother and his lover were fairly wealthy women, and after making the handsome golden-haired Sulla their heir, both conveniently died; leaving him sufficient funds to embark on a military career.

He became quaestor (an aide-de-camp with a particular responsibility for financial matters) to Marius, one of Rome's greatest generals. Marius was in his first consulship and had removed the property qualification for joining the legions, and built on other recent reforms. Sulla and Marius campaigned in Numidia against Jugurtha, a scheming and ambitious king whom Sulla was eventually able to capture by subverting one of Jugurtha's allies. Marius and Sulla received considerable kudos for bringing about the end of this difficult war, which had been dragging on for many years. Marius, however, became jealous of the fame of his subordinate, and tried to ensure he played little part in the wars against the Cimbri. The Cimbri were a large Germanic tribe, and Marius increased his fame yet further by preventing them from conquering north Italy, and indeed Rome itself. Sulla, meanwhile, had been furthering his reputation under the command of Lutatius Catulus, Marius' fellow consul, much to Marius' disgust. Tensions between the two men were only aggravated by the Social War of 90 BC, which followed almost immediately afterwards, when Rome's Italian allies rebelled against Roman hegemony. Sulla campaigned with great distinction, while the cautious Marius achieved little of note.

Taking advantage of Rome's distraction with war in Italy, the Pontic king Mithridates conquered much of Asia Minor, and even sent his forces into Greece. Sulla was chosen to march against him, igniting the frantic jealousy of Marius. Using his political connections, Marius engineered the annulment of Sulla's command amid riots that left one consul's son dead. Sulla fled to the army he had been gathering, and marched all eight legions against his own city 'to restore order'. Thus in 88 BC Rome was for the first time conquered by its own soldiers. Sulla's political enemies were put to the sword, and Marius fled for his life. Sulla then marched off to the Middle East, leaving his surviving enemies to regroup behind him. With the help of a grimly vindictive Marius these enemies retook Rome, instituted a reign of terror and declared Sulla an outlaw. Sulla, however, re-took Athens from the control of Mithridates (massacring most of the city's inhabitants) and thrashed a vastly larger Mithridatic army at Charonea in central Greece, despite not having the sanction of the Senate.

This forced Mithridates to the negotiating table, and peace was made. Mithridates agreed to give up his conquests and retire to his kingdom. Sulla was widely criticized for letting Mithridates off lightly, but Sulla's enemies back in Rome demanded his immediate attention. On his return to Italy Sulla was joined by Publius Licinus Crassus who shared Sulla's political views, and the opportunistic Gnaeus Pompey. Both men were to dominate Roman politics in the next generation. There was hard fighting in the surrounding countryside, but Sulla was victorious. Having re-conquered Rome, he declared himself dictator – the first in Rome for over a century. After several major massacres and individual random slayings, Sulla was prevailed upon to publish a list of his enemies so at least the rest of Rome could breathe peacefully. Like his march on Rome, these 'proscription lists' were later emulated by Sulla's successors, including the young Augustus Caesar. Augustus' adoptive father, Julius Caesar, narrowly escaped death by these proscription lists, Sulla only being persuaded to mercy by the pleading of numerous well-connected relatives.

As dictator, Sulla attempted to set the Republic to rights after the political storms of the previous 50 years. The depleted senate was increased to 600 members, and accession was regularized by making the quaestors elected each year into senators. This ensured a rough equality between the numbers entering the Senate and those senators who died in the course of each year. The conservative Sulla saw the tribunate as the route to power for demagogic rabble-rousers. Consequently he trimmed the powers of the office, and made the tribunate a political dead-end by barring its holders from further office. That done, Sulla stunned Rome by announcing that his work was complete, and in 80 BC he formally renounced the dictatorship. As he was consul for the next two years, he did not immediately become a private citizen. Whilst in office, Sulla had paid his debt to his men by seeing them discharged and rewarded with land in Italy, and his contentment was completed when his wife gave birth to twins. Oddly enough Sulla, who had regarded his life as ruled by chance (he called himself 'Sulla the fortunate'), saw his felicity as a sign of doom, for it had been prophesied that he would die at the moment when he was at the peak of power and fortune. Sure enough, he had barely time to put his affairs in order before he perished – the plague was affecting Rome at this time and he may have been a victim.

The day of Sulla's funeral was gloomy, but when his pyre was lit, a great wind blew it to incandescent heat, and the rain held off until Sulla's ashes had been collected and interred. In death as in life, fortune did not abandon her favourite.

26 | STABERIUS EROS

Schoolteacher

The early part of the 1st century BC saw Rome increasingly engaging with the Greek east, and slowly merging Greek and Roman culture into a single entity. One of the many catalysts of this process was a man called Lucius Staberius Eros. We first hear of him from the elder Pliny, who describes a ship which arrived from the east in 83 BC with an exceptional cargo of slaves. It is almost certain that the trader had specifically picked highly educated slaves, probably to meet the growing demand for such in Rome. One of these, Manilius, was to become famous as an astronomer and astrologer, and the writings of another, Publius Syrus, survive today. One of

Syrus' quotations, 'only the ignorant despise education', might be said to have reflected the views of a third member of the group – Lucius Staberius Eros.

It is not known if Staberius was a free man enslaved during the wars with the Pontic king Mithridates, or a *verna*, a slave from birth. He was certainly a man of considerable enterprise, for he carefully saved his *peculium* (the money allowed to slaves by their masters), and purchased himself with his own savings at a public sale. To do this, Staberius would have needed the consent of his master, but the biographer Suetonius says that he was allowed to do so 'because of his love for literature'. It is probable that this love was partly acquired through the tedious process of copying literary works by hand for his master's library. Fronto, a later scholar, says that Staberius is among those famous men who copied out the literary works of others.

Staberius now became a teacher of grammar. This was not a highly valued or well-paid occupation (despite their fame, some well-known grammarians died in extreme poverty), but Staberius was fortunate in attracting an elite clientele. When Sulla (no. 25) purged the Roman aristocracy of his enemies and confiscated their property, Staberius allowed the children of the proscribed to continue taking classes with him even though they now had no money. This was not only a financial sacrifice but a political risk, as Sulla had a decidedly terminal way with those he perceived as enemies. We know that Staberius survived at least long enough to teach Brutus and Cassius, the future assassins of Julius Caesar; indeed they might have first struck up their friendship in his classes. However, he thereafter disappears from the historical record.

27 | PASITELES
Roman sculptor

The end of the Social War in 90 BC marked a period when aristocratic Romans not only stocked their houses with plundered Greek art, but also turned to home-grown works. Rome was finally developing a native tradition in the fine arts. We know nothing of his background, but it is clear that Pasiteles was born around 100 BC in Magna Graecia (the general name for the Greek foundations, such as Naples, dotted about southern Italy). In 87 BC his community received Roman citizenship as part of the peace that ended the Social War, and soon afterwards the aspiring young artist moved to Rome.

Pasiteles had chosen well: there was now a flourishing market for sculpture. The rich wanted copies of famous pieces for their homes, and public figures wanted original statues in their new buildings. Pasiteles made works for the Temple of Juno in the Portico of Octavia, and the elder Pliny, a connoisseur, praised his ivory and gold statue of Zeus for a commission by the Roman aristocrat Metellus.

Not content to mimic the old masters, Pasiteles liked to model from life. He was once so absorbed in a caged lion that he failed to notice a panther had broken out of a nearby cage, and only narrowly escaped. Pasiteles loved to model in clay, which he called 'the mother of all sculpture', and unlike earlier artists who roughed out the clay model and did their finished work on the metal cast, Pasiteles tested every last detail in clay before committing himself. He also worked in gold, silver, bronze and marble. None of his works seem to have survived (although his name is on a statue base in Verona), but two of his pupils, Stephanos and Menelaos, proudly admit his influence on their extant works – now in the Villa Ludovisi, Rome.

Pasiteles found time to write in his later career, and listed the world's greatest works of art in a series of five books. Pliny called this 'a truly noble work', and almost certainly referred to it often. How and when Pasiteles died is not known.

Part 3

Life in Troubled Times

88 BC–AD 14

The ruined Republic gradually gave way to Rome under the military autocracy of the Caesars. The transition was a painful business, which at times plunged the state into near-anarchy, and there would be periods during the 1st century BC when it seemed as though Rome would be destroyed by its warring factions. From the time when Sulla (no. 25) led his legions against Rome in 88 BC, the state was constantly troubled by men such as Catiline (no. 31) who would follow his example, either to right what they considered to be the wrongs of society in their day, or simply for personal power and profit.

Between these attempted power-grabs by members of the Roman aristocracy, the Pontic king Mithridates VI briefly conquered Asia Minor and killed 80,000 Romans and Italians, and the rebel slave Spartacus pillaged Italy from end to end and back again. The rebel general Sertorius set up a rival government in Spain, and a Roman army was wiped out at Carrhae during a failed attempt to conquer the Parthian empire on Rome's eastern frontier. After this, the situation deteriorated.

This was an era of extreme violence, of a form not previously seen in Rome. During the Republic the Roman elite had fought their battles in the law courts, and the losers could expect exile at the worst. But conditions went sharply downhill in the final years of the Republic, when the battles became more literal, and the heads of the losers were displayed on spikes in the Forum. The Romans who had conquered their own state created 'proscription lists' of their enemies, men who could be killed with impunity, or even for reward. Often the 'crime' of these victims was simply that they possessed assets which the victorious generals needed to pay their troops or bribe the voters.

It was in such circumstances that the last generation of the Roman Republic grew up. Few of that generation were without relatives who had died violently in the troubles of the 80s BC, and this gave a lethal edge to the politics in the next generation. Cicero (no. 29), Brutus, Mark Antony, Cato the Younger, Pompey and Julius Caesar (no. 37) were among those who suffered violent ends, and all died victims of civil strife rather than at the hands of Rome's enemies. Yet these enemies were not quiescent. Even as civil war raged within, enemies such as Mithridates of Pontus assailed the state from without, while fleets of pirates roamed the seas, severely disrupting travel and maritime commerce. (The young Julius Caesar was among those captured and held to ransom by these pirates.)

The ordinary people of the empire suffered doubly – from the armies roaming their lands, from arbitrary confiscation and taxation, from venal governors such as Verres (no. 30) and by the rival dynasts as they gathered their resources for each new confrontation. It was weariness with this 'age of iron' (as the poet Horace (no. 38) described it) that made the people of the empire willing to embrace even a thinly disguised military dictatorship such as Caesar's if it meant peace, stability and an end to the constant political tumult of the ever-failing Republic.

Yet despite plots, rebellion and civil war, there were those who lived peacefully, and even prospered amid the chaos. Some, like Atticus (no. 35), stayed above the party infighting; others, like Tiro (no. 33), Cicero's slave, were beneath the notice of the mighty. Some, such as Agrippa (no. 40) or Nonius Balbus (no. 42), picked the right side, and were mightily rewarded for the risks that they had taken. Others, including the poet Horace, were caught within the maelstrom but emerged with their skins intact – if little else. And there were those, such as Cicero, who saw all that they had fought for go down in defeat, taking at the last even their lives. In its final years, the Republic was not a democracy, but a triumvirate ruled by three men: Mark Antony, Lepidus and Octavian, the heir of the assassinated Julius Caesar. Even this government lasted only as long as it took for one of the three – Octavian – to gather sufficient forces to destroy his rivals. Finally a new system emerged from the chaos, its development guided by the political genius of Augustus, as Octavian had become known (no. 39) – Rome's first emperor.

The return of peace yielded an unexpected dividend in the flowering of the literary arts during the reign of Augustus. The poets Ovid, Livy (no. 43) and Horace were not only contemporaries, but also knew each other personally. Their combined output, together with the work of almost a score of minor writers, has formed a body of literature known today as Latin's Golden Age.

One of the most interesting aspects of the collapse of the Roman Republic is the extraordinary loyalty of the provinces. For most of Rome's conquests, the issue was not whether they should make a break for independence or remain loyal to Rome, but which of the contending bits of Rome they should be loyal to. Despite the prevailing chaos, the Roman system of government had already put down deep and enduring roots. Already the city of the seven hills was evolving into a state in which being a Roman indicated not one's city of residence, but belonging to a particular social and legal system. Certainly many 'Romans' lived and died without ever setting eyes upon Rome, the city of which they were officially citizens.

28 | HORTENSIUS
King of the courts

Like his contemporary Atticus (no. 35), Quintus Hortensius Hortalus lived peacefully through the chaos of the late Roman Republic and died wealthy and respected. In fact, Hortensius proudly boasted that in an age of civil strife, he had never taken up arms against a fellow citizen. The chosen battlefield of Hortensius was the courtroom, and he was quite prepared to manipulate the truth when it suited the interests of his sometimes highly disreputable clients.

Hortensius was born in 114 BC to an ancient plebeian line of native Romans. His father was that rarest of creatures, an honest provincial governor, and his mother was of the line of Cornelia, mother of the Gracchi (no. 23). When the Social War of 90 BC broke out, Hortensius joined the army and served two campaigns. This interrupted an already promising legal career which had brought him to the notice of the leading orators of the day, and that included the exiled king of Bithynia as a client. However, Hortensius was neither so distinguished nor identified with a particular political faction as to become a victim of the chaos which followed the Social War.

As an aristocrat with excellent connections, Hortensius rose smoothly up the political ladder once the Sullans were firmly in command. Their conservative, pro-aristocratic policies (which the Romans called 'optimate') suited young Hortensius, and thereafter he was closely identified with this group. He maintained the family reputation for honesty as a quaestor in 81 BC, and was aedile in 75 BC. His flourishing legal practice paid for spectacular games staged for the Roman public, who responded by making him *praetor urbanus* in 72 BC. In 69 BC he was consul.

This political success was directly linked to success in the courts. As a lawyer, Hortensius was helped by an excellent memory and so splendid a courtroom presence that actors would attend court to take notes of his style. His speeches would today seem florid and pretentious, yet were delivered in a soft mellifluous voice which almost hypnotized jurors. Victory followed victory. An early client in 86 BC was young Pompey, charged with looting. He was acquitted – partly because he married the presiding judge's daughter. Apparently Hortensius was not above doing whatever it took for an acquittal. Cicero remarked on his technique in bribing jurors, who were given a special ballot to ensure that they voted as they had been paid to. His foppish dress and extravagant hand gestures while pleading gave Hortensius the nickname of 'Dionysia' – a notorious contemporary dancing girl.

Hortensius' most profitable clients were those accused of pillaging the provinces they governed for personal gain. Hortensius usually argued before a sympathetic audience, as Sulla had given control of the juries to the Senate, and plundering a province was most senators' greatest aspiration of achievement. He had no scruples in taking massive fees, which paid for a house on the Palatine Hill (later the home of Augustus) and two luxurious country villas.

Perhaps the turning point of Hortensius' career came when he and Cicero clashed in 70 BC, an exchange in which Hortensius was so overwhelmed that his client, the rapacious Verres (no. 30), fled without even awaiting the verdict. It did not help that Pompey had recently pushed through a law abolishing the senatorial monopoly on jury places. This made Hortensius oppose Pompey politically, a sentiment probably reinforced by Cicero's support of Pompey.

However, after his consulship of 63 BC, Cicero found himself increasingly sympathetic to the optimate viewpoint, and consequently was often on the same side as Hortensius in court. Murena, Sulla (son of the dictator) and one Rabirius were among the pair's famous clients. Although Cicero started referring to him as '*noster* [our] Hortensius', Cicero never quite trusted his colleague, and when he was exiled Cicero felt Hortensius, spurred by professional jealousy, was conspiring against his return.

The opposite was true. Hortensius disliked the triumvirate of Caesar, Crassus and Pompey and saw Cicero as a natural ally.

However, when he saw the direction political life was taking, he abandoned it altogether, and dedicated himself to leisure and the arts. He was an annalist of some distinction, and wrote elegantly indecent erotica. He collected fine wines and paid outrageous sums for works of art which appealed to him. As his nickname 'Hortalus' suggests, he was a keen horticulturist who also made pets of the fish he kept in massive fishponds.

He died of unknown causes in 50 BC. On Hortensius' first wife's death Cato had divorced his wife, Marcia, to secure a family alliance by marrying her to Hortensius, his fellow optimate. On Hortensius' death Cato remarried Marcia. Hortensius' daughter took up the family tradition of oratory and in 42 BC successfully opposed a tax on wealthy matrons. The male line of Hortensius was less successful. Oafish and degenerate, they were living in destitution at the time of the emperor Tiberius.

29 | CICERO
Rome's greatest orator

Cicero is something of a conundrum – his relentless self-promotion, his bombastic egoism and his ability to fall to self-pitying pieces in a crisis are as unappealing today as they were to Cicero's contemporaries two millennia ago. Yet Cicero seldom boasts of his oratory, although he was the greatest of Latin orators, and when he was caught in a crisis Cicero proved that courage is indeed 'grace under pressure'.

Cicero, the man who became pater patriae, the father of his country, was not born into the Roman aristocracy. He was from Arpinum, the home of Marius, another outsider who deeply influenced Roman politics. All we know of Cicero's mother is that she gave birth to him – the first of two sons – on 3 January 106 BC. Encouraged by their early promise, the father took his children to

Rome where he had political connections. Cicero did not stay long in the city, for we know he travelled to Greece as part of his education, yet was back to serve in the army during the Social War of 90 BC. 'I was there, a raw recruit', he commented later of a meeting between an enemy commander and his general, Pompeius Strabo.

The war over, Cicero came under the influence of the two great jurists of the day, the brothers Scaevola, and took to pleading cases. In his second major case, he defended Roscius of Ameria on a charge of parricide. Cicero successfully argued that his client was being framed by a henchman of Sulla who wanted Roscius' property. Boldly exposing corruption in Sulla's regime was not a particularly healthy activity, and Cicero decided to abandon Rome for Athens to 'continue his studies'.

Sulla died in 78 BC, and a year later, Cicero was back, climbing Rome's political ladder. He married the wealthy and aristocratic Terentia, and soon afterwards became quaestor (the most junior rank of magistrate). In 75 BC he served in Sicily and helped to ease a shortage of corn in Rome. He extracted corn from the islanders with such skill that they afterwards gave him a vote of thanks. But this success hardly registered with the Roman voters, and Cicero vowed thenceforth to remain in the public eye in the city. However, Cicero's friends in Sicily remembered him for his deft handling of the corn levy, and in 70 BC asked him to prosecute Verres (no. 30), a venal ex-governor of the island. Cicero argued his case so devastatingly that Verres went into exile without even waiting for the decision – a victory that immediately propelled Cicero to the top ranks of Roman advocates.

In 66 BC Cicero threw his political support as praetor behind Pompey the Great, the son of his old commander Pompeius. For the rest of Pompey's life Cicero was a loyal supporter, though his support was not always reciprocated. Cicero needed allies to make real his intention to become the first of his family to become a consul of Rome. At this time the consulship was almost the property of a small group of aristocrats, and no *novus homo* ('new man') had been elected for a generation. Cicero stood against the ambitious and decadent Catiline (no. 31), who was desperate for high office to clear his debts. Cicero showed the depth of Catiline's desperation when agents he had planted in Catiline's entourage uncovered his plot to overthrow the government. Catiline fled Rome, and Cicero had those conspirators arrested in the city put to death without trial. This execution was on his own authority and the legally dubious *senatus consultum ultimum*, a decree by which the senate ordered that the state should come to no harm.

Following this success, his inflated self-importance caused Cicero needlessly to antagonize the politically powerful and well-connected Clodius. In 58 BC Clodius responded by charging Cicero with illegally killing Roman citizens. Without attempting a defence, Cicero fled into exile. Being no stoic, Cicero wrote tearfully to his friend Atticus (no. 35), 'No one has ever had such misfortune as I, or had more right to wish for death… I would write more often if grief had not made me witless.' Given his performance at this time, it is perhaps unremarkable that his marriage broke down, and he and his wife Terentia divorced. (The single life clearly suited Terentia, as she died at the age of 103.)

His exile was brief, but Cicero returned to a Rome under the power of the Triumvirate of Caesar, Crassus and Pompey. His attempt to re-establish himself as a political force was sharply curbed by Rome's new masters, who forced him to use his oratory to defend their political protégés. In public, Cicero put a brave face on developments, but his private letters show his vituperative despair. He virtually abandoned politics and turned to study and philosophy while his beloved Republic crumbled about him. His appointment to the governorship of Cilicia he took not as an honour but as a second exile (he had been far more flattered when he joined the priestly College of Augurs in 53 BC). Nevertheless, his urge for self-promotion made Cicero elevate the storming of a barbarian stronghold into something worthy of a triumph in Rome. Rome was not interested, as Caesar had crossed the Rubicon and the civil war had begun. After a long prevarication, Cicero backed Pompey, though his bitter jokes about the conduct of the war suggests that the shipwreck of the Republican cause came as no surprise to him.

Caesar pardoned Cicero, as Cicero's son-in-law was one of Caesar's henchmen. However, Cicero's beloved daughter, Tullia, was first divorced, and later died in 45 BC, plunging Cicero into another orgy of grief. He was roused from this by Caesar's assassination in 44 BC, an event he greeted with delight. He threw himself back into politics, and became the principal foe of Mark Antony, Caesar's former second-in-command. Like Catiline, Antony was driven from Rome by Cicero's rhetoric. Unlike Catiline, Antony had friends outside Rome, and returned with an army of Caesar's veterans. Octavian, Caesar's adopted son and Cicero's protégé (later to be known as Augustus) promptly went over to the enemy, taking the Republic's last army with him. Cicero's death was the price that Mark Antony demanded for Octavian's admission to the alliance, and Octavian reluctantly agreed. Cicero fled, but his heart was not in it. Cornered by his pursuers in 43 BC at one of his villas by the coast, he faced his killers with dignity. Antony vindictively despoiled the corpse, but Cicero's inventive vilification of Antony's character has long survived this petty revenge.

30 | VERRES
Rapacious governor of Sicily

Gaius Verres was the most notorious of Roman magistrates, infamous for his greed and corruption, his career highlighting the extent of official misconduct in Rome's provinces.

Born around 115 BC he enjoyed a dissolute youth, indulging in drunken orgies and gambling, until in 84 BC he began his political, and criminal, career as quaestor to the proconsul Gnaeus Papirius Carbo. Verres accompanied Carbo to Cisalpine Gaul in 83 BC, their mission to raise troops to fight Sulla. Instead Verres embezzled the public funds that he was supposed to administer and deserted to Sulla, who pardoned his crime and rewarded him with property in Beneventum.

In 81 BC Verres was appointed acting quaestor to Gnaeus Dolabella in Cilicia. En route to Asia he plundered the cities he passed, notably stealing gold from the temple of Minerva in Athens, and taking ancient statues from the sanctuary of Apollo on Delos. Similar crimes followed his arrival in Cilicia, apparently with Dolabella's collusion. Word of their appropriations reached Rome and Dolabella was put on trial. In a remarkable act of betrayal, Verres took the stand against him, and Dolabella was convicted, while Verres himself was pardoned and used his ill-gotten gains to purchase the urban praetorship of 74 BC. He used this office to extort money and possessions from Roman citizens, and to bully and abuse them. At the end of his year in office he was given the province of Sicily to govern, a post that marks the spectacular climax of his criminal career.

The catalogue of his petty thefts is endless; he stole works of art by famous Greek artists, and silver vessels and furniture. He raged against those who attempted to thwart him. When a man named Diodorus fled Sicily rather than lose his fine chased silver, Cicero tells how 'Verres… was so thoroughly upset that everyone felt sure he had taken complete leave of his senses. Because he could not himself rob Diodorus of his silver, he talked of himself as "robbed of those lovely vessels", threatened the absent Diodorus, uttered open cries of rage, and now and then even shed tears.' He then prosecuted Diodorus in his absence on a capital charge. The story spread to Rome, prompting Verres' own father, an undistinguished senator, to write to him in anger – leading to a temporary cessation of his crimes.

Verres' activities were not limited to robbery. He used the slave revolt of Spartacus (73–71 BC) to extort money; slaves were falsely accused of plotting rebellion, convicted and ransomed back to their owners. Verres used a famine at Rome in 75 BC as an excuse to demand greater tithes from the Sicilian farmers, with the result that a large number were impoverished and forced to abandon their farms or even flee the island. Many went to Rome where they appealed for action against Verres' tyrannies.

The Sicilians turned to Cicero (no. 29) because, as quaestor in Sicily in 75 BC, he had gained a reputation for fairness. After three years in Sicily, Verres returned to Rome in 70 BC to face Cicero's prosecution. He expected to be acquitted – he had powerful friends, such as the orator Hortensius (no. 28) – and, it is claimed, perhaps spuriously, that he had boasted of setting aside the illegal profits of one year in order to bribe the court (senatorial juries were notoriously corruptible). To make his acquittal even more of a certainty, attempts were made to delay the trial until 69 BC when Hortensius would be consul. Cicero frustrated these ploys: 'I accuse Gaius Verres of committing many acts of lechery and brutality against the citizens and allies of Rome, and many crimes against god and man. I claim that he has illegally taken from Sicily sums amounting to 40 million sesterces.' In the face of such invective, Verres abandoned his defence and fled to Massilia (modern Marseille).

Verres was condemned in his absence by a senatorial jury cowed by the prospect of judicial reform, and under pressure from the crowds of spectators (including deputations from Verres' victims) who had gathered to hear the judgment. His exile was confirmed and his possessions were ordered to be sold to repay the Sicilian people. He had, however, managed to take much of his wealth with him, and he lived in comfortable exile until his death in 43 BC. Pliny the Elder records that 'Verres, whose conviction Marcus Cicero had procured, was … proscribed by Antony for no other reason than because he had refused to give up to Antony some pieces of Corinthian ware.' A fitting end, perhaps.

31 | CATILINE
Decadent revolutionary

The family of Catiline was ancient but never at the forefront of Roman affairs, and from the 3rd century BC it had slowly sunk into obscurity. Sergius Catiline was determined to reverse this trend. He had as his example Cornelius Sulla (no. 25), who had risen from similar obscurity to become master of Rome. Catiline was born in the last decades of the 2nd century BC, and in his youth was a zealous Sullan partisan. He is described by the historian Sallust (no. 32) as good-looking but somewhat gaunt, capable of incredible stamina and able to go for prolonged periods without food or sleep. His character was, by universal agreement, vicious and decadent. He was ferociously cruel, yet when it suited him he could be charming and courteous.

Even among the brutality of the Sullan purges, Catiline stood out. His brother-in-law was related to Sulla's political rivals, so he personally killed the man – slowly and painfully – then paraded through the city with the man's severed head. His promiscuous love life also attracted attention, not least his alleged affair with Fabia, a Vestal Virgin and sister-in-law of the politician Cicero (no. 29), a man who would later become first his bitter rival and then his mortal enemy.

Yet for Catiline a decadent lifestyle was no bar to public office. We next hear of him as a praetor, presumably elected through the influence of Sulla's supporters. It required a massive financial war-chest to reach the upper magistracies of Rome, and Catiline is believed to have borrowed heavily. After his year in office, he went to Africa. As governor, he apparently arrived in a rich province as a poor man, and left an impoverished province as a very rich man. So alleged the indignant Africans, who followed the unscrupulous Catiline back to Rome, and used Sulla's own legislation to demand their money back through the courts.

The case dragged on through 65 and 64 BC. As an accused man, Catiline was unable to stand for the consulship. His evident frustration at this situation led to rumours that he planned a coup with two wild young noblemen, Piso and Autronius. If so, the plot came to nothing, and eventually a friendly prosecutor, Publius Clodius, was persuaded to make the African case go away. Catiline married the heiress Aurelia Orestilla, 'about whom decent men could commend only her beauty', Sallust remarks somewhat snidely.

Free to stand for election in 63 BC, Catiline was infuriated by his defeat to Cicero, a *novus homo* whose family had never previously held the consulship. The two men became open enemies, and Cicero quickly found a spy in the enemy camp. One of Catiline's closest accomplices had a lover named Fulvia, who was sufficiently intrigued by his boasts of imminent wealth to enquire where it would come from, and was so appalled by the answer that she went to the authorities. It appeared that Catiline was conspiring with Sulla's disaffected veteran soldiers, and stashing arms in secret depots around the country.

Cicero excoriated Catiline in a series of speeches, laying bare his rival's decadent lifestyle and illicit political ambition. Yet Catiline also had his supporters (among whom, it was rumoured, was an old Sullan partisan, the millionaire Licinius Crassus, and a young, extravagant and near-bankrupt demagogue called Julius Caesar). Accordingly Catiline again presented himself for election in 62 BC and, partly through Cicero's efforts, was again defeated. With his financial reserves running out, and Cicero hounding him in the senate, Catiline was cornered and desperate. He left Rome, allegedly planning to go into exile. However, he tried to gain the support of a Gallic tribe which had sent envoys to Rome to protest against Roman misgovernment. Instead the envoys gave Cicero letters from Catiline's supporters that showed that Catiline was plotting revolution and seeking allies.

Tension ran high in Rome. Cicero arrested Catiline's allies in the city, and had them put to death without trial, though these included sons of the highest nobility. In response, Catiline unilaterally awarded himself the consular honours he had never achieved. This was illegal, but legality hardly mattered as Catiline went into open revolt at the same time. In early 62 BC the rebel forces were caught between two consular armies, and Catiline died fighting. His body was eventually found under a pile of dead enemies still showing 'the indomitable spirit which had animated him in life'. Catiline had been contained, but the fact that his cause had found support from so many different levels of Roman society showed how divided and deeply dysfunctional the Roman state had become. Revolution had been postponed, rather than quashed.

32 | SALLUST
Disappointed demagogue

Gaius Sallustius Crispus was born in 86 BC in Amiternum (modern Aquila) in the Sabine lands of central Italy. Despite his fervent desire to play his part in the political machinations of times in which he lived, his career was a disappointment. He retired from politics and devoted himself to writing history, where he proved to have a much greater talent.

Nothing is known of Sallust's family, though we can assume that they were members of the local aristocracy. Nor is it known whether Sallust himself grew up in Amiternum during the tumultuous 70s and 60s BC. It is known, however, that he was the first of his family to embark on a political career at Rome: 'My earliest inclinations led me, like many other young men, to throw myself wholeheartedly into politics.' He became Tribune of the Plebs in 52 BC.

Politics in this period were corrupt and openly violent, and Sallust plunged headfirst into the fray. He was among three tribunes who prosecuted Milo, the leader of well-organized gangs of thugs, for the murder of Clodius (a rival demagogue), and took the opportunity to attack Cicero (no. 29) for also defending Milo. The tribunes themselves were immune from prosecution while in office, but at the end of their term Cicero took his revenge. Sallust's two colleagues were prosecuted. Strangely, Sallust escaped this fate – possibly due to the protection of Julius Caesar (no. 37). His political enemies appear to have bided their time, and may have been behind Sallust's later expulsion from the Senate in 50 BC. Cassius Dio records the event, but gives no explanation for it. In later years stories of immorality became attached to the expulsion. In particular it was claimed – without a scrap of evidence – that Sallust had been caught in adultery with Milo's wife, beaten up and forced to pay to be released.

Sallust turned to Caesar. From 49 to 45 BC he fought for Caesar in the civil wars. He revealed a talent for organization when put in charge of supplies during Caesar's African campaign, and received as his reward the governorship of the newly created province of Africa Nova. He used his office to plunder the province. Although this was the usual practice of Roman administrators in the provinces, Sallust went rather too far: 'This officer took many bribes and confiscated much property, so that he was not only accused but incurred the deepest disgrace.' On his return to Rome he faced charges, but they were hushed up by Caesar, possibly in return for a massive bribe.

Sallust's political career had ended in infamy, though he claimed it was his choice to retire. He had been led astray by the 'prevailing corruption' and after 'suffering manifold perils and hardships, peace of mind at last returned to me, and I decided that I must bid farewell to politics for good'. He was about 40 years old. Turning to history for solace, he wrote with bitterness, adopting a much-criticized and somewhat hypocritical moralizing tone. He had strong views about politics and politicians, and his readers are left in no doubt what they are. His first work was *The Conspiracy of Catiline*, which he himself had witnessed (no. 31). This was followed by *The Jugurthine War*, an account of Rome's campaigns in Africa in the years before Sallust's birth and in his eyes the start of a chain of events that would lead to the civil wars of his day, 'because it was at this time that the first challenge was offered to the arrogance of the Roman nobles'. Thereafter followed the *Histories*, a year-by-year account of Roman history starting in 78 BC (only 12 years were completed). These works were written over a period of about seven years and broken off at Sallust's death in 35 BC. They have a common theme – the decline and fall of the Roman Republic. Often criticized for omissions, inaccuracy and idealism, Sallust's works were recognized in antiquity as a great literary achievement though their historical value has been debated ever since.

There is no evidence that Sallust ever married, and he died without children. His sister's grandson inherited his name and his estates – including the '*Horti Sallustiani*' in Rome, which he developed into a magnificent palace and gardens. The younger Sallust achieved the political success that his great-uncle had once aspired to, becoming a confidant of Augustus (no. 39). But it is the historian whom posterity remembers.

33 | TIRO
Cicero's slave and amanuensis

Historians chronicling the fall of the Roman Republic owe a huge debt to Tiro, the former slave who neatly tabulated and documented the papers of his master and patron, Cicero, and so gave us a detailed – sometimes day-to-day – report of one of the crucial periods in world history.

It is uncertain when Tiro was born – some reports suggest around 103 BC, but there are indications it could have been up to 20 years later. He first makes his appearance in the historical record as part of the household of Cicero in Rome, a household into which he may well have been born as a slave. He became Cicero's right-hand man, handling his correspondence, social life and everyday affairs.

He was highly literate, and fondly regarded by the whole family. Cicero's brother Quintus once joked that even Cicero would not be able to justify Tiro's laxity in not writing to him more often: 'you will have to call Marcus [Cicero] to your aid, and… though he should compose a speech after long study and a great expenditure of midnight oil, don't be too sure of being found innocent.' While he was away Cicero himself wrote to Tiro sympathizing about the bouts of poor health to which his slave was prone.

After receiving his freedom in 53 BC Tiro continued to work for Cicero, and went with him to Cilicia when Cicero was made governor there in 51 BC. After Cicero was killed on the orders of Mark Antony, Tiro became his literary executor, preparing the great man's speeches, philosophical works and letters for posterity. Medieval authorities believed that Tiro invented the form of shorthand that bears his name (Tironean notation), and though modern historians are more sceptical, Cicero's household were definitely innovators in the development of speedwriting.

Tiro wrote on his own behalf, as we have references by other writers to his work on grammar and a biography of Cicero to which Plutarch referred. Tiro retired to a small estate that he had purchased near Puteoli, and there seems to have lived out the remainder of his long and happy life, dying, according to various authorities (including St Jerome) at some time around his 100th birthday.

34 | CLODIA
Aristocrat and wild child

If Cicero (no. 29), our only available source, is to be believed, Clodia Metelli was beautiful and imperious, and wielded far more influence in politics than a good Roman woman ought to. Thanks to his histrionics, Clodia is often considered to be the promiscuous wild child of Rome, ultimately deserving of her public vilification in court.

1 Fourth-century mosaic of a Roman house on a lake.

11 The Roman Empire at its greatest extent in AD 200.

III Actors, from a mosaic now in the Sousse Museum, Tunisia. Roman actors wore masks on stage, each representing a stock figure in comedy, farce or tragedy. This helped the audience immediately to identify the protagonists in any particular production.

IV Mosaic of a chariot race. This dramatic and often violent sport was a Roman obsession, from the regal period to the very last days of the empire. Here the lightness of the chariot and lack of protection for the charioteer can be clearly seen. Crashes were frequent and sometimes fatal, but a top charioteer could become very wealthy.

∨ Statue of Augustus as a Roman general. This famous statue was found at the Villa of Livia at the Prima Porta and the cuirass depicts a major triumph of Augustan diplomacy, when the Parthians returned to Rome the standards lost at the Battle of Carrhae. The Cupid at Augustus' leg is a reference to his alleged descent from Venus.

VI This painting by Juan Antonio Ribera y Fernandez (*c.* 1806) depicts the moment when Cincinnatus was called from the plough by a delegation of the Senate.

VII A master physically chastizing his slave. The master wears a toga, indicating that he is a Roman citizen, while the slave makes no attempt to defend himself, knowing that this could invite further punishment, perhaps even death.

VIII A scene of masked comic actors, found in the House of Casca Longus at Pompeii. A girl looks on in horror and is held by a youth, while an old slave makes the sign of the horns to avert evil.

IX Classical-imitation mosaic of Archimedes, Marcellus' ingenious opponent at Syracuse, about to meet his death. His inventions had stymied the Roman siege for two years, but Marcellus regretted his killing.

x The triumph of Marius – an occasion which must have grated with Rutilius Rufus, who did much to create the conditions that brought it about. A captive Jugurtha stands defiant in his chains before the conqueror's chariot, while the inscription (top) quotes lines on the occasion by the historian Florus. The artist, Tiepolo, has included his own portrait among the admiring throng.

Clodia was the elder sister of one of Cicero's most dangerous enemies, Publius Clodius Pulcher. Hers was an old and powerful patrician family – the Claudii; but, in a political move, both brother and sister had renounced their patrician rank and adopted the more popular forms of their names. The second part of Clodia's name, Metelli ('of Metellus'), distinguished her from her two sisters who, in Roman fashion, were also called Clodia. It referred to her marriage to Quintus Metellus Celer, consul of 60 BC. The marriage does not seem to have been a happy one. Metellus opposed Clodius' attempt to become Tribune of the Plebs, and Clodia chose to side with her brother instead of her husband. She became one of her brother's inner circle of advisors after her husband's death in 59 BC, yet she was not above passing on information about her brother's activities to Cicero via their common friend Atticus (no. 35). Her motives for doing this are unknown, but she was clearly playing her own game.

Clodia chose not to remarry after Metellus' death. She was wealthy and capable of looking after her own affairs, as she was already known as an astute businesswoman. She owned several houses in and around Rome, and probably a villa in the Campanian holiday resort of Baiae. With a wide circle of friends, she was one of Rome's leading socialites and enjoyed a luxurious lifestyle.

Some time after 59 BC she is alleged to have had an affair with the politically ambitious Marcus Caelius Rufus, who had rented a house near hers on the Palatine Hill. The affair was clearly over by 56 BC – Caelius was brought to trial by Lucius Sempronius Atratinus, and Clodia appeared as a witness for the prosecution. The precise charges against Caelius are unclear, but appear mainly to relate to the murder of an Alexandrian diplomat called Dio. Added to this, however, were accusations that he had stolen gold from Clodia and had tried to poison her.

Caelius engaged Cicero, who was inspired in his defence. Virtually ignoring the charges against Caelius he shifted the focus to Clodia. Caelius' lax morals were excusable because he was young (the young should be allowed some leeway, after all) and he had been enticed by Clodia, an older woman; he had not attempted to poison Clodia, but she had probably poisoned her husband; she was in effect a high-class prostitute, leader of Rome's decadents and she was undoubtedly sleeping with her brother. Indeed, from Baiae came 'the report that there is one woman so deeply sunk in her vicious depravities that she no longer bothers to seek privacy and darkness and the usual veil of discretion to cover her lusts. On the contrary, she actually exults in displaying the most foully lecherous goings on amid the widest publicity and in the glaring light of day.' Cicero could not have been more successful. By playing on hostile Roman stereotypes of 'bad' women he destroyed Clodia's credibility. Caelius was acquitted and Clodia's name was blackened.

But the story does not end here. In his speech defending Caelius, Cicero referred to Clodia as a poet. Clearly she was educated and cultured, and it appears she wrote verse too. Another poet was at work in this period. Catullus, who is famed for his racy love poetry, wrote a series of poems charting his affair with a girl named Lesbia from its start to its bitter end. She is adulterous, promiscuous and cruel, and his portrayal of her is increasingly vulgar and venomous.

> Caelius, my Lesbia, that Lesbia,
> that Lesbia whom alone Catullus
> loved more than himself and all his own people,
> now in the crossroads and back alleys
> she peels the grandsons of great-hearted Remus.

In the 2nd century AD Apuleius identified Lesbia as a 'Claudia', from which the jump has been easily – and frequently – made to Clodia Metelli. Was Clodia really Lesbia? Modern scholarship argues against this today. But one thing is clear: the historical figure of Clodia has been coloured by the poetic construction of Lesbia. Cicero ruined her reputation in Rome; Catullus (and Apuleius) ruined it for posterity.

35 | ATTICUS
Friend to the powerful

The 77 years of Titus Pomponius Atticus' life almost exactly covered the most turbulent period of Roman history, beginning with the Germanic invasion of Italy (approximately 105 BC, five years after his birth) and finishing in 32 BC with the imperium of Augustus. Atticus lived in tranquillity through revolutions, plots, civil wars, assassinations and purges, despite the fact that he was closely associated with most of the protagonists. He was an equestrian, the rank of the Roman nobility below the Senate. His family had been so for generations, and Atticus determinedly remained one, though he was regularly invited to higher rank.

When Atticus was in his early twenties, his family relationship with the tribune Sulpicius and his personal friendship with the son of Marius meant that he was in danger of being associated with the Marian cause, at a time when the followers of Marius were locked in a bloody war with Sulla (no. 25). Since his father had died early and bequeathed him a modest fortune, Atticus decided to keep both fortune and person intact by selling up and leaving Rome for the relative tranquillity of Athens. While endearing himself to the Athenians by his generosity, Atticus avoided the bloodshed and purges of Rome's first civil war.

Sulla was so grateful to find a 'Marian' who was not against him that the two became personal friends when Sulla visited Athens. It helped that Atticus was an agreeable character, with a knack of forming friendships that were stronger than politics. He remained friends with his uncle, the notoriously difficult Caecilius, and subsequently became sole heir to his substantial fortune. It was about this time that Atticus realized the changeability of fortune in Roman affairs. He often used his wealth discreetly to assist those currently on the losing side, and reaped their gratitude when the political tide turned.

When the Sullans were firmly in control Atticus returned to Rome. He had been friends with Cicero since childhood, and his sister Pomponia married Cicero's brother Quintus. Consequently, when Cicero's political enemies forced him into exile, it was Atticus who gave Cicero financial and moral support. However, despite his friendship with the leading politicians of the day, Atticus never accepted favours or high office which would identify him as a member of one party or the other. He also kept his resources highly liquid, avoiding investment in large estates or other property which was easy to locate and seize.

Consequently, he remained equably in Rome during Caesar's invasion of Italy. Atticus made sure that he was seen to assist the Pompeians, but to such a limited extent that Caesar was deeply grateful for his inactivity. Likewise, he managed the difficult feat of remaining on good terms with Caesar's assassins Brutus and Cassius, and also with Caesar's heir, the young Octavian. Mark Antony was a special case, insofar as he and Cicero loathed each other so much that helping one was seen as direct hostility to the other. So when Cicero had Antony hounded from Rome, Atticus instead stood by Antony's wife, protecting her from vindictive lawsuits and attempts to seize her property. When Antony returned to Rome as a triumvir, he reciprocated by removing Atticus' name from the list of Cicero's friends to be proscribed. Atticus' unfailing political instinct kept him from becoming too close to Antony. Instead, Augustus' victory left Atticus so close to the centre of power that his daughter married Agrippa, Augustus' right-hand man. (And Vipsania, Atticus' granddaughter, married the emperor Tiberius.)

Despite his wealth, Atticus lived relatively modestly on the Quirinal Hill. His major expense was entertainment – no surprise in someone whose prosperity and tranquillity depended on his friendship with the powerful. The administrative skill which he so studiously declined to put at the disposal of the state was used in maintaining his wealth, and that of a number of rich and well-connected friends who put their affairs in his hands – another investment which paid dividends, both in securing political allies and because many of these Romans left substantial bequests to Atticus in their wills.

As a hobby Atticus traced the family trees of Roman aristocratic families. These and the annalistic records he compiled of treaties, battles and other major events in Roman history have not survived, but were almost certainly consulted by Roman historians such as Plutarch and Livy. Eventually, dying from what appears to have been bowel cancer, Atticus decided to make a dignified end by starving himself to death. His funeral was somewhat less modest than he planned as almost the entire aristocracy of Rome insisted on attending.

36 | SERVILIA
Caesar's lover, Brutus' mother

Few people reflect the tangled affairs – both personal and political – of the late Republican aristocracy better than Servilia, though she herself survived safely to old age and seems to have died peacefully. During this period members of the small group of Roman elite families tended to divorce and remarry often (one historian has called the practice 'serial polygamy'), so almost all of Rome's leading politicians were related in some way. This gave a family flavour to their bitter political struggles.

Servilia's family claimed to be older than Rome itself, being one of the aristocratic clans transplanted to Rome in the mid-7th century BC. Servilia was born around 100 BC. Her uncle was Livius Drusus, a highly influential tribune and an ancestor of Livia, the wife of Augustus. Servilia's mother was married to a Cato, and from this marriage came Servilia's half-brother, Marcus Porcius Cato, known to posterity as Cato the Younger. Servilia herself was born from a marriage to Quintus Servilius Caepio, once an ally and later an enemy of Drusus. This enmity caused a sensational divorce which led to young Servilia staying with her uncle until he was murdered in 90 BC.

As was the aristocratic custom, Servilia seems to have married young. She gave her husband, Marcus Junius Brutus, a son in 85 BC when still in her mid-teens. Her husband was killed during political troubles in 77 BC, by Pompey the Great's soldiers. Servilia then married Decimus Junius Silanus and had three daughters with him, named, thanks to the imaginative Roman naming system, Iunia(s) First, Second and Third.

Servilia's family were deeply involved in politics. Cato opposed Pompey, who was allied with Julius Caesar. This was unfortunate, as Servilia was Caesar's lover. During the debate on the Catiline conspiracy (no. 31), Caesar received a note which Cato claimed proved Caesar was corresponding with Catiline's supporters. Cato forced the note to be read aloud, only to find that it was from his half-sister suggesting a romantic meeting with Caesar after the debate. This romance had been of such duration that some suspected Caesar of having fathered Marcus Brutus, Servilia's son. This is generally discounted on the grounds that Caesar would only have been 15 at the time, but then, so was Servilia.

Caesar's victory in the civil war of 49 BC complicated Servilia's life yet more. Cato killed himself rather than accept Caesar's rule, whereupon her son made a point of marrying Cato's daughter. Brutus had opposed Caesar, forcing himself to ally with Pompey, the man who had killed his father, but Caesar had forgiven him, partly for Servilia's sake. Indeed, such was his fondness for his long-time paramour that when selling off lands confiscated from his enemies, he gave some to Servilia at a scandalous discount. ('Even cheaper than it seems' remarked Cicero, 'since a third got knocked off', a reference to the rumour that Caesar had seduced Servilia's daughter Iunia the Third.)

Caesar's assassination showed how comprehensively Servilia's family was split. In the Julian corner were Servilia, Caesar's mistress, and Iunia the Second, wife of Lepidus, Caesar's second-in-command. For the opposition were Caesar's assassins Brutus, son of Servilia, and Cassius, Servilia's son-in-law, who was married to Iunia the Third (and if rumour of an affair with Caesar was true, certainly might have given Cassius some extra motivation).

Once Caesar had perished, Servilia threw herself wholeheartedly into supporting her son, showing a flair for politics that won Cicero's grudging admiration. When her cause and her son died (by his own hand) at the Battle of Philippi in 42 BC, Servilia retired into private life, protected by Atticus (no. 35) and her daughter's marriage to Lepidus, who was now one of the three most powerful men in Rome. It is not known when Servilia died, but her clan continued until at least AD 189, having endured over seven centuries.

37 | JULIUS CAESAR
Glory and infamy

Gaius Julius Caesar was the man who finally overthrew the Roman Republic. Others had set the wheels in motion, but it was the recklessness and ruthlessness of Caesar that hammered the final nails into the Republican coffin, and secured his own fate – assassination at the hands of his outraged peers.

Caesar was born in 100 BC, on 13th of Quintilis (renamed July after 44 BC), into an ancient patrician family that claimed descent from Aeneas, the Trojan hero of Virgil's *Aeneid* and the son of the goddess Venus. Caesar was only 15 when his father died of a heart attack or stroke while lacing his boots one morning. A year later Cinna, the leader of the Marians, gave his daughter Cornelia to Caesar in marriage, and at the same time Caesar was designated for the office of *Flamen Dialis*. But with Sulla's (no. 25) victory in 82 BC, Cinna's acts were annulled and Caesar's priesthood taken from him. Sulla demanded that Caesar divorce Cornelia; Caesar chose to flee

Rome instead. Eventually hunted down, his life was spared through the intercession of his mother who appealed to Sulla through her kinsmen. According to Suetonius, Sulla's words on this occasion were prophetic: 'You are saving the very man who will be the ruin of everything you and I have fought for and hold dear.'

Others took Caesar less seriously, at least initially, partly because of his foppishness. He was notoriously concerned with his appearance and was always neatly groomed. It was even alleged that he depilated parts of his body – an accusation related to sexual impropriety, and one that would be made frequently. In 80 BC, for example, he had dallied at the court of King Nicomedes of Bithynia, and was later accused by Cicero and others of having had an affair with him. Yet he also had a reputation as a ladies' man, and was notorious for his love of luxury. According to Plutarch, Caesar was 1,300 talents in debt before he had held any public office.

After Sulla's death in 78 BC, Caesar attempted to make a name for himself as a lawyer and orator in Rome. Aiming to hone his skills (he would later be described by Quintilian as one of the greatest orators of his day), Caesar returned to the east in 75 BC to study rhetoric with Apollonius. There he was captured by pirates and ransomed for 50 talents; upon his release he manned some ships, captured the pirates and crucified them.

Back in Rome, in 69 BC Caesar served as quaestor, and the following year was assigned to duties in Spain. Here he came across a statue of Alexander the Great and famously lamented that by the age of 33 Alexander had conquered much of the known world while he, Caesar, had so far achieved nothing. Returning to Rome, Caesar developed close political ties with the powerful and wealthy Crassus, and courted popularity with the people, causing deep suspicion among the aristocracy and incurring massive debts in the process.

This set the scene for an audacious act. In 63 BC Caesar campaigned for the office of Chief Priest (*pontifex maximus*). This was normally the culmination of a long and distinguished political career, yet Caesar had held only a junior magistracy. His candidacy outraged the political establishment. When Caesar left his home on the morning of the election, he declared to his mother, 'you will next see me as *pontifex maximus*, or not at all'. But Caesar had no reason to worry: massive bribery had secured his election. It had also made him some powerful enemies.

The situation in Rome was becoming increasingly violent. In 62 BC the demagogue Clodius unlawfully entered Caesar's house where the *Bona Dea* festival, at which men were prohibited, was being celebrated. The festival had been organized by Caesar's wife, Pompeia (Cornelia had died in 69 BC), and Caesar used this as an excuse to divorce her – in his own words, 'Caesar's wife must be above suspicion', yet she was now suspected of having an affair with Clodius. But Caesar's main concern was probably that her family lacked powerful political connections that could aid him in his career.

Caesar's next move was to agitate for the recall of Pompey to deal with the Catiline threat (no. 31). It is not clear to what extent Caesar and Crassus had themselves become embroiled in Catiline's conspiracy, but Caesar appealed for clemency for the conspirators and was himself physically threatened just outside the Senate. When he attempted to leave Rome the following year to take up his propraetorship (special command, or governorship of a province allocated by the Senate at the end of a praetor's term of office) in Spain, his creditors prevented him. Only when Crassus vouched for him was Caesar able to take up his military command; and the need to repay his debts no doubt fuelled the many campaigns against the Lusitani in which he now engaged. Indeed, the considerable war booty he amassed eventually satisfied his creditors.

Caesar returned to Rome hoping to celebrate a triumph and stand for the consulship. His triumph was effectively prevented by Cato, but Caesar was elected consul in 60 BC. Recognizing the deep loathing felt for him by the Senate, Caesar entered into a secret alliance with Pompey and Crassus, now known as the 'First Triumvirate'. The three agreed that no one of them would take any political action that could be disadvantageous to the others. Then

Caesar gave himself proconsular command of Cisalpine Gaul and Illyricum for four years (see pl. XII). As proconsul he was immune from prosecution – essential since his many enemies immediately challenged the legality of the laws he had passed.

Caesar was not authorized to conquer Gaul. His own rhetorical descriptions of his campaigns in Gaul were intended to justify his actions; Caesar was 'defending' Rome's allies against migrating tribes. A transparent excuse, but sufficient for a ten-year campaign in Gaul (extending briefly to Britain) from March 58 BC. While absent from Rome, Caesar was dependent on the support of Pompey and Crassus, and initially the situation suited all parties. In 56 BC an attempt was made to recall and prosecute Caesar, which was headed off by a meeting and renewal of the triumvirate at Lucca. In consequence Pompey and Crassus took the consulship, and Caesar's command was renewed for five years. However, Crassus died fighting the Parthians, and Caesar found himself increasingly isolated and at odds with Pompey, both personally and politically. Caesar's daughter, who had married Pompey when the First Trium-virate had been formed, died at this time after a difficult childbirth. It became clear to all that if Caesar returned to Rome as a private citizen he would be prosecuted. Accordingly he tried to stand for the consulship in absentia, but Pompey, joining with Caesar's enemies, stepped in to prevent him.

In 49 BC the Senate ordered Caesar to demobilize his legions and return to Rome for prosecution, and drove his main supporters from the city, including the tribune Mark Antony. Caesar – claiming to be defending his tribucian rights – marched his legions on Rome. By crossing the Rubicon (the boundary between Cisalpine Gaul and Roman Italy) in January 49 BC and bringing his army into Italy, Caesar declared war on Rome and the Republic.

His progress was swift and by February most senators had fled Rome. Caesar pursued Pompey to Greece, eventually defeating him at the Battle of Pharsalus in 48 BC. Crossing to Egypt, Caesar then settled a dispute over the Egyptian throne, installing Cleopatra as queen and fathering a son by her. Then a lightning campaign against Pharnaces II in Asia produced the famous epithet, 'I came, I saw, I conquered'.

Finally returning to Rome as its absolute master, Caesar held a triumph – ironically a celebration of his victory over his fellow citizens – and turned his attention to administration (including the reform of the calendar). Honours were heaped upon him, even by his enemies who undoubtedly hoped this would stir up discontent.

In February 44 BC Caesar declared himself dictator for life – in stark contrast to Sulla who had laid down his dictatorship and whom Caesar considered a political illiterate. He adopted the dress of Rome's ancient kings, but he rejected the royal diadem when offered it by his ally and subordinate Mark Antony. Some ancient sources suggest that he had been testing the waters to see if the Roman people would accept a king, but it is not known if Caesar coveted the kingship. One story was that the Sybilline oracle had declared that only a king could defeat the Parthians – and Caesar planned to set off on a Parthian campaign on 18 March.

It was undoubtedly a good move to leave Rome. The majority of the Roman aristocracy was hostile, and Caesar may have suspected a plot. If so, he was correct. Around 60 senators conspired under Marcus Iunius Brutus, a descendant of the original liberator of Rome (Brutus, no. 5), and Gaius Cassius Longinus. On the Ides (15th) of March 44 BC Caesar's wife Calpurnia awoke from a nightmare and begged Caesar not to attend the Senate that day. It was only when his friend, Decimus Brutus, made light of Calpurnia's fears that Caesar departed for the Curia of the Theatre of Pompey, where the Senate had gathered. On the way he was handed a scroll containing details of the plot, but did not read it, not realizing its importance. Once at the Curia, Caesar was surrounded by members of the Senate. One pulled the toga from Caesar's shoulder, a signal to the conspirators who rounded on him with daggers from all sides (see pl. XI).

Naively, the conspirators seem to have believed that once Caesar was dead, the Republic would return to 'normal'. Instead Rome plunged into the further series of civil wars that ultimately led to its first real emperor, Augustus. And the memory of Caesar was not vilified as expected. Caesar had been ruthless, bloodthirsty and had effectively destroyed the Republic, yet he was declared a god.

38 | HORACE
Poet and freedman's son

It is an oddity of Latin literature that very few of its greatest exponents were born in Rome. Rome's greatest lyric poet, Quintus Horatius Flaccus, was no exception, being born on 8 December 65 BC near Venusia in southern Italy.

Horace's father was a freedman of Venusia, and since Horace talks of being brought up in the old Italian way, his father may have been enslaved during the Social War of 90 BC. Horace's father was a collector of taxes, probably of indirect taxes from auctions – and given the frequent purges that were such a feature of political life at the time, this would have been a profitable living. Certainly it was enough for the purchase of the smallholding where Horace was born, and later, when his son entered his teenage years, the father could afford to get him a good education in Rome. Horace writes of his father with respect bordering on reverence, and implicitly contrasts his father's 'gentle severity' with schoolteacher 'the severe Orbilius'.

At the age of 18 Horace went to study in Athens. He describes himself at this time as short, sociable, inclined to sudden bad temper, but easily calmed. His health was weak, as were his eyes. His eyes, he tells us, were dark, as was his hair. The young man's studies were interrupted by news of the assassination of Julius Caesar. The idealistic Horace joined the Republican cause, and may even have met Brutus on his way east after his expulsion from Rome. Horace must have made a good impression as he was made an officer at the level of those of equestrian rank, a flattering promotion for the son of a slave. Nevertheless as military careers go, Horace's was short and inglorious. He was on the losing side at the Battle of Philippi, in the part of Brutus' army which was put to rout. He talks of losing his shield, 'terrified as I was', and being saved by 'swift Mercury'. Mercury was the god of poets, though here the poet is probably making a joking allusion to the god's winged feet.

The following years were hard for Horace. His family estates were confiscated, and he had to take up work as a clerk. He lived frugally, and passed his spare time in writing poetry. It is probable that some of his bitter satires, the *Epodes*, date from this period, and likewise some of his more heated amatory verses. According to one source, it was a satire on Augustus' close confidant Maecenas that brought him to that great man's attention. Whatever the reason, the art-loving Maecenas soon offered Horace his patronage, and purchased for him the property of which Horace wrote rapturously: 'I petition the gods no longer, nor do I require of my friend in power any larger enjoyments, I'm content with my Sabine farm alone. Day is driven on by day, and the new moons hasten to their wane.'

From here, Horace's life seems, by his own account, to have been idyllic. Rich enough now to count himself a member of the equestrian order, he commuted from his farm in the hills near Tibur (modern Tivoli) to exchange the quiet of a rural existence for nights spent hobnobbing with the cream of Roman society. (This may have been the basis of his poem on the town and the country mouse.) He put on weight, and Augustus himself teased the poet about his pot-belly and love of *la dolce vita*, to which the poet goodnaturedly responded that teetotallers produced poor poetry: 'the sweet muses smell of wine by morning.' According to his biographer Suetonius, Augustus even offered Horace the post of personal secretary, and took it in good part when he was turned down. The nearest Horace was to come again to personal danger was on his own farm, when a tree unexpectedly fell over and nearly killed him.

His later years produced some of Horace's finest poetry. Through the *Odes* he had become recognized as the greatest lyric poet in the golden age of Latin literature. At Augustus' urging he produced the *Carmen Seculare*, a book of verses which embraced the growing prosperity and peace in his time. In his later life Horace was no longer the fiery idealist who had fought at Philippi, and helped himself liberally to the pleasures of his day. 'It is said,' remarks Suetonius, 'that he was highly over-sexed; apparently he had a room lined with mirrors so that he could observe himself coupling with prostitutes from every angle.' Perhaps such exertions took their toll. He died suddenly, on 17 November 8 BC, at the age of 57, leaving his affairs so disorganized that it fell to his heir, the emperor Augustus, to sort out the poet's estate.

39 | AUGUSTUS
Master of the empire

When, on 23 September 63 BC, Rome's future ruler was born, no one paid much attention. Rome was gripped by the Catiline conspiracy and Cicero's efforts to head off revolution (no. 31), and neither his mother, Atia, nor his father, Octavius, were powerful or distinguished. Atia's mother was a Julia, sister of Julius Caesar – who was at that time an aspiring and impoverished junior politician. Octavius himself was the first of a long line of equestrians to ascend to senatorial status, and he was to become praetor in 61 BC. The boy was brought up in the town of Velitrae, not far from Rome. Though named Gaius Octavius after his father, history knows the boy as Octavian (see pl. XIII), a name he never used.

Although sickly, young Octavian showed considerable promise. Julius Caesar became the boy's closest male relative after Octavius died, probably around 59 BC. Caesar's interest was further sharpened by hearing the polished funeral oration Octavian gave for his grandmother Julia, though at the time he was only 12. Political enemies claimed that Octavian also became Caesar's catamite, an accusation which was furiously denied.

By the time Octavian was 16 and officially a man, Caesar was at war. Octavian's mother forbade him to accompany Caesar on his African campaign as the climate was unhealthy, but he insisted on joining Caesar in his war against Republican die-hards in Spain. Young Octavian was highly ambitious, and unreservedly supported his great-uncle's cause. In return, Caesar sent Octavian to virtual exile in Illyria, 'for his education'.

This was not the snub it seemed. The real reason became apparent in 44 BC when Caesar was assassinated and his will made Octavian his adoptive son and heir. Although Caesar had ensured that the youth was safely out of Rome with a friendly legion nearby, Octavian's danger was no less for not being immediate. As Caesar's heir, Octavian was automatically a major political figure whom rivals would eliminate as a matter of course.

Octavian accepted the challenge and returned to Rome. There he discovered that Mark Antony, Caesar's former second-in-command, had out-manoeuvered Caesar's assassins with unexpected deftness and was now master of Rome. Antony's enemies, especially Cicero, saw Octavian as a counterweight to Antony, though Octavian took careful note of Cicero's quip that he should be 'raised, praised – and erased'. Aided by Cicero's rhetoric, this faction succeeded in driving Antony from Rome. Antony thereafter made common cause with Lepidus, the Caesarian governor of Gaul. As both consuls had died in battle against Antony, the legions insisted that they be led by Caesar's son, and that son should be consul.

The opposing armies met near Mutina in north Italy. Rather than destroy each other, as their enemies hoped, Octavian, Antony and Lepidus settled down to divide Rome's empire between them. Thus in 43 BC the Second Triumvirate was formed. (The first had been an unofficial alliance between Crassus, Pompey and Caesar; see no. 37.) The new triumvirate ruthlessly executed without trial all men they even suspected of being enemies, including Cicero. This was both a political purge and a fund-raising exercise – many 'enemies' were innocent of everything except having more wealth than connections. Caesar's assassins had fled to the east and were just as ruthlessly raising money to overthrow the triumvirs, so money was desperately needed.

The clash came at Philippi in Greece in 42 BC. Antony crushed the formidable Cassius, but Octavian (again suffering ill-health) was beaten by Brutus, and it took a further engagement for the triumvirs to prevail. Consequently, at the age of 21, Octavian became one of the three rulers of the empire (see pl. v).

After Philippi, Antony took control of what he saw as the prime real estate, Rome's eastern provinces, while Octavian took Italy and much of the west. Lepidus found himself the junior member of the triumvirate, shouldered aside to Africa.

It was Antony's plan to cover himself with glory by conquering Parthia, thus fulfilling Caesar's dream, and avenging a massive Roman defeat of 53 BC at Carrhae, when an attempted Roman invasion of the neighbouring empire failed ignominiously. Octavian was left to deal with a faction-ridden Senate and Italians made impoverished and surly by unceasing civil strife, taxation and the settlement of veteran soldiers on their lands – the latter a tradition which Octavian followed, to great resentment.

Hostility towards Octavian was increased by the activities of Sextus Pompey, a son of Caesar's former rival, who had set himself up with a fleet and was disrupting the Roman corn supply. Antony's wife, Fulvia, decided that the time was ripe to raise Italy in revolt on her husband's behalf. She and her allies (including Antony's brother Lucius) briefly took Rome, but prompt action by Octavian and his general Agrippa (no. 40) forced the rebels to take refuge in the fortress town of Perusia (now Perugia in present-day Umbria). On hearing of Octavian's troubles Antony immediately gathered a fleet and returned to Italy. He was probably disappointed to find when he got there that the rebellion had been defeated, and the rebels given little mercy. Antony's wife was also dead 'due to the privations of the siege'.

Antony accepted the story without question, partly because this allowed him to patch up the alliance by marrying Octavian's sister, Octavia, and partly because of his increasingly personal interest in Rome's ally and Caesar's former mistress, Cleopatra of Egypt, whose fortunes were becoming increasingly linked with Antony's. Suddenly things looked brighter for Octavian. When Lepidus attempted to reassert himself by bringing an army over to Sicily, Octavian displayed great personal bravery by walking to his rival's camp, and winning over Lepidus' soldiers by force of personality alone. Agrippa crushed Sextus Pompey at sea, and Octavian gleefully exploited Antony's love life to portray his rival as a lust-besotted tool of Cleopatra's imperial ambitions. Consequently, the Roman people became increasingly wary of Antony's entanglement with the Egyptian queen, and there were rumours that Antony intended to transfer the capital of the empire to Alexandria. When Antony's invasion of Parthia failed, Octavian used this growing public antipathy to declare war on Egypt, knowing that Antony would support Cleopatra and civil war would result.

In 31 BC, the two sides met in Greece. The decisive battle was fought at sea at Actium, and was a decisive victory for Octavian and his admiral Agrippa. Antony and Cleopatra later committed suicide, leaving Octavian master of the empire.

Octavian began his reign as Rome's first emperor by categorically asserting that he was not, in fact, an emperor. Rather, he was the restorer of liberty, the man with a mission to set a near-shipwrecked Republic to rights. For this reason he changed his name to distance himself from his adoptive father (who had made himself dictator for life). He declined the name of Romulus (Romulus had been a king, after all), and settled for Augustus, a name meaning 'distinguished and revered'.

Like a true aristocrat, he had married several wives, but in 38 BC he wed the highly aristocratic Livia. He remained married to her for the rest of his life. Livia set an example as a good Roman *materfamilias*, living modestly and weaving her husband's attire. Julia, the fruit of Augustus' marriage to Scribonia and his only child, was brought up so strictly that she was later to rebel spectacularly, scandalizing Rome with her wanton infidelities.

In his dealings with the Senate, Augustus set up the government known today as the Principate. In a series of settlements in 27, 23 and 19 BC he went through the motions of handing back control of the empire to the Senate, but carefully retained certain powers which became the constitutional basis of his rule. However, Augustus insisted that he did things simply through his *auctoritas*: personal authority based on respect. It is perhaps the greatest tribute to Augustus' political skill that he made the job of being emperor look easy: his successors were to find that it was anything but.

It helped that despite his constant ill-health Augustus proved remarkably durable. The Republic had effectively ended when Caesar crossed the Rubicon in 49 BC. By the time Augustus died in AD 14 only the very old could remember the chaos that had preceded the peace and stability of his rule. Long life, however, was not without disadvantages. Augustus considered first Marcellus, his nephew, as a successor, then Agrippa, then Agrippa's sons. As these died, one after another, he finally adopted the dour but competent Tiberius, son of Livia, as his heir.

In person the man was very different from the cold and ruthless politician. Although strict with his family, Augustus was indulgent to his friends, and enjoyed amorous liaisons and gambling. He wore a broad-brimmed hat to protect himself from the sun, and seems not to have taken himself too seriously. When he was being presented with a petition, he told the man delivering it 'for goodness sake, you are not giving a titbit to an elephant!'. On his deathbed in Campania in August AD 14, he asked 'did I play my part well?' using the conventional request of a departing actor asking for applause.

Augustus is one of the few emperors who speaks to us directly, through the *Res Gestae* ('Things Accomplished') which he posted outside his tomb. Though ingenuous in places, and a work of propaganda throughout, it describes momentous achievements by the man who was Rome's greatest citizen.

40 | AGRIPPA

Augustus' second-in-command

Perhaps the most striking rise to power in the late 1st century BC – with the exception of Augustus himself – was that of his close friend and confidant Marcus Vipsanius Agrippa. Agrippa's family were wealthy enough to hold equestrian rank, but had no significant political influence. Born *c.* 63 BC, Agrippa's good fortune was to be educated with Octavian (no. 39), the great-nephew of Julius Caesar (no. 37). Suetonius relates how, as students in Apollonia in 44 BC, the pair visited the astrologer Theogenes. Theogenes predicted an 'almost incredible career' for Agrippa. Octavian feared that his own career would be less eminent until, to his amazement, Theogenes threw himself at his feet. Agrippa would be great, but always second to Octavian.

Shortly afterwards, Julius Caesar was murdered. Octavian and Agrippa returned to Italy together, and began their climb to power. First Agrippa helped Octavian levy troops in Campania, a force that helped Octavian to membership of the Second Triumvirate in 43 BC. In the same year, Agrippa entered the Senate by becoming Tribune of the Plebs. His friendship with Octavian earned him consulships in 37 BC (despite being well below the legal age limit), and again in 28 and 27 BC.

Agrippa is most famed as a brilliant general, particularly since Octavian himself was a poor commander. Agrippa probably first saw combat in 45 BC at the Battle of Munda against Gnaeus and

Sextus Pompey (sons of Pompey the Great), and fought alongside Octavian and Mark Antony at the defeat of Caesar's assassins at Philippi. He was left to defend Rome from Sextus Pompey while Octavian was in Gaul in 40 BC, and then in 39 or 38 BC he was sent to crush a rebellion in Aquitaine, using this as an opportunity to cross the Rhine (the first Roman since Julius Caesar to do so) in order to intimidate Germanic tribes. He capped his success by marrying Caecilia Attica, the daughter of Titus Pomponius Atticus (no. 35), one of the wealthiest men in Rome. But he refused a triumph claiming, according to Dio, that he was unwilling to celebrate while his friend was in trouble. Octavian was struggling in Italy, and had been humiliatingly defeated at sea by Sextus Pompey. Agrippa came to his friend's rescue, drilling his navy in an artificial lake near Cumae, then destroying the enemy fleet and earning himself the unprecedented honour of a naval crown decorated with the beaks of ships. Antony was quick to praise Agrippa's role, claiming that Octavian had lain in a stupor looking at the sky throughout the entire battle.

Agrippa's greatest achievement came in 31 BC, when he led Octavian's fleet to victory over Mark Antony and Cleopatra at Actium. Octavian was now sole ruler of the Roman empire, and rewarded Agrippa with marriage to his niece, Claudia Marcella Maior (Attica had either died or been divorced). Agrippa's position was such that when, in 24 BC, Augustus (as Octavian had become known) fell ill it was Agrippa who presided at the wedding of Augustus' daughter Julia to her cousin Marcellus. The young Marcellus was being groomed for power and, as Augustus' health deteriorated further, it was expected that he would be named as heir. Instead, Augustus handed his ring to Agrippa, to Marcellus' dismay. Recognizing the animosity between the two upon his recovery, Augustus decided to send to send the former to Syria. Agrippa instead travelled to Lesbos. The motives for his voluntary exile are unknown but he was probably offended by Augustus' preference for Marcellus. He returned to Rome after Marcellus' death in 23 BC.

Although there is no evidence that he ever sought to be anything other than a loyal friend to Augustus, it is alleged that Maecenas (another important member of the emperor's inner coterie) now advised Augustus to neutralize Agrippa's power by making him his son-in-law. Accordingly in 21 BC Agrippa divorced Marcella and married Julia. Their sons – Gaius and Lucius – were adopted as Augustus' heirs.

Like Augustus, Agrippa made his mark on Rome itself, helping to transform the city into a monumental capital worthy of an empire. Agrippa built new aqueducts and repaired old ones, paved the streets and cleaned and enlarged the sewers. He built public baths and laid out gardens for the use of the people of Rome. At the entrance of his new temple, the Pantheon in the Campus Martius, he put statues of himself and Augustus – partners in creating a new Rome. Shortly before his death, he ordered the construction of the Porticus Vipsania, upon which would be displayed his crowning glory – a marble map of the Roman empire. Unsurprisingly, Agrippa was a popular figure. His unexpected illness and death in Campania in 12 BC was viewed as a calamity, and accompanied by many portents – owls flitting about the city, lightning strikes and buildings destroyed by fire (including the hut of Romulus). A distraught Augustus found space for his old friend in the mausoleum built for himself. Agrippa left his fortune to Augustus, and a gift to the people of Rome – funds enough to allow free entry to the baths he had built for their use. As Cassius Dio states, 'such was the end of Agrippa, who had in every way clearly shown himself the noblest of the men of his day and had used the friendship of Augustus with a view to the greatest advantage both of the emperor himself and of the commonwealth'.

Agrippa helped to establish the new Roman order. How he felt about this is unknown – his autobiography, though referred to by some ancient writers, is lost. But his legacy remains.

41 | JULIUS ZOILOS
Octavian's loyal freedman

After Julius Caesar's murder in 44 BC, his supporters flocked to his adopted successor, Octavian. Gaius Julius Zoilos was one of many of Caesar's freedmen who rose to prominence in their home cities during the next decade, becoming Octavian's trusted agents in troubled times.

Zoilos is not known from the literary sources, but both his career and his relationship to Octavian can be inferred from inscriptions in his home town, Aphrodisias (in modern southwest Turkey), where Zoilos' high standing is illustrated by a lavish funerary monument. For this reason little is known of Zoilos' early life and career. He was probably enslaved during the turbulent 70s BC and purchased by Julius Caesar. After his freedom he remained a loyal client of Caesar, and as part of the dictator's entourage he became immensely rich. Soon after Caesar's death he returned to Aphrodisias, having established a close relationship with Octavian. His loyalty is especially notable given that Aphrodisias lay within the territory governed at that time by Brutus and Cassius, Caesar's assassins, and later by Mark Antony. In the theatre of Aphrodisias, an inscribed copy of a letter of 39/38 BC from Octavian states, 'You know how fond I am of my Zoilos'. As Octavian's agent in the city, it is unsurprising that Zoilos became a prominent figure, and the Caesarian connection may have had something to do with the privileges (including freedom and exemption from taxes) with which Aphrodisias was rewarded for resisting a Parthian-backed invasion in 39 BC.

During the 30s BC Zoilos paid for the construction of the aedic-ulated marble stage-building of the theatre, where his name and his status as Octavian's freedman and a Roman citizen were inscribed twice. He constructed part of a new temple to Aphrodite, and was involved in other building projects (for which only fragmentary epigraphic evidence remains). In return, he was honoured with at least two public statues and made lifetime priest of Aphrodite and of Eleutheria ('liberty'). The theatre inscription records that he was *stephanephoros* ('wreath-bearer', a title sometimes given to magistrates permitted to wear a wreath on public occasions) ten times in succession, and in the temple inscription he is saviour and benefactor of his city.

On his death Zoilos was given a grand tomb, lavishly decorated with an unusual series of marble friezes representing him surrounded by gods and personifications, such as Roma, Loyalty and Valour. He was neither exceptional nor the most influential of Octavian's freedmen, but loyal and competent. Aphrodisias benefited greatly from his civic generosity and influence at Rome.

42 | NONIUS BALBUS
Benefactor of Herculaneum

Marcus Nonius Balbus was a prominent citizen of Nuceria and Herculaneum in Campania in the age of Augustus, to whom exceptional honours were decreed in recognition of his civic benefactions and political achievements.

Balbus was the first of his influential Nucerian family to enter the Senate. This was achieved partly through matrimonial alliance – he married Volasennia Tertia, probably the daughter of an Etruscan family of senatorial rank – but his rise may also have been due to the influence of Octavian (no. 39). It is difficult to be certain as the only available sources are inscriptions. We do know that Balbus was Tribune of the Plebs at Rome in 32 BC and used his position to help Octavian against Antony's supporters in Rome. This act may have led to his appointment as proconsul of the province of Crete and Cyrene. The date of Balbus' proconsulship is debated, but it was probably *c.* 26/25 BC, and relates to the Augustan territorial settlement after the Battle of Philippi in 42 BC. Octavian settled some of his army veterans at Capua in Campania; lands on Crete were expropriated and given to the Capuans as part of the settlement (yielding, according to Dio, an annual income of 1.2 million sesterces). As proconsul, it was Balbus' job to administer over this settlement and, as a leading Campanian, there was no one who was better suited to look after the Capuan interests on Crete. Yet the delicate way in which he apparently handled the situation earned him the gratitude of the Cretans (the cities of Knossos and Gortyn had been involved in a boundary dispute which was now settled). Remarkably, a series of dedications were made by the Cretans and set up in his hometown of Herculaneum. No other proconsul of this province was ever honoured in the same way.

Back in Herculaneum, Balbus built a new basilica, a new gate and city wall, and probably baths. The people of that city were rightly proud of their leading citizen, and voted him honours on at least three separate occasions. Statues of Balbus, his mother, his wife and possibly his daughters were found inside the theatre, and equestrian statues of Balbus and his son flanked the entrance to the basilica. The inscription on a marble altar (actually his cenotaph), crowned with Balbus' statue outside the sea gate, records that after his death an equestrian statue was set up in his honour in the forum, that his *bisellium* (magistrate's chair) was to be placed in the theatre during performances, that customary athletic games were to be extended by a day in his honour, and that the annual procession of the *Parentalia* (Festival of the Dead) was to start from his cenotaph. Balbus was Herculaneum's patron, and even after death he was present at its major festivals and in its public buildings.

43 | LIVY
Historian of Rome

Titus Livius, known today as Livy, is someone of whom we would like to know more, both about his life and his works. His history is the most definitive source we have for early Rome, and his description of the war with Hannibal is essential reading for historians. Yet many would willingly swap the surviving works of Livy for those that have been lost. Livy's *Ab Urbe Condita* ('From the Foundation of the City') was written in 142 books, of which numbers 1–10 and 21–45 alone have survived. His work on the later Roman Republic is lost, though it was apparently both accurate and unbiased.

Livy, like many great 'Roman' writers, was not a native of the city. He spent most of his life in Rome, but was born in Padua (or, as may be inferred from a verse of the poet Martial, in a hamlet nearby), and he returned there to die. Even the span of Livy's life is uncertain. All that is definitely known is that he was born in the 50s BC, and died about 60 years later. Internal evidence in his texts suggests that he began writing late in life, probably in his mid-forties. His lucid prose, and his ability to pick his way through the different, contradictory and sometimes frankly incredible accounts of Rome's history rapidly brought him to the attention of the powerful, many of whom were aware that they were shortly to be immortalized by history themselves. Foremost among them was the emperor Augustus, who seems to have been on friendly terms with the historian, notwithstanding that Livy was on occasion so sympathetic to Augustus' opponents that the emperor jokingly called him a 'Pompeian'. Sadly, the books that deal directly with Augustus and his bloodstained rise to power are now lost, so Livy's impartiality must be taken on trust.

Livy was criticized in later ages for not verifying his sources, but in at least one case he hints broadly that he carefully avoided checking facts which might prove contrary to Augustan propaganda.

Although not a tool of the establishment, Livy shared its aims of edification and moral regeneration. A contemporary refers to Livy's 'Paduaness', which is perhaps a dig at the historian's straight-laced morality, which Augustus was attempting to restore in Rome.

In assembling his facts Livy seems to have used most of the histories available in his time. Where these agreed he reported the 'facts', where there was controversy he sometimes picked the version he considered the best (as opposed to the most trustworthy – Livy was a writer, not an academic), and sometimes he gave both versions, inviting the reader to choose. Livy was impressed by the Greek historian Polybius, and particularly on eastern affairs follows him so closely as to be merely Polybius' translator. Later historians get annoyed by Livy's habit of inserting long, polished and unhistorical speeches into the text – but Livy's contemporaries were impressed by the same feat.

Such was Livy's fame in later life that one admirer was said to have come from Cadiz in Spain with the sole purpose of seeing his hero in the flesh, and having done so, promptly went home satisfied. Livy's books were widely distributed, though a complete set transcribed on parchment would have cost the same as a respectable villa. Many made do with summaries or the chapter heads (called epitomes), and it is from these that we have a tantalizing idea of the contents of the missing books. The 'lost Livys' have been sought for centuries. A complete set was last known to exist in the 6th century, but modern science is still retrieving fragments from old manuscripts.

Livy is known to have had a wife, but other details are scarce. An inscription which archaeologists have unearthed from Padua may refer to Livy, in which case his lady was called Cassia Prima. The inscription also refers to two sons, and we know Livy wrote to one son urging him to study Demosthenes. Either this son or another son is mentioned as the author of a geographical work, and a later writer refers to Livy's daughter, who married a rhetorician called Lucius Magius.

The picture that emerges from the sources, and from Livy's own writing, is of a genial, talented individual who rubbed shoulders with the mighty (he encouraged the future emperor Claudius to write history, though there is no evidence that he was, as has been suggested, Claudius' personal tutor), yet kept his feet firmly on the ground. If, as many hope, more of Livy's work remains to be discovered beneath the desert sands or in some neglected palimpsest, one of Rome's greatest historians may yet have more to give.

44 | EUMACHIA
First lady of Pompeii

The destruction and burial of Pompeii has given to posterity a wealth of information about daily life in a Roman town, and tantalizing glimpses into the lives of many of its most prominent inhabitants. Eumachia is one of the most famous of these, a woman whose political influence and high social standing in the Augustan period are clear from various inscriptions and buildings discovered in the town.

Eumachia's family appear to have made their money by exporting wine, since amphorae with the stamp of Lucius Eumachius, her father, have been found in Mediterranean ports such as Carthage. Their wealth gave them status and influence, and naturally Eumachia married the son of another prominent Pompeian family, Marcus Numistrius Fronto. He, or his son of the same name, was *duumvir* (chief magistrate) of Pompeii in AD 3, a fact commemorated by Eumachia in two identically worded inscriptions found on a building in the forum:

Eumachia, daughter of Lucius, public priestess, in her own name and that of Marcus Numistrius Fronto, built at her own expense the *chalcidicum* [porch], *crypta* [covered

passage], and porticus, and dedicated them to Augustan
Concord and Piety.

These inscriptions relate to the construction and dedication of
the largest and most prominent building in the forum of Pompeii
(known to us today as the 'Eumachia Building'), which Eumachia
– a woman – had been allowed to erect. Although her only public
role was that of priestess (probably of Ceres), the highest office
open to a woman, there is no doubt therefore that she wielded
significant influence in local affairs, possibly due to the wealth and
social connections she must have inherited from her father. Not
only that, her name was permanently associated with the building,
a reminder to all of her act of beneficence and a great boost to the
political kudos of her husband or son. It is interesting, too, that
she chose to dedicate her building to Augustan Concord and Piety,
virtues central to the new imperial ideology that were commonly
celebrated on buildings constructed in Rome and throughout Italy
in this period. Eumachia draws attention both to her status within
Pompeii and to her allegiance to the new Roman order.

Eumachia's prominence within the town is further highlighted
by another inscription in the Eumachia Building, set up by the
Fullers' Guild:

To Eumachia, daughter of Lucius, public priestess, from
the fullers.

A statue of Eumachia dressed as a priestess (with head covered)
accompanied the inscription. Similar statues of Livia, Augustus' wife,
have been found leading some to speculate that Eumachia's statue
was a deliberate copy, an attempt to emulate the most powerful
woman in the Roman empire. We have no idea why the fullers
should honour Eumachia in this way. It has been suggested that
the Eumachia Building was their guild headquarters, or even a
functioning fullery, but actually there is no evidence to confirm

how the building was used and many different theories have been put forward. At the very least it would appear that Eumachia was a patroness of the Fuller's Guild and had performed some act to advance their interests. Like many of the elite, she is likely to have maintained wide-ranging business interests.

Eumachia was buried in Pompeii's largest and most imposing tomb, located just outside the Nuceria Gate and measuring almost 14 square metres. Herms (carved heads or busts) of the deceased family members were displayed in niches on the façade of the tomb, which also featured a frieze depicting fighting Amazons. It was usual for prominent public priestesses to be buried at public expense or on land given by the town council, yet the inscription in Eumachia's tomb reveals that she built the tomb for herself and her household. The reason for this is unknown, but no one who passed the tomb could have doubted her prominence among Pompeii's elite.

45 | HILARION OF OXYRHYNCHUS
Killing a girl child

The ancient world sometimes seems very similar to the modern. People face the same personal dilemmas, and struggle with the rent or bureaucracy. But occasionally it is jarringly and disturbingly different. This contrast is perfectly encapsulated in a letter from Hilarion to his wife. Hilarion was from Oxyrhynchus in Egypt, some 250 miles from Alexandria on the west bank of the Nile. There was a constant traffic between the two cities, as Oxyrhynchus was poorer, and had a large population of illiterate native Egyptian workers. These went to work in the port city of Alexandria and corresponded with home through the medium of scribes who both wrote letters to dictation and read them to the recipients. These letters, preserved under the dry desert sands, have been a window into the past and the lives of everyday citizens.

On 17 June 1 BC, the following letter was sent:

Hilarion to Alis his sister, heartiest greetings, and to my dear Berous and Apollonarion.

Know that we are still even now in Alexandria. Do not worry if when all the others return I remain in Alexandria. I beg and beseech of you to take care of the little child, and as soon as we receive wages I will send them to you. If – good luck to you! – you bear offspring, if it is a male, let it live; if it is a female, expose it. You told Aphrodisias, 'Do not forget me'. How can I forget you? I beg you therefore not to worry.

The 29th year of Caesar, Pauni 23

The reference to a 'sister' may have been literal; brother–sister marriage was far from unknown as it helped those without dowries, or poor families which needed to avoid dispersing their meagre resources. Hilarion's concern and love for his wife is as obvious as his calm matter-of-factness in deciding the fate of the child. 'Exposure' meant literally the leaving of the infant on a rubbish tip to die or be picked up by anyone who felt the urge. However, Hilarion was not being uniquely, or even unusually, cruel in this respect. Unwanted children were a fact of life, and households which could not support them had no choice but to be rid of them. Girls were especially vulnerable as they were considered less productive, and required dowries.

46 | VIRGIL
Rome's greatest poet

The man known today as Virgil was in his own time Publius Vergilius Maro. He was among the creators the golden age of Latin literature, and his epic poem the *Aeneid* standardized the legend of the years before Rome's foundation. Virgil was a prime propagandist for the Augustan regime, and even today his poems speak for imperial Rome.

> Your task, O Roman, is to rule and bring to men the ways
> of government, to impose upon them the arts of peace,
> to spare those who submit, and to subdue the arrogant.

In Virgil's time the Romans needed reminding about peace and good government, for there had been little of either over the previous century. Rome was lurching into the final rounds of civil war that preceded the rule of the Caesars when Virgil was born in 70 BC. His upbringing was in the small town of Andes, near Mantua, and his love of the countryside is shown in the vivid rural imagery which illuminates his poems. His parents may have been of peasant stock, but if so they were at least wealthy enough to ensure a decent education for their son at Cremona and Mediolanum (Milan).

It is quite possible that Virgil's family lost land to the confiscations of the triumvirs. His first collection of poems, the *Eclogues*, are dated to the late 40s BC and refer to the misery that these confiscations caused. However, the poetic skills deployed in the *Eclogues* brought him to the attention of Maecenas, the leading literary patron of the day.

The next set of Virgil's poems, the *Georgics*, published soon after Augustus' victory at Actium in 31 BC, seem to reflect his conversion to the Augustan point of view. The serenity of bucolic life in these resonates with the tranquillity Augustus promised. Certainly the *Georgics* were vastly influential with the opinion-formers of the day, and echoes from Virgil can be found in much of the poetry of the 20s BC. We know little of his life apart from what he alludes to in his poetry, and chance references to him by contemporaries. (Horace mentions a journey with him through central Italy.) The biography written in late antiquity by Donatus has details from an account by Suetonius, but also contains interpolated material that led to Virgil's medieval reputation as a Magus with supernatural powers.

In the 20s BC, Virgil was at work on his masterpiece, a poem that combined the picaresque aspect of the *Odyssey* and the martial theme of Homer's other masterpiece, the *Iliad*. Virgil described the wanderings of the Trojans, led by Aeneas, after the fall of Troy and how they finally found and fought for their new homeland in Italy. Throughout the poem the gods are intensely interested in the fate of Aeneas and the divine destiny of his people is repeatedly emphasized – such as when Aeneas travels to the underworld to meet a succession of Rome's future heroes. Ascanius, Aeneas' son, is often called Iulus, a reference to the Julian family's claim to descent from Venus, Aeneas' mother. Virgil's treatment of his female protagonists, like the tragic Dido of Carthage, together with his choice of metaphor have aroused considerable speculation as to the poet's sexuality. (Sources say that he was nicknamed 'The Virgin', or alternatively that 'he took his pleasure with boys'.)

Interest in Virgil's epic was intense. Even Augustus himself pestered the poet for updates and sneak extracts, for he was a painstaking writer with an output alleged to be a mere two-and-a-half lines a day. The attention distressed the poet, who was so shy that when recognized in public he would duck through the nearest available building to get away. Eventually he decided to escape to Greece and finish his work in peace. En route he met Augustus on the latter's return from the east in 19 BC, and decided to accompany him back to Italy. He fell ill during the journey, but insisted on pushing on. By the time he reached Brundisium he was failing fast, and he died there, the *Aeneid* still unfinished. His tomb is believed to be in the Piedigrotta district of Naples.

Part 4

Romans and Caesars

AD 14–75

The transition from Republic to empire introduced a new cast of characters to the drama that was Rome. Although reduced in power and number, the old aristocratic families such as Sulpicia's (no. 47) still lingered on, but were joined by a new class of power-brokers in the imperial court as power shifted slowly but inexorably from the Senate to the Palatine, home of Rome's first dynasty, the Julio-Claudians. The early emperors of Rome were a mixed bag both in character and ability, ranging from the coldly brilliant Augustus (no. 39), the stolid and unpopular Tiberius, the flamboyant and malicious Caligula (no. 51), the eccentric Claudius and the bad and decadent Nero. That the empire functioned while under Julio-Claudian rule and that of their successors was not simply due to the fact that most emperors worked conscientiously at their jobs (a fact their biographers tend to gloss over), but because by and large they chose competent subordinates such as Pallas and Frontinus (nos 52 and 59). Even if we discount as fantasy that Augustus was poisoned by his wife Livia, Tiberius (possibly suffocated), Caligula (stabbed), Claudius (poisoned, though possibly accidentally), and Nero (suicide) can testify that being emperor was a very dangerous occupation. However it was even more dangerous to be a potential emperor while someone else had the job, a fact that contributed to the deaths of many leading senators and to the Julio-Claudian clan managing to almost wipe itself out completely within three generations, to be replaced by the Flavian and Antonine dynasties at the end of the 1st century AD.

The Roman people acquiesced to life under military dictatorship, which was fundamentally how Rome was now ruled. This was simply because while not engaged in killing off their peers, the Caesars did far more for the average citizen in ruling Rome than the Senate had in its final chaotic and bloodstained decades. The ferocious exactions of tax-collectors in the provinces were reined in (though this did not stop egregiously stupid and greedy imperial officials from goading Boudicca to rebellion in Britain), and, with the exception of a brief bout of bloodletting in AD 69, the state was spared the devastation of civil war. This period saw a further flowering of literature in the generations after Virgil (no. 46), with the magisterial histories of Josephus (no. 60) and Tacitus, the engaging letters of Pliny, and the vitriolic satires of Juvenal and Martial (no. 63) – a period which is sometimes referred to as the 'Silver Age' of Latin.

Soon after his defeat of Cleopatra in 31 BC, Augustus with great ceremony closed the doors of the Temple of Janus – something the Romans did only when the state was at peace, and which had only happened once before, and then in Rome's legendary past under King Numa. However, the doors were soon opened again, for Rome continued to expand through annexation and military conquest. While the Germans stubbornly resisted assimilation, and wiped out a Roman army in the Teutoburg forest, other areas such as Judaea (Pontius Pilate, no. 50), Britain (Frontinus, no. 59), and Mauritania (Caligula, no. 51) were brought within the empire. The steady expansion of Rome's frontiers was matched by an increase in the number of Roman citizens, for Rome had almost completed its metamorphosis from a city-state to a trans-national entity. The city of Rome absorbed floods of immigrants from Spain, Gaul, Greece and Asia Minor (the last causing the poet Juvenal to complain that the river Orontes now flowed into the Tiber). But even as Rome became more foreign, more Romans lived in foreign parts – even Juvenal is alleged to have finished his days in Egypt. Many men have engaged in circular migration, by which they came to Rome as immigrants and returned to their native provinces as rich and respected citizens.

For most of antiquity, war or the threat of war had been an everyday reality for the majority of people living around the Mediterranean. For generations it had been the job of almost every non-servile male to do a spell of military service for the state. Now, as the *Pax Romana* took hold, war became almost exclusively a job for full-time professional soldiers like Tiberius Claudius Maximus (no. 69). It was something which happened on distant frontiers far from the everyday lives of most citizens – unless it was recreated for their delectation in the ever-bloodier spectacles of the arena, where those who died were sometimes prisoners of war, but also professional fighters.

With the ending of the mercifully brief civil war of AD 69, the stage was set for the long decades of peace and prosperity which were ineradicably to embed Roman law, language and culture within the communities of southern Europe.

47 | SULPICIA
Teenage poet

It's my bloody birthday, and I've got to spend it in
   the dreary countryside
Without Cerinthus! What's better than being in the city?

Any teenage girl expected to spend a boyfriend-free birthday at
her uncle's country house might have felt this way. Sulpicia's minor
tantrum has survived for 2,000 years because she expressed herself
in such unique elegiac poetry. Love elegies in Roman literature
were traditionally a male genre, which Sulpicia turns on its head
with a subversive role reversal of the poet and his object of desire.
Six of Sulpicia's verses, all intimate glimpses into a real or imagined
relationship, have survived in a book by the Latin poet Tibullus.
These six poems total 40 lines, which is not much to build a reputation upon, but Sulpicia's approach to writing love elegies has
such spontaneity, vivacity and blatant eroticism that her verses still
seem fresh today.

The indiscretion is sweet, it's hiding it that's bitter
Let them say of me
I've been a worthy woman with a worthy man.

Sulpicia was probably the daughter of the aristocrat Servius Sulpicius
Rufus, and the uncle she refers to is Mesalla, a close confederate of
Augustus. Cerinthus is a discreet pen-name for her lover, if indeed
he existed at all. (Cerinthus is also a type of wax, such as that on
the tablets to which Sulpicia committed her verses.) Yet Sulpicia
certainly makes her relationship seem real.

I'm glad you are so relaxed with me,
That I can get to see

The type of man I almost allowed to have me
Go chasing after that low-class tramp
And forget Sulpicia,
Daughter of the Servian family.

What became of Sulpicia, and whether she eventually married her Cerinthus is unknown. There was another Sulpicia who wrote poetry during the reign of Domitian (AD 81–96), so it seems that Sulpicia may indeed have passed her talents to a later generation.

48 | ANTONIA AUGUSTA
Imperial matriarch

The younger Antonia and her elder sister (also named Antonia) were the fruit of a political alliance. Their father, Mark Antony, had married their mother Octavia, sister of Octavian (no. 39), in 40 BC to cement the Second Triumvirate (formed in 43 BC). As the favourite niece of her uncle Octavian, Antonia was destined to play a prominent part in what would become Rome's first imperial family. Yet, unlike many of her female relatives, her reputation is unsullied; Antonia rose above the sordid world of politics and intrigue, and became a shining example of Roman matronly virtue.

Antonia was born in Athens on 31 January 36 BC, but was taken to Rome by her mother shortly afterwards. She never knew her father, who divorced her mother in 32 BC and killed himself in 30 BC, shortly after the Battle of Actium. She was, however, permitted to inherit from him, and became a wealthy woman, with properties in Italy, Greece and Egypt. A central pawn in her uncle's dynastic plans, in 16 BC she was married to Drusus, second son of Augustus' wife Livia. Together they had an unknown number of children, of whom three survived – Germanicus, Livilla and Claudius. Drusus was a highly successful general and his family travelled with him on his campaigns. In 9 BC they were with him in Germany when he died after falling from his horse.

The sources, including Valerius Maximus, agree that Antonia had been a loyal wife. 'Antonia, too, whose feminine merits surpassed the masculine fame of her family, balanced her husband's love with outstanding loyalty. After his death, in the flower of her age and beauty, she slept with her mother-in-law [Livia] in lieu of a husband.' Although only 27 years old, Antonia resisted her uncle Augustus' suggestions of remarriage, choosing to remain a widow.

Widowhood did not, however, mean obscurity. Antonia was a formidable matron of the imperial family, and her son Germanicus was groomed for power, finally being adopted by Tiberius, Augustus' heir. Germanicus died in AD 20, probably of malaria, though suspicions abound that Tiberius, who felt threatened by his adopted son's popularity, had had a hand in his death. Tacitus, who is hostile to both Tiberius and Livia, claims that they prevented Antonia from attending Germanicus' funeral, so that they too could stay away, and so conceal their joy at her son's death.

After Livia's death in AD 29, Antonia became the family matriarch, opening her home to her grandchildren (Caligula and Drusilla) and son (Claudius) who had all previously lived with Livia, and it is claimed by Suetonius that she once caught Caligula (no. 51) and his sister in an incestuous act. Her daughter, Livilla, also did not subscribe to her mother's virtuous ways and had an affair with Sejanus (no. 49), Tiberius' right-hand man. Antonia discovered a plot against Tiberius in AD 31, instigated by Sejanus and involving her daughter; she wrote to Tiberius at Capri and informed him, allowing him to act against the conspirators. He now gave Antonia, whom he had previously respected, his full confidence and in his gratitude spared Livilla's life. It would appear, however, that Antonia could not come to terms with her daughter's crime – it is claimed that she starved Livilla to death. Antonia was equally disdainful of the sickly Claudius, her other surviving son, who stammered and limped. According to Suetonius she frequently called him 'a monster: a man whom Nature had not finished but had merely begun'.

When Caligula became emperor he sponsored a senatorial decree that awarded her in one go all the honours given to the empress Livia in her entire lifetime. She used her position to attempt to influence him, but he spurned her advice, and shortly afterwards may even have done away with her. Suetonius writes:

> When his grandmother Antonia asked him to grant her a private audience he insisted on taking Macro, the Guards Commander, as his escort. Unkind treatment of this sort hurried her to the grave though, according to some, he accelerated the process with poison and, when she died, showed so little respect that he sat in his dining-room and watched the funeral pyre burn.

Antonia died in AD 37.

One of Claudius' first acts as emperor, despite his ill-treatment by Antonia, was to institute public sacrifices and games to his parents, during which the image of his mother was paraded in a carriage. Stern and unloving she may have been, but she had, as Josephus noted, 'kept her life free from reproach'.

49 | SEJANUS
Tiberius' sinister henchman

According to the historian Tacitus, in the ninth year of his reign (AD 23) the emperor Tiberius suddenly became tyrannical. The reason for this, in Tacitus' opinion, was the influence of Aelius Sejanus, the only man to whom the emperor spoke 'freely and unguardedly'. Sejanus rose to great heights at Rome, and his fall from grace was spectacular.

Sejanus was an Etruscan, born in Vulsinii. His father was Lucius Seius Strabo, an equestrian who had risen to the rank of joint commander of the Praetorian Guard under Augustus. As a young man Sejanus somehow acquired the wealth necessary to become part of the entourage of Augustus' grandson and heir, Gaius Caesar. (Tacitus suggests his increased fortune can be attributed to a homosexual affair with a rich debauchee.) He went on to share office with his father as Praetorian Prefect, and shortly after Tiberius' accession in AD 14 he was sent to Pannonia with Tiberius' son Drusus to put down an army mutiny. From AD 17 he was sole Praetorian Prefect, and in AD 21 his daughter was betrothed to Claudius' first son. The Romans believed Sejanus to be ambitious, and his actions – such as concentrating the Praetorian Guard into a single camp just outside Rome – tend to support their conclusion (see pl. XVI). Tacitus records: 'Of audacious character and untiring physique, secretive about himself and ever ready to incriminate others, a blend of arrogance and servility, he concealed behind a carefully modest exterior an unbounded lust for power.'

Tiberius himself described Sejanus as 'the partner of my labours', and allowed statues of him to be placed in theatres and public places. Sejanus' power was such that Drusus was moved to resentment and suspicion about his motives, and even struck him on one occasion. Sejanus' response was to seduce Drusus' wife, Livilla (he encouraged her by divorcing his own wife). Together Sejanus and Livilla are accused of slowly poisoning Drusus in AD 23. Emboldened by success, Sejanus began to move against Agrippina (wife of Germanicus and mother of the children who were next in line to succeed Tiberius), by charging her friends with treason and immorality. But when in AD 25 he asked Tiberius' permission to marry Livilla he was refused. Although he detested Agrippina, Tiberius was not yet ready to split the imperial house by allowing Sejanus to become part of the family. But his confidence in Sejanus was intact, and would be increased still further by a dramatic incident in AD 26. Tiberius and Sejanus were dining at a villa called 'The Cave' (located at modern

Sperlonga) when there was a rockfall. 'Sejanus, braced on hands and knees, face to face, warded the falling boulders off Tiberius.'

Tiberius had been persuaded to withdraw from Rome in AD 26 and take up residence on Capri. Then in AD 29 Livia, his formidable mother, died, and with her death a moderating influence – on both Tiberius and Sejanus – was removed. Agrippina was accused of having a disobedient spirit and her son Nero Caesar of homosexuality; they were both banished to remote islands. Her second son Drusus was accused of sleeping with the wives of distinguished men and was imprisoned in Rome. Sejanus was given proconsular power and honoured with more statues and games. Dio tells us that 'Sejanus was growing greater and more formidable all the time, so that the senators and the rest looked up to him as if he were actually emperor and held Tiberius in slight esteem'.

All Sejanus' rivals for power – with the exception of Gaius (known to posterity as Caligula, no. 51), Agrippina's youngest son – had now been removed. His position seemed unassailable, yet his downfall came swiftly. Tacitus and Josephus (no. 60) claim that Sejanus conspired with Livilla to overthrow Tiberius, and that their plot was exposed to Tiberius by Antonia (no. 48). Dio instead suggests that Tiberius finally became alarmed at the extent of Sejanus' power and suspected a conspiracy. Too frightened to move openly against Sejanus, Tiberius used subterfuge to undermine him in the Senate and with the people, and began to elevate Caligula, making him a priest and publicly praising him. Finally a letter from Tiberius denouncing Sejanus was read out in the Senate and he was dragged off to prison. That same day he was executed, his body abused by the people and afterwards thrown into the Tiber. His three children and many close associates were also killed, and his lover Livilla disappeared, allegedly starved to death by her mother when it was revealed to Tiberius that she may have poisoned his son.

Sejanus was certainly one of the most powerful men of his day, but whether the crimes and ambitions attributed to him were true will never be known. The ancient sources were universally hostile to him. As Tacitus himself admits, 'Sejanus, too much loved by Tiberius and hated by everyone else, passed for the author of every great crime; and rumours always proliferate around the downfall of the great.'

50 | PONTIUS PILATE
Governor of Judaea

Few Romans of the early imperial period are as readily remembered today as Pontius Pilate, yet apart from those moments when he is mentioned in the Gospels, the man himself is a shadow. Fortunately, we know that the Pontius Pilate described so memorably in the Gospels was a real person, for he is referred to also by the near-contemporary writers Tacitus and Josephus (no. 60).

The name Pontius was not unknown to the Romans. Two centuries before the birth of Christ, the Romans fought a drawn-out series of wars with the mountain people of central Italy known as the Samnites. The name Pontius first appears among these enemies of Rome, and later among Roman aristocrats and soldiers from the region. Despite his birth being claimed from points as scattered as Spain and Scotland, it seems likely that Pontius Pilate was a Roman of central Italian stock.

Pontius Pilate first appears in history as prefect of Judaea in AD 26. The duties of a prefect were fiscal, principally involving the supervision of tax collection; civil, since he, together with the Jewish authorities, was responsible for law and order; and judicial, in that he occasionally sat in judgment, particularly in capital cases. He was not, however, as Tacitus tells us, a procurator. Procurators were a later imposition in Judaea when the region had become formally assimilated into the Roman empire. An inscription found at Caesarea in the 1960s refers to 'Pontius, prefect of Judaea', thus establishing him beyond doubt both as a prefect and as a real historical figure. Caesarea was Pilate's base in Judaea, though as a prefect he travelled frequently. Like later procurators he commanded no more than a few auxiliaries and irregular troops. The legions were under the command of the higher-ranking regional official, the governor of Syria, and he was keeping them to himself while tensions remained high with the Parthian empire. Without substantial military backing, Pilate had to enforce his will by his authority and the reputation of Rome.

Pilate's predecessor, Valerius Gratus, had spent the previous decade attempting to reconcile Roman rule with Jewish sensibilities. Almost as soon as he took up office Pilate discovered how sensitive those sensibilities were. He was moving some troops into Jerusalem, and aware that the depictions of the emperor on the military standards might give offence, he had the men brought in at night. Nevertheless, once it was known that the standards were within the sacred city, Jewish envoys petitioned so earnestly for their removal that Pilate acceded. He probably felt on firmer ground when he dedicated some ornamental shields in the city, for these were fully in compliance with custom and practice. Nevertheless, this too was felt to be a Roman imposition. With Pilate standing firm on his rights, the Jewish people went over his head to the emperor, who ordered the shields to be withdrawn to Caesarea.

Despite his reported conduct at the trial of Jesus, Pilate was no pushover. When the Jewish people came close to a riot after he appropriated temple funds to pay for a 70-km (45-mile) long aqueduct, he mixed his own plain-clothes troops among the rioters. When matters came to a head, he ordered his men to produce the clubs hidden under their tunics and disrupt the riot. Josephus complains that there were many fatalities from the incident. It is quite possible that, some time after AD 32, Pilate tried someone he considered a would-be pretender to Herod's throne, who was causing unrest during the Passover; especially if he felt the man in question was leading an apocalyptic cult. This at least was the view of Tacitus: 'Chrestus, from whom the name [of Christians] has its origin, was executed during the reign of Tiberius by one of our procurators, Pontius Pilatus. That temporarily checked this nasty superstition.' It is unlikely that the incident troubled Pilate enough to write to the emperor about it, let alone commit suicide, as later reports claim.

Pontius Pilate next fell out with the Samaritan people, when he blocked the advance of a mob up Mount Gerizim where a religious demagogue had promised to retrieve the sacred vessels of Moses. According to Josephus the bloodshed amounted to 'a pitched battle'. Thereafter Pilate was recalled to Rome, allegedly on the instructions of Vitellus, then governor of Syria. Even if Vitellus had this authority (which is doubtful) Pilate need not have been in disgrace. He had served for ten years, when three or four was usual. He left his post in AD 36 and returned to Rome soon after the death of Tiberius in AD 37. It is quite possible that Pilate himself died soon after, because when Philo's embassy came to Rome in AD 41, its members seemed able to denigrate his memory without fear of a personal rebuttal.

51 | CALIGULA
Bad or mad?

Gaius Julius Caesar Augustus Germanicus – to give Caligula his full name – was Rome's third emperor. The first, Augustus, was of Rome's ancient Julian family. The second, Tiberius, was a Claudian, a family almost as ancient, and with an even more venerable history. Great things were expected of Caligula, the first emperor to combine the two lines (his mother was a Julian, his father a Claudian).

That father was Germanicus, a hugely popular general and nephew and heir to the emperor Tiberius. Born in August AD 12, Caligula was the youngest boy of three brothers and three sisters. He gained the nickname of Caligula ('little boot') from an army camp in Germany. There, dressed as a miniature Roman soldier, he became something of a mascot for the troops. Such was their fondness for him that his father used him to quell a mutiny, lifting him up to the mutineers and asking if they really intended to harm him.

The fortunes of the family changed abruptly in AD 19. Germanicus had travelled east on official business when, in September after a visit to Egypt, he fell sick and died. The evidence suggests malaria contracted in Egypt, but Agrippina, Germanicus' wife, was convinced that Tiberius had ordered the poisoning through jealousy. Her barely concealed hostility proved the ruin of her family, as the ageing Tiberius became ever more suspicious of all around him, a suspicion nurtured by Sejanus (no. 49), the emperor's ambitious henchman. Agrippina eventually died in exile, and Caligula's older brothers were killed.

Caligula survived, partly through the protection of two formidable matriarchs, Livia, mother of Tiberius, and Antonia Augusta (no. 48), the emperor's sister-in-law. At the age of 19 he was brought to Tiberius' retreat in Capri, mainly because he was almost the last surviving politically acceptable heir to the empire.

Tiberius passed away in AD 37 (with the help, it was rumoured, of a pillow over his face). After almost two decades of living in daily fear for his life Caligula was again the centre of adoring crowds. Little wonder that after a promising start, the young man collapsed with what might have been a nervous breakdown brought on by the sudden easing of the massive stress he had been under. For over a month his very survival was in doubt. When he finally recovered from his delirium, he was confronted with another terrible truth – the empire had carried on running smoothly without him. It may have been the realization that he was dispensible which drove Caligula's new policy, which was that of explicitly subordinating the Senate to the emperor. Previously, the military autocracy of the Caesars had pretended that the Republic of Rome was restored, and that the Senate was back in charge. Caligula ripped through this pretence and demanded that he be worshipped as a god, promoting himself above the pretensions of even the most ambitious senator.

Caligula blamed the Senate for its acquiescence in the killing of his mother and brothers, and the Senate hated him in turn for his flamboyant disregard of convention (which the general public rather enjoyed). As a 'god' he considered himself above the rules that bound normal mortals, and his behaviour became increasingly erratic.

The history of Caligula's reign was written by senators who passionately loathed him for the public contempt he showed them, and these senators made full use of Rome's rich tradition of political invective to destroy his memory. (In the same tradition Cicero, for example, cheerfully accuses his enemies of drunkenness, incest, sodomy and parricide even when these had nothing to do with the point he was making.) As this tradition makes Caligula a homicidal maniac, it may never be known how many political enemies – real or imagined – he genuinely had killed (fewer than 30 of his victims are named). That he made his favourite horse a consul of Rome is a myth of later generations, but he certainly threatened it, and such was his contempt for the Senate, he was certainly capable of it.

Between spells of dressing alternately as a god and a woman (says Suetonius), Caligula took himself on a rapid trip to Germany for a confrontation with the military commander there – a man so sure of the backing of his troops that he had earlier been able to defy Tiberius. Caligula's swift and uncompromising approach wrong-footed the commander, who was speedily executed and replaced by a competent subordinate. Then Caligula departed again. Political conditions were right for an attack on Britain, which was suffering internal chaos, and Caligula had raised new legions, XV and XXII Primigenia, for just this purpose. However, turbulent weather prevented the army from crossing, and the frustrated young emperor ordered his catapults to fire instead at the sea, and the troops to gather shells from the shore as the spoils of this 'victory'.

The rest of Caligula's foreign policy comprised the annexation of Mauretania and dealing with strife between Jews and Greeks in Alexandria. He adjudicated mainly in favour of the Jews, but horrified them by ordering that his image be placed in the temple in

Jerusalem. What is startlingly absent from his brief reign are signs of raving insanity in either domestic or foreign policy. Perhaps he came closest when he closed off the bay of Baiae with a pontoon bridge of boats and drove across on a chariot. However, this was the highlight of a stupendous party, and Caligula's way of sneering at the prediction that he would more easily ride a horse across the bay than become emperor. The project was undoubtedly very expensive, as were all of Caligula's tastes, but it is dubious that he 'drained the treasury' as reported. Firstly, he compensated by putting up taxes (one of his few unpopular moves with the people), and secondly, Caligula's successor, Claudius, still had enough money to invade Britain – and even a small war costs more than a lot of extravagance. In short, the mad emperor's fiscal, domestic and foreign policies were neither mad, bad nor ruinously expensive.

How Caligula's reign might have turned out (almost certainly badly) will never be known. He was assassinated at the age of 28 by members of his own guard, their ringleader (allegedly) incensed by jokes Caligula made about his sexuality. There was also a political motive, for the assassins afterwards went to the palace and killed Caligula's wife and baby daughter. (Even Caligula's critics grudgingly admitted that Caligula's wife appeared to love him deeply, and he was an excellent father.) His assassination was bitterly resented by the common people, and the Praetorian Guard forced the Senate (which had been hoping to restore the Republic) to put Claudius, Caligula's last surviving relative, on the throne.

52 | PALLAS
An ex-slave takes charge

The emperor Claudius never fully trusted the Roman Senate, perhaps with reason. The Senate as a whole resented their loss of power, and many individual senators felt they could do better as emperor.

Consequently, Claudius relied to an unprecedented degree on his own household to help govern the empire. This gave immense power to his financial secretary, Marcus Antonius Pallas. Yet Pallas had started as a slave to Antonia Minor, a powerful member of the imperial family. Antonia freed him some time in the AD 30s and became his patron, as was customary. On Antonia's death, that patronage passed to Claudius. Claudius used him to manage his personal budget, which was a major responsibility as at this time the emperor's budget was larger and in far better financial health than the official treasury.

By then Pallas was already wealthy, as Antonia seems to have left him land in Egypt. As a shrewd investor working at the financial heart of the empire, Pallas soon became phenomenally rich, though he was astute enough to be scrupulously honest in his official duties, which protected him from the frantic jealousy of the Senate. To make the extraordinary powers of this ex-slave more palatable, a dubious genealogy was published claiming Pallas was descended from the kings of Arcadia in Greece. Felix, the younger brother of Pallas, was less honest, and after serving as a moderately disastrous procurator in Judaea (where St Paul appeared before his court), he was hauled back to Rome to face a plethora of charges for bribery and embezzlement.

Pallas worked closely with Narcissus, another influential freedman, and the pair became immensely rich. It was said that the financial problems of the empire would be resolved overnight if Pallas and Narcissus would only include Claudius in their partnership. When the wild and self-destructive Messalina unilaterally divorced Claudius and remarried, Pallas and Narcissus worked together to stabilize the regime and to ensure that Messalina was executed. Pallas was also influential in persuading Claudius to choose as his next wife his niece, Agrippina (no. 53). Despite allegations that Pallas and Agrippina were lovers, it is more probable that they shared a desire for influence over Claudius. This association meant that Pallas survived the change of regime when Claudius was poisoned.

Narcissus did not, so Pallas briefly became more powerful than ever. But as Agrippina's influence at Nero's court waned, so did that of Pallas. It did not help that Pallas was famously snobbish, haughty and high-tempered, and so had few personal friends.

Nevertheless, Seneca, another advisor of Nero, defended him when he was accused of treason, and he escaped conviction. Pallas retired from public life and died in AD 63. It was generally believed that Nero poisoned him, since as Pallas' current patron Nero would inherit a share of his vast wealth.

53 | AGRIPPINA
Claudius' wife, Nero's mother

The family tree of the Julio-Claudian emperors is a complex affair in which branches fork, twine about themselves, and abruptly reappear on a completely different part of the trunk. The central point of reference often used by those trying to render it intelligibly on paper is Agrippina Minor (see pl. XVII), great-granddaughter of Augustus, great-niece of Tiberius, sister of Caligula (no. 51), niece (and wife) of Claudius, and mother of Nero. She was also a granddaughter of Marcus Agrippa (no. 40), who gave her his name.

Agrippina Minor was a daughter of Germanicus (born AD 15), and she shared in the tribulations of the family after his death. At the age of 13 she was married to her second cousin, Gnaeus Domitius Ahenobarbus, a man known for his vicious temper. However, the marriage may not immediately have been consummated, for she bore her only child, Domitius Ahenobarbus Nero, nine years later in AD 37, and her husband passed away soon after in AD 40.

By then her brother Caligula was running the empire in his own unique way. Later reports suggest that Agrippina threw herself into the debauched life of the imperial court, prostituting herself at her brother's instructions, and even sleeping with him on occasion. Incest was regularly attributed by political enemies in Rome, and truth here is hard to determine. Certainly family relations deteriorated after the revelation of a murky political plot that Agrippina and one of her sisters allegedly cooked up with an imperial favourite to replace their erratic and dangerous brother. The 'plot' was discovered, Agrippina was accused of debauchery with the favourite, who was executed while in Germany. Agrippina was forced by Caligula to carry his ashes back to Rome, and thereafter she and her sister were exiled. There Agrippina allegedly made her living by diving for sponges to sell.

Exile was actually a rather safe place to be while Messalina was wife of Claudius, Rome's next emperor. Messalina was determined that her son, Britannicus, would be the next emperor. It is not certain how much Claudius knew of the mini-massacre Messalina insti-gated among potential rivals, but certainly Agrippina's return from exile in AD 41 put her right in the firing line. Looking for allies, she married her former brother-in-law, the wealthy C. Sallustius Crispus Passienus (who died conveniently soon after making Agrippina his heir). Assassins made a failed attempt to kill the young Nero. These were probably hired by Messalina, whose uninhibited debauchery was losing her influence at court. Perhaps through desperation, Messalina unilaterally divorced her imperial husband in AD 48 and remarried a leading senator. This was seen as an attempted coup, and the pair were dead almost before their wedding dinner had gone cold.

With the help of Pallas (no. 52) Agrippina became the wife of Claudius, who had been politically wounded by the Messalina debacle. Because of her ancestry, Agrippina was still extremely popular with the people, and for a while she was seen almost as co-ruler with her new husband. She received unprecedented honours and used her new-found power to promote her own son over Claudius' child Britannicus. As a mark of the respect in which she was held, her birthplace in Germany was given her name, becoming Colonia Agrippinae (modern Cologne). It was uncertain how long Agrippina could maintain her position, which is why, when Claudius died from eating poisoned mushrooms in AD 54, many decided that Agrippina intended to consolidate her position and maintain her new authority through her son. At first this strategy was successful, and Nero allowed himself to be guided by his mother and Seneca, the tutor whom Agrippina recalled from exile. When Nero started to reveal his true nature, Agrippina resorted to ever more desperate measures to regain control. When she showed signs of transferring her support to Britannicus, Nero had his step-brother poisoned. This lack of family feeling was followed by an attempt to kill Agrippina herself. The murder weapon was a boat which Nero had built as an engineered death-trap. Agrippina avoided the collapsing ceiling and the attempts by the crew to kill her, and made the long swim back to land.

In a panic, Nero resorted to tried and tested techniques. A centurion was sent to kill Agrippina, who bitterly ordered the man to direct his first strike at her womb. She died in AD 59, having packed her eventful life into just 44 years.

54 | LOCUSTA
Imperial poisoner by appointment

Roman literature is littered with stories of poisons and poisonings. The wealthy were poisoned by their heirs, husbands by their wives, and men by their political enemies. But it is women who are particularly associated with the art of poisoning – Cato (no. 17) even claimed that all adulteresses were poisoners. The first reported case of poisoning involved the death of many leading Roman citizens in 331 BC; a group of 20 Roman matrons were allegedly found in the act of brewing poisons and drank their own concoctions in order to escape justice. There are many examples of women accused of poisoning their husbands or prominent politicians, and the most famous of all is the professional poisoner Locusta.

During the 1st century AD, the period in which Locusta plied her trade, poisonings were common at the imperial court. Tiberius' son Drusus and adoptive son Germanicus were supposedly victims of poison. The emperor Caligula was reported by Suetonius to have kept a chest full of poisons: 'It is said that when Claudius later threw this into the sea, quantities of dead fish, cast up by the tide, littered the neighbouring beaches.' Nero supposedly considered poisoning the entire Senate at a banquet.

Little is known of Locusta's background beyond the fact that she was an 'expert poisoner'. She had recently been condemned for poisoning, and was selected by Agrippina to kill Claudius, her husband. The most common version of the story is that a plate of Claudius' favourite food – mushrooms – was poisoned. When this did not immediately dispatch him, a doctor put a feather dipped in poison down his throat (under the pretence of inducing vomiting).

After this deed it appears that Locusta was returned to custody, but she was swiftly recalled to service by the new emperor Nero, who wished to dispose of his main rival – Claudius' young son, Britannicus. Like Claudius, Britannicus was poisoned at dinner but the effect – that of a mild laxative – was not fast enough for Nero. Summoning Locusta to his chambers, Nero flogged her. She was forced to rebrew her concoction several times until it killed a pig on the spot. It was then given to Britannicus. Tacitus reports that 'speechless, his whole body convulsed, he instantly ceased to breathe'. Nero informed his guests that Britannicus was prone to epileptic fits, but apparently his skin turned black – a sure sign of poisoning.

As for Locusta, Nero pardoned her of her crime and rewarded her with extensive country estates. Such was her notoriety that she established a school of poisoning, to which Nero sent students. But her immunity lasted only as long as Nero's reign. She was executed by his successor, Galba, in AD 69.

55 | CORNELIUS PULCHER
A patron of the Isthmian Games

One of the most influential figures in an ancient city was the *eugertes*, literally 'the do-gooder'. These civic benefactors were (usually) men who improved the facilities of the city and the lives of its citizens, ostensibly out of the goodness of their hearts, but more realistically as a way of glorifying family, ostentatiously displaying wealth, and promoting their chances of obtaining elected office.

Among the more interesting of these benefactors was a man called Cornelius Pulcher (though by another reading of the inscription on which he appears, the name Cn. Publicius Regulus is also possible). This man was a native of the Greek city of Corinth. However, 'Greek' here is a geographical description, as the Greek city was comprehensively flattened in 146 BC by the Romans, who later erected a very Roman colony on the site. The Corinthians had formerly celebrated games honouring Poseidon at his sanctuary at the isthmus. To Cornelius Pulcher fell the honour of restoring the games to their former venue, probably in AD 43.

We can make a number of deductions about the man from this fact. He was a provincial, a citizen of Corinth, very wealthy, and a leading politician. We can be sure of the last as the competition to be the man who staged the games (the *agonothete*) was intense in a normal year – in the year when the games returned to their old sanctuary the competition was fierce. It is evident that the games were successful, as the son raised an inscription to commemorate the event. This inscription tells us much of what we know about the return of the games to the isthmus, though archaeological evidence such as the date of the rebuilding of certain venues corroborates this, as do issues of Corinthian coins showing the victor's garland of pine.

The games featured both cultural and athletic events, some of which were only open to maidens (*parthenoi*). The ladylike Hedea, daughter of Hermesianax of Tralles, seems to have triumphed in the ladies' chariot racing (armed) event, if the record of her victory is contemporary (as it seems to be). After the Isthmian Games, the citizens plunged into a further round of events at the Caesarean Games in Corinth. These were again organized by the indefatigable *eugertes*, who rounded off the momentous occasion by treating all the citizens of his city to a sumptuous banquet.

56 | NUMERIUS QUINCTIUS
Actor

NVMERIVS QVINCTIVS ·)) · L · COMICVS
SIBI · ET · QVINCTIAE · PRIMILLAE
COLLIBERTAE · ET · CONIVGI · SVAE
VIXI · CVM · EA · AN · XXX

The highly compressed and cryptic text above tells us much about Roman life and the relationships between masters and servants and men and women in society at the time. First, we can see it is in part a memorial to one Numerius Quinctius. This man was a freed slave, as the same line shows with the letter 'L' for *libertus*, which means 'freed man'. We know he was a slave in the household of some branch of the noble Quinctian family (descendants of Cincinnatus, no. 9) because on being freed he took their name, as was traditional. Roman inscriptions tend to be very compact and conventional – stonemasons cost money, and slabs of good stone were not cheap either. If, as has been argued, the abbreviation for 'a woman' was ')' then Quinctius is saying that he was freed by two women. These would have been members of the Quinctian family, and therefore (by another Roman convention) named Quinctia. To a Roman this would be obvious, so there was no need for the names to be repeated. Thus the rudimentary ')' showed no disrespect to women in general or Quinctius' manumitters in particular.

Quinctius was freed at the same time as his wife Primilla (they are *collibertae*), who is called Quinctia not because she is married to Numerius, but because they were both freed from the Quinctian household. On being freed, Numerius made his career either as an actor or writer of comedies (*comicus*). It was not uncommon for actors to be slaves and to continue with their profession when freed. The profession was one of very low status in Rome, and many actors were regarded as just a step above prostitutes. Some comedies were elegant and witty, but many were bawdy, burlesque pantomimes staged for undiscerning holiday crowds.

Quinctius has erected this stone partly to his own memory, and that of those who freed him, but also to his wife, proudly pointing out, as Romans with happy marriages were wont to do, that he had lived with her (*vixi cum ea*) for 30 years.

57 | ANTONIA CAENIS
Vespasian's mistress

Antonia Caenis was a slave, and her career reveals yet again that personal connections were vastly more important in Rome than one's station in life. Caenis was born in the opening years of the 1st century AD. Possibly she or her family were from Thessaly, and her name is an allusion to a famous contemporary poem by Ovid which refers to:

Young Caenis, then a fair maiden of Thessaly:
Caenis the bright... A princess.

Roman slave owners often changed their slaves' names to whatever they felt best, and history does not record how Caenis felt about being named after a woman who changed genders after being raped and eventually comes to a bad end. Although Roman women did not usually have two names, the 'Antonia' shows that Caenis was a slave in the household of Antonia, daughter of Mark Antony, and was eventually freed by her mistress, and so, as was conventional, she added the name 'Antonia' to the single name she had possessed as a slave.

Unlike many slaves, Caenis was literate, and while in the household of Antonia she was ordered by her mistress to write a highly significant letter to the emperor Tiberius. At the time Tiberius was in Capri, and unaware of the extent to which his subordinate Sejanus (no. 49) was gathering power into his own hands. It appears that Antonia denounced Sejanus in this letter, and, aware that discovery could have fatal consequences, Antonia ordered Caenis to destroy all traces of the document. Caenis responded: 'It is useless for you to tell me to do this, Mistress, for each and every document you have ever dictated to me is ineradicably fixed in my mind.' If true (and Dio uses this quotation as an example of her 'superb memory'), then Caenis may have had an eidetic (photographic) memory – a useful trait in a secretary, especially one whom Dio calls 'exceptionally loyal'. By some reports Caenis took the incriminating message personally to the emperor, who then organized the downfall of his treacherous henchman.

After receiving her freedom, Caenis took up with Flavius Vespasian, a general who was in and out of imperial favour. (Caligula had Vespasian's tunic stuffed with street refuse when Vespasian failed in his duty to keep the streets clean. Nero put him into semi-exile, allegedly for falling asleep during one of his theatrical performances, but later restored him to command in Judaea.) It may well be that Vespasian met Caenis through the emperor Claudius, whom she certainly knew from the household of Antonia, Claudius' mother. Caenis became Vespasian's mistress, though their relationship was interrupted by Vespasian's marriage. Some time before AD 69 Vespasian's wife died, and the pair resumed where they had left off, though Vespasian was now emperor. His son Domitian never accepted Caenis' place in the household. On one occasion, when

Caenis returned from a trip abroad and came to greet Domitian, he held out his hand to to be kissed as an emperor's son by a servant.

Interestingly we are told that Caenis had returned from Histria, probably the city on the Black Sea, which was hardly a pleasure resort for imperial mistresses. This suggests that Caenis was no imperial bimbo, but an active and trusted official of the imperial retinue. Vespasian had dedicated himself to rebuilding the imperial fisc after the ruinous reign of Nero and was not scrupulous as to how he did this. Caenis was widely believed to be the intermediary through which procuratorships, generalships and priesthoods were marketed. Dio suggests that the influence of Caenis could be purchased to avert the possibly fatal consequences of imperial displeasure, and afterwards she and Vespasian split the profits between them.

Archaeologists claim to have found a bath house with lead piping bearing her name, and her house by the Porta Nomentana. Unlike Macedo (no. 65), this freed slave was apparently kind to her servants, as attested by a memorial which calls her 'the best of patrons', and another testifying to the happy marriage of her slave Helpis Caenidiana. Caenis herself (described as 'Vespasian's wife in all but name') died some time before AD 75, having diplomatically avoided the opprobrium heaped on Claudius' imperial freedmen, and is rightly considered one of the most exceptional women of her era.

58 | PETILIUS CERIALIS
Trouble with testosterone

Quintus Petilius Cerialis was perfectly suited for the wild times of the mid-1st century AD. His particular mix of ability and luck often rescued him from sticky situations into which his impetuosity and carelessness had landed him in the first place. He was a favourite of the army, and as much at home on the barbarian frontiers of the empire as in the imperial palaces.

Born around AD 30, Cerialis married the sister of a medium-ranked general, Flavius Vespasian. Cerialis served in Britain in AD 60, and was one of the few Romans on hand when Boudicca's rebellion erupted. Cerialis gathered together a scratch force to try to prevent Boudicca from taking Colchester, but had failed to appreciate the size of the revolt. His tiny force was overwhelmed, and he barely escaped with his life.

Back in Rome in AD 68, Cerialis, like Vespasian's son Domitian (no. 57), was left personally exposed by his brother-in-law's claim to the imperial throne. Cerialis escaped from Rome disguised as a peasant (Domitian had to go into hiding), and joined a friendly army advancing on the capital. He took charge of a unit of cavalry, and immediately led it in a foolhardy attempt to take a Roman suburb. He was soundly defeated.

Once Vespasian was established in power, he sent Cerialis to suppress a dangerous revolt by the Batavians on the Rhine frontier, which Cerialis managed competently. However, on one occasion when the Roman camp was attacked at night, Cerialis had to fight his way into the besieged camp to take command. He had been 'otherwise engaged' in a villa a few miles away, and was consequently severely under-dressed when he engaged in battle.

His amorous interests allegedly saved his life when Cerialis later made a trip upriver to inspect a bridgehead. A special Batavian boat squadron towed his command vessel away under the noses of the Roman sentries, but that night Cerialis was ashore, attending to 'an Ubian lady'. In AD 71 Cerialis was again in Britain as governor, practising his particular brand of diplomacy on Cartimandua, deposed Queen of the Brigantes. We last hear of him (or possibly his son) in AD 83, consul of Rome with the emperor Domitian.

The historian Tacitus calls Petilius Cerialis 'rash' and 'no lover of delay', and his conduct on campaign 'disgraceful', but he cannot deny that Petilius had a successful life, and lived it to the full.

59 | FRONTINUS
Rome's master of aqueducts

The antics of the imperial court during the 1st century AD have both fascinated and appalled later generations. Yet it is evident that for the Roman empire not to have comprehensively fallen apart during these years, there must have been capable people minding the shop while Caligula frolicked at Baiae, or Nero went chariot racing in Greece. Sextus Julius Frontinus was one such administrator. What we know of him is mostly what the man tells us himself in his works. The character that emerges from his writing is rather austere, precise and slightly humourless, a man so fond of detail that he occasionally takes his eye off the big picture. His pride in Rome and its citizens shines clearly through in his work. 'Compare these, if you would, with the pointless pyramids, or the pretty but useless constructions of the Greeks!' he exclaims of the Roman aqueducts which were his pride and passion. A military man himself, he also quotes with approval Scipio's comparison of himself with barbarian warlords: 'My mother gave birth to a general, not to a warrior.'

We know the rough parameters of Frontinus' life, for in his *Histories* Tacitus tells us that he was a senior magistrate, the *praetor urbanus*, in AD 70. Given the legal minimum age for this position, he was probably born between AD 30 and 35. Like any Roman aristocrat of his day, he had a cosmopolitan outlook and was fluent in Latin and Greek. More exceptionally, he also had a sound grasp of mathematics. On the other hand, again like many Romans who served the empire, Frontinus also wielded a sword. It is likely that he saw his first military action soon after AD 70 in the suppression of the revolt of Batavian auxiliaries on the German frontier. He was consul in AD 74 or 75, and thereafter served as governor in Britain, taking over from the flamboyant Cerialis, his old commander during the Batavian revolt. While in Britain, Frontinus continued to push Rome's western frontier into Wales, engaging in the traditional

Roman gubernatorial pastimes of building and fighting – in this case battling the Silurian tribe and constructing the road that still bears his name, the Via Julia. (Short sections of this road remain and can still be walked today.) He began writing on his return to Rome, starting with the *Stratagems*: a list of dirty tricks to play on the simple-minded enemy, which the methodical Frontinus had no doubt painstakingly compiled while teaching himself the art of war from histories of ancient campaigns.

It is probable that Frontinus took over the administration of Rome's aqueducts in the 90s, on his return from serving as pro-consul in the province of Asia. He tells us that the post had long been a sinecure of Rome's old elite, though this should not be taken to imply that he himself was such a placeman, since he was specifically charged with cleaning out practices that had seen the public water supply corruptly diverted to private use. It was a task ideally suited to Frontinus' precise and painstaking character, and he promptly became immersed in the details of Rome's water supply. His work *De Aquis* has passed these details on to posterity, delighting modern historians who are more accustomed to heady rhetoric and grandiloquent prose from their sources than cold, hard technical facts. As Frontinus himself tells us, what we have in *De Aquis* are the working notes which he put together as he tried to get to grips with this new challenge. 'This book may be useful to my successor, but I have prepared it for my own guidance.'

His diligence was rewarded by a further appointment to the consulship in AD 98, and again in 100, when the emperor Trajan himself served Rome's other consul, giving Frontinus an imperial colleague. We know that Frontinus was also a member of the elite College of Augurs, the priests charged with divining the intentions of the gods. Two of the great writers of his day, Tacitus and Pliny the Younger, seem to have known Frontinus personally, and the poet Martial abandoned his usual excoriating style to dedicate an affectionate verse to him:

In Anxur, Frontinus, I lived in calm seclusion by the
sea, and closer to Rome, I lived in a villa at Baiae by the
beach where Cancer flames. It had a wood that lacked
tormenting crickets, and a river-like pond. There you and
I found time to cultivate the poetic Pierides.

Now almighty Rome grinds us down, and I never have a
day to call my own. I am tossed about in the ocean of the
city, and waste my life in pointless labour.

(It is possible that Frontinus was a patron of Martial, which may
explain the latter's restraint.)

It has been speculated that an inscription in Germany dedicated
by a Julia Frontina is evidence that Frontinus had a daughter, and
the date of the mid-80s is appropriate, but otherwise nothing is
known of his family. Pliny quotes one of Frontinus' sayings in his
Epistles: 'the memory of a man's life will be preserved for as long
as his actions merit.' Frontinus died in about 104, and he is still
remembered as Pliny described him – as one of the best men of
his generation.

60 | JOSEPHUS
Crossing the cultural divide

In time, those peoples conquered by Rome both acquired Roman
culture and added aspects of their own culture to what it meant
to 'be Roman'. The process was sped up by the rapid adoption of
Roman ways by local aristocrats, who often went on to become fully
integrated members of the Roman elite. Few people demonstrate
this process in action more comprehensively than the writer born
Joseph ben Matthias, who fought the Romans as a young man,
was captured, and died many years later in Rome under the name

of Flavius Josephus, friend of the emperor, and champion of his native culture.

Josephus was born in AD 38 while Caligula (no. 51) was emperor. Even at the time of his birth, there was friction between the Jewish peoples, their Hellenistic neighbours and their Roman overlords, and throughout Josephus' youth this tension stretched towards breaking point. He spent this period in Jerusalem. He was the scion of one of the noble families, and would normally have expected to step into one of the high priesthoods of the Jewish state when he became an adult. His childhood was spent preparing for this, and Josephus immodestly informs posterity that he was a child prodigy, with rabbis and other learned men coming from all across the city to consult him on fine points of religious law. In his late teens his learning and family status led to Josephus being included in a diplomatic embassy to Rome. Consequently his name would have been known to the Roman high command – something which probably later saved his life.

Judaea, where Josephus lived, was strategically important to the Romans. It was the communication nexus of the Middle East, commanding the land routes between Egypt and Asia Minor, the hinterland of Syria, the province abutting Parthia, Rome's rival empire to the east. It was not a happy place. Banditry was rife, and as the Romans made provincials pay for their own defence, taxes were rising. This taxation was vehemently opposed by the zealots, Jewish religious nationalists who were against Roman rule, and also by the more fanatical *sicarii* who resisted to the point of terrorism, assassinating Jews whom they felt were in any way assisting the Romans. The favoured weapon of this group was the dagger (*sicarius*), giving the members their name.

As a member of the Jewish establishment, Josephus felt more antipathy towards these groups than he did to the Romans, but nevertheless, when the foment in Judaea boiled over into open rebellion in AD 66, Josephus joined the rebels. He was given command of the province of Galilee, an area of mixed peoples and cultures in the north of Judaea, and ordered to defend it against Rome. This proved impossible, for the Romans arrived in force, their legions commanded by Vespasian, a general with military experience in Britain.

Josephus masterminded the defence of the fortified town of Jotapa, and when the town eventually fell, he and his companions faced the choice of suicide or surrender. Determined not to surrender, the group drew lots so that each would kill the other. By an extraordinary coincidence, the last survivors of this lethal lottery were Josephus and the most amenable of his companions. The pair surrendered. (Josephus says that his survival was due to almost miraculous chance, and those who might have disputed his version were dead.)

The Romans knew from long experience that the only way to control a province was to gain the co-operation of the local aristocracy, so Vespasian gladly accepted Josephus' surrender. It thus came about that Josephus watched the next Roman siege – of his home town Jerusalem – from the opposite side, as an involuntary guest of the Romans. By now Vespasian had departed to make his bid for the imperial throne, leaving operations to his son Titus.

When Jerusalem fell in AD 70, Josephus went to Rome with his new patrons. He took the name of Flavius after the family name of Vespasian. However, he never abandoned his Jewish heritage. Instead he made it his life's work to present the Jewish point of view to his new homeland. His writings, especially the *Jewish Antiquities* and the *Jewish War*, are still essential reading for students of the ancient Middle East, as is his *Contra Apion* – a rebuttal of a Hellenistic anti-semitic tract.

Josephus had two sons, Justus and Simonedes, and appears to have been married three times. It is not known when he died, but it was peacefully in his own bed – a notable achievement for a man who had lived in troubled times.

61 | AMAZONIA

Female gladiator

A Roman matron was meant to be virtuous, almost prudish, shy and retiring, and so modestly clad that even her ankles were covered by her dress. However, the women of the early Roman empire seem to have been particularly good at avoiding this typecasting, few more so than the sword-swinging ladies such as Amazonia who fought in the arena.

Although it is certain that there were female gladiators in ancient Rome and the provincial cities, it is uncertain how common female fighters actually were. Even more controversially, it appears that these fighters were often not unfortunate female slaves coerced into fighting each other for the titillation of the audience, but genuine equal-opportunity combatants who were taken as seriously as their male counterparts.

Juvenal, the satirist, ridiculed the topic in the late 1st century AD.

> Listen to her grunt and groan as she gets down to it,
>   parrying, thrusting;
> Look at her neck drooping beneath her weighty helmet …
>   and the practice being over,
> Armour and weapons are discarded
> While she squats to use the can.

Not only were some of these women volunteers, but the sources suggest ladies of noble birth may have been among them. Under the emperor Tiberius, a law known as the Larinum decree forbade the female relatives of those 'who had ever had the right to seating reserved for the knights' to appear as gladiators. Information about female gladiators in the ancient sources is scanty, and the first explicit reference to female fighters actually appearing in the arena comes from the reign of Nero, but this refers to women casually, regarding the exceptional thing about the combatants being that they were Nubians.

Amazonia was exceptional in that the sculpture on which she is commemorated appears to be from the Hellenistic city of Halicarnassus, on the seaboard of Asia Minor. Arenas were more common in the west of the empire, but by the end of the 1st century a gladiatorial career was evidently possible in the Greek east, and indeed some eastern cities actively petitioned the emperor for permission to hold games.

Whatever her social class, Amazonia would have had to swear away her rights in the 'gladiatorial oath', allowing herself to be burned, bound, beaten and to die by the sword. (The burning may be a reference to the habit of touching a hot iron against the skin to check that a combatant was not shamming death.) Once sworn in, the gladiator took her *nom de guerre*, generally choosing one from mythology. References to the Amazons were unsurprisingly popular among female fighters. Like her male counterpart, Amazonia would have been under the care of a trainer, a *lanista* (literally 'a bladesman').

Occasionally women fought in mock combats (Domitian pitted them against dwarves), but sometimes they fought against men (in one case they appear to have done so in chariots in a reenactment of the exploits of Boudicca of the Iceni). However, Amazonia seems to have been a serious fighter, one of those who fought in the early evening, when the star attractions appeared in the arena.

The picture shows her matched against one Achillea. The pair are fighting without helmets, though this may have been so that their features can be shown in the picture. It is uncertain whether the heads of spectators appear at the bottom, or if these are the helmets, included for purposes of identification. (The shame of their profession meant that many gladiators preferred to be recognized by their distinctive helmets rather than their faces.) Both of the female combatants shown here have the kit of their male equivalents, which suggests that, like the male gladiators of this class, they fought with bare chests.

Each female gladiator has a curved shield (*scutum*) and a short stabbing sword. Each arm has protective armour (*manica*) and there are greaves on the legs. This armour was designed to make debilitating wounds less likely while leaving the wearer vulnerable to a killing stroke.

In this case, both fighters were allowed to leave the arena alive. This was usually the reward for a particularly thrilling fight, as appears to have been so here, since the citizens saw fit to commemorate the engagement on stone. It is believed that gladiators, even slave gladiators, had the incentive of keeping their prize money. Nevertheless, it was a risky way to get rich. Recently a grave was uncovered in London of a young woman who may have been a gladiator. If so, she would be a contemporary of Amazonia's whose luck ran out.

62 | EPICTETUS
The philosopher slave

A strength of Roman society was that a person of ability could make his mark, no matter what his social station. However, even in this context Epictetus is remarkable. His origins were lowly, being a slave of a recently freed slave (*epictetus* means 'acquired'). How he came to that situation after being born in Hierapolis in Asia Minor is unknown. It did not help that Epictetus was lame – one claimed this was through being tortured by his master, others more prosaically suggest rheumatism. As a way of coping with his troubles, Epictetus turned to the Stoic philosophy which teaches 'pain is inevitable – suffering is optional'. He studied under Musonius Rufus, probably still a slave, and shared his lessons with many leading Roman citizens. Epictetus was considered enough of a philosopher to be banished in AD 89, when Domitian concluded that Rome had too many bearded and subversive layabouts.

By now a freedman, Epictetus set up school in Epirus in Greece, where his reputation ensured him a clientele of top Romans. (The historian Spartianus says the emperor Hadrian treated Epictetus 'with the greatest friendliness'.) As befitted his philosophy, he was blunt with these aristocrats. 'If a man is dependent on others for favour and advancement, call him a slave', and 'But you say this is not worthy of you... well, you know what you are worth, and if you are going to sell yourself, you owe it to yourself to get a good price.'

Some of his quotes refer to God as a single deity, but there is no evidence that Epictetus had ever heard of Christianity. Indeed some of his teaching, such as that on suicide, directly contradicts Christian doctrine. Christianity regards suicide as a sin, Epictetus considers it a convenient option. 'When they are tired of a game, even children know to cry "enough". I will stay in a smoky room, but if the smoke is excessive I will leave. The door is always open.'

Arrian, a student, collected Epictetus' sayings into the *Enchiridion* ('Handbook'), giving advice on morality and public conduct which influenced the *Meditations* of Marcus Aurelius and is still relevant today. While we know that Epictetus lived a long life there is no sign of a family, and he probably died in the early 2nd century AD.

63 | MARTIAL
The art of epigrams

'We feel no respect for the character of the man... his name is crushed by a layer of cold-blooded filth spread ostentatiously over the whole surface of his writings, too clearly denoting habitual impurity of thought, combined with habitual impurity of expression.' So wrote a 19th-century biographer of Martial, Rome's foremost epigram-matist, the author of over 1,500 short verses in a style uniquely his own. Some of these verses are touchingly tender, others are sharp observations of social life, and many are breathtakingly vulgar.

Marcus Valerius Martialis was a Roman in that he was a Roman citizen, but he was born in Spain, one of a generation of 'Spaniards' who were to profoundly influence political and intellectual life in Rome. Others born in Spain at or about this time included the philosopher Seneca, the epic poet Lucan and the emperor Trajan. Almost all we know of Martial is from what he tells us in his works – even his name may be a pen-name taken from *Martialis*, the month of his birth. From a verse celebrating his 57th birthday, we can place his birth at 1 March, probably AD 40. His parents, according to a somewhat dubious inscription, were Fronto and Flaccilla. Both appear to have died early, leaving their son to make his way to Rome when he was in his mid-twenties.

Martial's early days in the big city were smoothed by other Spaniards such as Lucan who were already there. These helped him make friends at the highest level (at one time being invited to dine with the emperor Domitian). He turned down lucrative offers of employment, for example in the law courts, in favour of the relatively impoverished but bohemian life of a poet. His first work was the *Liber Spectaculorum*, an awed account in verse of the opening of the Circus Flavius (today called the Colosseum) in the reign of the emperor Titus. Shortly afterwards Martial turned his attention to the epigram – a form of writing which had meant simply 'an inscription' but which he re-defined as a set of short, pithy lines leading to a pointed conclusion. It was a style which lent itself well to puncturing the decadence and pretension he saw around him.

> Lesbia boasts that she never screws anyone for free.
> It's true. When she wants sex
> She has to pay.

Verses such as this delighted and appalled the Romans, and almost every generation since. Martial himself was well aware of this reaction to his poetry, remarking of Rome's most famous paragon of feminine purity, Lucretia:

Blushing Lucretia would have closed my book
While Brutus was there,
But when he was gone
She'd have read.

Poetry paid well for Martial, who acquired a house on the Quirinal, and like Horace (no. 28), a small Sabine farm. Unlike Horace, Martial complained bitterly that his house was too small, his farm too unproductive, and his patrons too stingy. 'Everyone wants a second Augustus in Rome. Well, a second Maecenas [billionaire patron of Horace and Virgil] would suit me.' On another occasion Martial indignantly notes that a former patron is now sending gifts to his lovers instead. 'Oi! You are having it off on my money!' His popularity was not confined to Rome – the poet claims that he was devoured in Britain and Gaul, indeed he retired to Cisalpine Gaul once his writing had become successful. But he could not stay away from Rome for long, and in the end he spent some 35 years there. Eventually he retired back to the haunts of his youth in Spain, in the company of one Marcella who was either his bride or his patron.

No daughter of the the lofty Capitoline could rival you;
You tell me not to yearn for Rome and you, in yourself,
    create the city for me.

Martial died some time around AD 104, and his friend Pliny noted his passing in an undated letter. Martial himself wrote of how he wished to spend his last days.

A bed that's modest, yes, but which someone warms
Sleep that makes the dark hours short
Needing to be yourself, and nothing more
Neither fearing your end, nor wanting it.

Part 5

Citizens of the Empire
AD 75–200

In the second century of the Christian era, the Empire
of Rome comprehended the fairest part of the earth,
and the most civilized portion of mankind. The frontiers
of that extensive monarchy were guarded by ancient
renown and disciplined valour. The gentle but powerful
influence of laws and manners had gradually cemented
the union of the provinces. Their peaceful inhabitants
enjoyed and abused the advantages of wealth and luxury.
The image of a free constitution was preserved with
decent reverence: the Roman senate appeared to possess
the sovereign authority, and devolved on the emperors
all the executive powers of government.

These lines, from the first chapter of Gibbon's *Decline and Fall
of the Roman Empire*, give an idealizing picture of Rome at the
height of its power and prosperity. Yet as Gibbon was well aware, even
at this point the deep-seated flaws at the heart of the Roman social
and economic structure were slowly toppling the massive edifice.

However, to the people of the time it did not seem so. The goddess
Felicitas ('Good Fortune') appears on a goodly number of coins of
this period, signifying, as one inscription put it, 'the happiness of our

times'. Under Trajan, the Roman empire was to reach its greatest extent, and though Trajan's successor Hadrian pulled back from those frontiers where Trajan had perhaps over-committed Rome, life within the borders had assumed a pattern that its members happily assumed was permanent. Rome was at peace, her frontiers were secure, and the major enemy the empire had to fight was the plague, brought by returning soldiers from the east. The empire was now cosmopolitan, and a surprisingly homogenous society. Men such as Cornelius Pulcher (no. 55) and women such as Metila Acte (no. 74) lived their lives in the belief that the *Pax Romana* would extend, forever serene and unchanging, across the known world.

Disillusion soon followed. Marcus Aurelius (no. 75) was followed by his inept son Commodus, who used brutality and arrogance to cover his lack of basic competence. A brief and brutal civil war resulted in a brisk change of emperors until the Severan dynasty took power. Events were followed and discussed with interest by ordinary Romans such as Blandina Martiola in Gaul (no. 70), but the repeated changes in government only affected the daily lives of Rome's citizens to the extent that taxes were raised to pay for the soldiers on whom the emperor was becoming ever more dependant. Nevertheless, there was a sense, reflected for example in histories of the Roman senator Cassius Dio, that Rome's Golden Age had turned to one of 'iron and rust'.

Yet political change at the top reflected subtle changes that permeated Roman society. The Severans were Romans, but they were Romans from Africa, and they were to be succeeded by a dynasty of Roman emperors from Syria. Rome was now essentially a single state that stretched across most of Europe, Asia Minor and the northern shores of Africa. Local variations abounded, but this state had a common culture, and shared religion and language (though Greek was more common in the east and Latin in the west). This was particularly the case among Rome's upper classes. A 'Roman' such as Aulus Gellius (no. 76) could feel as much at home in Athens as in Rome, Alexandria or London.

Being Roman was now not a question of geography but of culture and a particular viewpoint, which regarded the prevailing social order as not only the best available in the known world, but even as the natural state of affairs from which alien cultures had somehow become perverted. There was much to be admired in foreign peoples, as Tacitus made plain in his descriptions of Germany and later writers were to do with the Persians, but the intention of these writers was to use foreign virtues as exemplars for those who they felt already existed among the Roman people, but who could use more encouragement. The overall superiority of Roman culture was not in question.

During this period the language and law of Rome became so fundamental to the peoples of southern Europe that they are still called 'Latin' peoples almost two millennia later, and their languages – Italian, Spanish, French and even Romanian – are collectively called 'Romance' tongues. Equally importantly, the memory of this peaceful era of greatness, however distant and distorted it became over time, remained an important part of the European collective consciousness. Charlemagne and his successors in the later Holy Roman Empire were united by a desire to recreate the unified Europe of the Antonines (the family from which Marcus Aurelius (no. 75) came), and it is a desire still reflected today among some supporters of the European Union.

This feeling of sharing a common culture and purpose helped to fortify Rome's empire against the storms that were to afflict it when the long peace of the Antonine era came to an end, and Rome was wracked from within by civil and religious conflict and by repeated invasions from without.

64 | PLINY THE ELDER
Scholar and man of action

Gaius Plinius Secundus packed into his 56 years more writing and research than could be expected of any two men, yet he combined this with a career as an admiral, soldier and imperial procurator. Any moment in which Pliny was not writing or reading he regarded as a waste of time. He chided his nephew for walking around Rome, when he could study from a litter, and even in his bath he was either dictating or having material read to him.

He was born in north Italy in AD 23 or 24. He came from a wealthy family with senatorial connections, and as did any Roman youth of high ambition, he made his way to Rome. He was there during the reign of Caligula (no. 51), for he reports personally seeing Caligula's wife Lollia Paulina dripping with gems. His parental connections obtained him a military command, and he exchanged the fleshpots of Rome for the forests of Germany.

From AD 47 Pliny took part in various campaigns against the Germanic tribes. He served in the cavalry, and combined his love of action and scholarship into a treatise, doubtless based on practical experience, on how to throw spears from horseback. While in Germany Pliny made the acquaintance of one Titus Vespasian, another officer with a promising future.

Back in Rome, Pliny tried a career in law, but soon gave it up. He still produced several literary works in this most fallow period of his life, but they were uncontroversial. Rome was under the tyrannical emperor Nero, and Pliny seems shrewdly to have decided to pass his reign on the sidelines of public life. Things changed in AD 69, a turbulent year which ended with his old comrade Vespasian as emperor, and Pliny entered into administrative and literary work.

'He would get up at midnight; or an hour later in winter, two at most. Consequently he was often sleepy, and would sometimes doze off while working. He'd be off to visit Vespasian (another

night-owl) before dawn, and then get down to his official duties…
in summer, by way of relaxation, he would often recline in the sun,
and have a book read to him while he took notes. He made extracts
of everything,' recounts his nephew Pliny the Younger. As was
common in Rome, the elder Pliny adopted his nephew when the
latter's father died, and much of what we know of Pliny comes from
his nephew's experience.

During the early 70s he was imperial procurator in Spain, Gaul
and Belgium, a job with responsibility for the imperial finances in
each province. He collected facts as he travelled, and assembled
these into a huge encyclopedia called the *Naturalis Historia* (Natural
History), which ran to 31 books on geography, botany and biology,
with some anthropology included. He did this in his spare time, as
on his return to Italy he became commander of the fleet at Misenum
– effectively admiral in charge of the western Mediterranean.

Then, in AD 79 on 24 August, the most spectacular natural event
in Roman history occurred. Vesuvius erupted, right next door to
Pliny's naval base in Campania. It was just after lunch on that day
when Pliny's sister called attention to a mushroom-shaped cloud in
the direction of Pompeii. Pliny, acting both as a scientist and a civil
servant, immediately boarded a fast boat to investigate, and while en
route received confirmation that Vesuvius was erupting. His mission
immediately changed to a humanitarian one, and he ordered the
fleet to assist with evacuation by sea of as many as possible (though
being Pliny, he continued to dictate scientific observations as he
worked). He stayed overnight at a villa in Stabiae, and apparently
slept peacefully through the earthquakes and pumice storms. But
on rising he seemed distressed. The party set out for the shore with
pillows tied to their heads for protection from falling stones and ash.
Although it was now daytime, it was pitch black, and the sea was
too wild for sailing. Pliny lay down, called for water, choked, and
died. Perhaps he was overcome by sulphuric fumes, or perhaps his
heart failed after his exertions. (Pliny found exercise a distraction
and his nephew admits he was 'pretty fat'. Fortunately the younger

Pliny stayed home doing exercises his adoptive father had set him, and to him we owe the above report, a description of a natural disaster so precise that even today volcanic eruption clouds of this kind are called 'plinian'.)

His death deprived Rome of a fine scholar. Pliny not only tried to examine facts at first hand, but had a refreshingly cynical attitude to his sources, not being afraid to take issue even with Aristotle, for centuries the undisputed authority on the natural world. Equally refreshingly, he quotes his sources, noting disapprovingly that some contemporaries copied others wholesale and without attribution. Tacitus in turn paid Pliny the compliment of being one of the few authorities he himself quoted in his own work.

65 | LARCIUS MACEDO
Master killed by his slaves

Slavery permeated almost every aspect of Roman life. Slaves worked in the empire's mines and estates, and citizens made them labour on their farms or in their houses (see pl. vii). As the Romans conquered, they enslaved. In 168 bc, for example, 150,000 inhabitants of Epirus in Greece were sold into slavery after their state capitulated to the Romans. Population estimates are controversial, but it has been suggested that by the end of the 1st century bc there were two to three million slaves in Italy. Tension was inevitable, and occasionally – and dramatically – it exploded. The revolt led by Spartacus (73–71 bc) is a prime example, one that nearly brought Rome to her knees. The situation was eased to some extent by the hope of manumission – freed men and women enjoyed a limited form of citizenship, and their children were full citizens. But, outnumbered by slaves and aware of past rebellions, Rome's citizens feared what would happen if their unpaid workforce rose up against them. This is what happened to Larcius Macedo in the later 1st century ad.

Pliny the Younger reported the shocking event in a letter to his friend Acilius. Larcius Macedo had once been a slave himself. He had been freed and had prospered, rising to hold the position of praetor, and becoming the wealthy owner of a large *familia* of slaves. Yet despite his own background, he was a cruel master, and one day his slaves reacted against their mistreatment.

He was taking a bath in his villa when some of his slaves surrounded him: 'one of them grasped him by the throat, another hit him in the face, another in the chest and stomach, another (what an unpleasant thing to mention!) in the groin. When they saw that he had lost consciousness, they threw him onto the boiling hot bath-floor to see if he was still alive.' Believing he was dead, they carried him out, pretending that he had fainted from the heat of the bath. They fled, however, when the wailing of his concubines and ministrations of some of his more faithful slaves roused him. Most of the slaves were caught, but some were still free when Pliny wrote his letter. Their fate would have been grim. In a case a few years earlier (AD 61), an entire household of 400 slaves had been tortured and executed because they had failed to prevent some of their number from a murderous attack on their master. Larcius himself survived only a few days after the attack, but died in the knowledge that some of his attackers at least had been tortured to death.

According to Pliny, there had been an ominous sign of Larcius' fate prior to the events, again while bathing. In a public bath in Rome, one of Larcius' slaves accidentally touched an equestrian. This man turned and hit Larcius so hard that he almost fell to the ground. For Larcius, the baths were first a place of insult, then of death.

In most cases, the lot of domestic slaves was better than that of those condemned to work down the mines or on large agricultural estates. But they had absolutely no rights, and their experiences ultimately depended on the nature and disposition of their master. The elder Cato (no. 17), for example, was notorious as a cruel master and recommended that elderly and sick farm slaves be sold when they were no longer useful, and Cassius Dio reported that many people didn't bother to treat their sick slaves and some even threw them out of the house completely. In contrast, Cicero (no. 29) believed that it was his duty to act justly towards his slaves (even though they were still to be made to do their work!), such as the loyal Tiro (no. 33).

Pliny was himself a humane master who had once even purchased a small farm as a retirement house for his old nurse. Yet he was deeply shocked by Larcius Macedo's violent end, even though he admitted that he had been a tyrant to his slaves. His reaction sums up the anxiety felt by many Romans, who were heavily outnumbered by their slaves:

> So you see how exposed we are to all sorts of danger, insult and humiliation. And it is not the case that anyone can feel himself secure because he is indulgent and mild – masters aren't killed with a just cause, but as the result of sheer criminality.

66 | MINICIUS ACILIANUS
The prospective husband

'So, you want me to look out for a suitable husband for your niece?' Thus Pliny the Younger, senator, lawyer and scholar in the age of Trajan begins a letter to his friend Junius Mauricus. It is evident that while he is flattered to be asked, Pliny is by no means surprised by the request. It was normal in Rome for marriages to be arranged by older members of the family, and indeed, Pliny was – very happily – wed to his wife, Calpurnia, because it proved impossible to withstand an aged aunt's suit on her niece's behalf.

'I know the very man,' Pliny says, and offers for consideration Minicius Acilianus, a native of Brixia, a province famous for 'old-fashioned modesty and simplicy'. As is proper, Pliny describes the potential husband's father and distinguished relatives, concluding 'you will find nothing in his family which is unworthy of yours'. The man himself is vivacious, amiable, hard-working and modest. Pliny cheerfully adds that Minicius has already scaled the ladder of Roman magistracies to praetor, 'so you will be spared the trouble and expense of soliciting those honourable offices for him'.

Lest one should think that looks are unimportant, Pliny says the virginal young lady would receive an elegant husband 'with graceful and patrician manners, a well-bred countenance and a ruddy, healthy complexion'.

And finally, Pliny feels he ought to mention that the man is extremely rich. Of course, he adds hastily (lest he imply that the prospective bride's family is either hard-up or money-grabbing), this is unimportant in comparison to character in a prospective husband, but since children must be cared for (Pliny understood that child-bearing and the continuation of the family was the main reason for a marriage), the fact should be given consideration.

It is certain that, as a respected senator, Pliny was often asked to suggest potential marriage partners for others. That he chose to publish this particular letter on the topic suggests that Minicius Acilianus was something of a pin-up boy among potential spouses – the ideal husband-to-be.

67 | DOMITIAN
The paranoid emperor

The emperors Vespasian and Titus were emphatically good with people and personal relations. The third and last Flavian emperor, Titus Flavius Domitianus, equally emphatically was not. He was born on 24 October AD 51 in Rome, just as his father Vespasian was made consul-elect, a sign of improving times for his struggling senatorial family. Domitian was ten years younger than his brother Titus, and had a somewhat solitary childhood. His father was often away on campaign, and was joined in Judaea by Titus to help fight the Jewish war. Domitian remained in Rome, and was bitter that his father declared himself emperor while his youngest son was still living amid Vespasian's new enemies. When taking refuge in the Capitol failed, Domitian escaped disguised as a priest of Isis, and only declared his whereabouts when Rome was safely in Flavian hands.

Domitian was highly intelligent (he chose Minerva as his patron goddess), but deeply reserved and resentful of the friendships his father and brother formed so effortlessly. He only grudgingly accepted his brother's right to succeed his father and the pair were never close. When Titus was on his deathbed, after reigning from just AD 79–81, his brother dropped everything to rush to the side of the Praetorian Guard, the largest military force anywhere near Rome. Safe among the men who had a strong influence over the choice of Rome's next emperor, Domitian waited anxiously for his brother to breathe his last, and for himself to be proclaimed in Titus' place.

As emperor Domitian was meticulous and conscientious. He took a keen interest in finance, and did his best to halt the debasement of the coinage – the empire struggled to support a highly expensive army at a time when foreign wars no longer paid their way as they had under the Republic. Domitian keenly enforced the special tax that Jews had to pay for living in Rome, and he made sure that the tax was also paid by those 'living as Jews but who did not declare themselves to be such' – almost certainly an early reference to Christians. Domitian was a keen defender of the old Roman religion, and had the chief Vestal Virgin buried alive for being unchaste. He was also an enthusiastic supporter of the games, and took delight in the unusual and bizarre, staging fights involving strangely matched opponents such as women against dwarves, or battles by torchlight. He had little personal skill with the sword, but was a keen archer. He would sometimes make a slave stand some distance away, and shoot arrows into the wood between the slave's outstretched fingers.

Aware of the high cost of military campaigns, Domitian kept the empire in a defensive stance. He pulled troops back to secure lines in Britain, and declared a spurious triumph for a minor war against the Chatti in Germany. The serious campaigning of his reign was in Pannonia, where Domitian personally took the field against the Sarmatians and Dacians who were causing trouble right across the Danube basin. Trajan's later conquest of Dacia was probably based on Domitian's painstakingly built foundation.

Domitian had a tendency to micro-manage the empire. For example, when a corn shortage was accompanied by a surplus of wine, Domitian drew up a careful roster of which vineyards should be replaced by cornfields (a measure which was never put into effect). The Senate felt disenfranchised by government conducted by the emperor and his close companions. An increasing amount of responsibility was taken away from the Senate and given to the equestrians, who Domitian felt had less chance of making a bid for power. For Domitian, in turn, neither liked nor trusted the Senate. He knew that his own dynasty were to some degree usurpers, and that any senator stood a chance of taking his place. During his reign some 35 senators were executed – a modest sum by Julio-Claudian standards – and we cannot know how many were genuinely guilty of treason, for as Domitian complained, the only way that a plot against him would be considered anything but paranoia would be if it succeeded. Consequently an atmosphere of fear and distrust filled the corridors of power. Domitian was rumoured to spend hours alone in his rooms, catching flies and stabbing them with a specially sharpened pen. The columns of the imperial peristyles were mounted with highly reflective stones polished to a mirror-like finish so that Domitian could see what was going on behind him as he walked along. The emperor's only trusted confidante appeared to be a dwarf with a grotesquely swollen head who Domitian liked to keep beside him at the games.

The history of Domitian's reign was therefore mostly written by men who loathed him, so it is hard to obtain a balanced picture of his achievements. Despite this, the attention Domitian gave to his mother city achieved grudging recognition. Shops which had been spreading across thoroughfares were cleared back, a degree of modesty was enforced at popular theatrical entertainments, and a huge building programme was begun. After two major fires and a recent civil war, parts of the capital had become distinctly down-at-heel.

Domitian's downfall was caused by his own suspicious nature. He executed his manifestly harmless cousin Flavius Clemens, after which no one, including his own wife Domitia, felt safe. (Domitia had already been exiled and recalled once in his reign.) On 18 September AD 96, Domitian was increasingly uneasy, fearing something horrible would happen on the fifth hour of the day. When that hour came, his retinue assured him that it had already passed, so a relieved Domitian went for a bath, where an assassin was lurking. On sighting the killer, Domitian yelled to a boy slave to grab the dagger stashed nearby under the imperial pillow. The dagger turned out to have a hilt, but no blade. Grappling with his armed assassin, Domitian attempted to claw the man's eyes out with his lacerated fingers. He yelled to the boy to get help, but all the doors had been locked from the outside.

Thus at the age of 45 Domitian met the death he had dreaded. His memory was damned by the Senate, and only a cursory attempt was made to unearth the details of the plot which undoubtedly involved highly placed senators and the imperial family itself. Few of the statues of the man who liked to be addressed as 'Master and God' now survive. His death marked the start of an era of almost unbroken success and prosperity for Rome.

68 | AGRICOLA
Governor of Britain

Gnaeus Julius Agricola's life and career show how international Rome had become. Although his father was a Roman senator, he was born in Gaul, and his mother had estates in southern Italy. Agricola served in Syria and Scotland, and had the option of also serving on the Danube or in North Africa. His son-in-law, Tacitus, wrote Agricola's biography, but apart from stock cliches about his modesty and brilliance, this yields little insight into the man or his personality. Nevertheless, thanks to Tacitus, we know more of Agricola's life than we do of any contemporary Roman of equivalent rank.

Despite his name (which means 'farmer'), Agricola was above all a military man. He was born on 13 June AD 40, the same year that his father was executed by Caligula (no. 51). Agricola was to spend much of his career in Britain, which he first visited as a young soldier. He arrived at an inauspicious moment. 'Never indeed had Britain been more excited, or in a more critical condition. Veteran soldiers had been massacred, colonies burnt, armies cut off.' This was the rebellion of Boudicca, which was put down by the governor Suetonius Paulinus, who took a personal interest in the promising young man under his command. Agricola learned much from Paulinus, appreciating not only the man's military ability but also how his treatment of his enemies as less than human intensified their resistance.

Agricola went to Rome in AD 63, where he met and married the noble Domitia Decidiana and was appointed quaestor to the province of Asia. Although responsible for the finances of this wealthy province under a particularly corrupt governor, Tacitus assures us that this father-in-law resisted all temptation to illicitly enrich himself. Evidently his wife accompanied him for she bore Agricola a daughter, Julia, and a son who died soon after birth. The next steps on the senatorial career ladder were tribune, and then praetor. Agricola was competent but utterly undistinguished in these roles – his low profile was probably wise, given that the murderous Nero was emperor. Agricola's mother was killed in the civil war of AD 69 which followed Nero's overthrow, and Agricola gave his support to Vespasian, the man opposing his mother's killers.

Vespasian became emperor, and Agricola took command of the legion XX Valeria Victrix in Britain. He campaigned against the Brigantes, and when his command ended in AD 75 he was made a patrician and given the governorship of Aquitaine in Gaul. In AD 77 Agricola was recalled to Rome where he became consul. At this time he guaranteed his reputation with posterity by betrothing his 15-year-old daughter to Tacitus. Agricola and his son-in-law must have frequently discussed Britain, as Tacitus is able to describe the country (which he never visited) at length:

Their sky is obscured by almost non-stop rain and cloud, though it never gets bitterly cold... the soil will produce all the usual crops, and a lot of them. These grow quickly, but ripen slowly. Both effects have the same cause – both air and soil are excessively damp.

Tacitus was no admirer of Roman imperialism – his famous aphorism 'they create a desert, and call it peace' appears in Agricola's biography at the very point when his father-in-law's peace-making extended to northern Scotland. Agricola had returned to Britain as governor in AD 78, though exceptionally young for so senior a post. He immediately launched a programme of Romanization in the areas which Rome held and renewed military activities, putting down a rebellion in Wales and pushing northwards, consolidating the military position with forts as he advanced. There is a tempting suggestion that he may have led a military expedition to Ireland in AD 82, and Agricola later told Tacitus that the island could be easily conquered.

In AD 84 Agricola had his most northerly victory, fighting the 'large red-headed' Caledonians at the Battle of Mons Graupius. Though he won the battle using only his auxiliary soldiers, Agricola could not follow up his victory, as the enemy melted away into rough highland terrain with their numbers still largely intact. After this inconclusive battle Agricola commanded the fleet to sail about Britain, finally proving that it was an island.

Tacitus claims that the emperor Domitian (no. 67) was bitterly jealous of his general's achievements. Agricola was indeed recalled the following year, but he had already served longer than was usual. Although granted triumphal ornaments by the emperor, the survivor of Nero's reign immediately sensed the atmosphere of the imperial court, and carefully declined all further offers of advancement. He was mooted for command in the Danube area where the military situation was dire, and actually awarded a governorship in Africa which he turned down, pleading, possibly justifiably, poor health. He retired to his family estates in Gaul, where, aged 53, he died on 23 August AD 93.

69 | TIBERIUS CLAUDIUS MAXIMUS
Roman cavalryman

The Roman army of AD 100 was the most formidable fighting machine ever seen in the ancient world. Its backbone was composed of veteran soldiers such as Tiberius Claudius Maximus, whose tombstone has delighted historians with its complete curriculum vitae of his distinguished career.

As he enrolled before AD 85, we can assume Tiberius was born in around AD 65 and enrolled, as was usual, at around 20 years old. His birthplace was in Philippi in Macedonia, a military colony, so it is quite probable that Tiberius was from a family of career soldiers. He may have received preferential treatment through his family connections with the army, since he seems to have immediately become a legionary cavalryman – one of that body of horsemen attached to every legion.

The legion was VII Claudia, originally stationed in Dalmatia, but which had recently moved to Moesia in the Danube basin because of tension with Dacia and Sarmatian raiders. One of Maximus' early responsibilities was managing a fund which the cavalrymen kept separate from the savings fund of the legion as a whole, probably because the cavalrymen had better financial resources and different needs. From there Tiberius became a *singularis*, someone under the personal command of the legionary legate, though the exact duties of this post are obscure.

Tiberius first saw action during Domitian's bid to restrain the growing power of the kingdom of Dacia. That the emperor (no. 67) personally led the campaign shows how serious this threat had become. Tiberius was given an award for his exemplary conduct in the field. Despite this imperial recognition (or perhaps because of it – Domitian was not a popular emperor with Rome's ruling class), it appears that Tiberius' career languished until the soldier-emperor Trajan took command and started looking for competent men to promote for his coming Dacian campaign. Thus ten years after he had received his award from Domitian, Tiberius became a junior officer and saw his pay rise to 700 denarii a year – a very respectable salary. Either at this point or earlier he had transferred to the second Pannonian cavalry, a separate unit but one which often operated together with VII Claudia.

Tiberius was part of a troop of cavalry with the special role of *exploratores*, legionary scouts. Though usually second-in-command, he was in charge on the day when he reached the pinnacle of his military career. The Dacians had been defeated, and their king, Decebalus, was on the run. It was the task of Tiberius and his troop to track him down, capture him if possible, but otherwise to kill him at all costs. Decebalus killed himself by cutting his own throat, probably because the Romans were quickly closing in on him. Tiberius managed to reach the king before he had expired, allowing the Romans to claim that their fierce enemy had died a Roman captive.

On his tombstone, Tiberius proudly displays the moment. His light cavalry cloak billows out behind him, and he brandishes a sword toward the falling Decebalus. In his other hand he holds two spears and an oval shield, which together with a helmet and chain mail shows that he was well-armed and protected. Beneath this moment of history, Tiberius shows the two awards he had won in the Dacian campaign. (Roman military valour was generally recognized by the awards of torques (neck rings) or distinctive arm bands called *armillae*.)

Tiberius was still in the Second Pannonian cavalry when it went east to fight in Trajan's Parthian war. He received another award for his service there, but he must have known this would be his last campaign. He had now served out his enlistment period, and was serving as a *voluntarius*. This was not particularly unusual – the cavalry and auxiliaries often stayed under arms for 25 to 30 years, as opposed to the 20 years served by a legionary.

At the end of the Parthian war in 115, Tiberius decided to retire from the military, receiving an honourable discharge from the provincial commander. The second Pannonian cavalry went back to Dacia in 118, but by then Tiberius had returned to his home town of Philippi to live out the rest of his days.

70 | BLANDINA MARTIOLA

A plasterer's wife in Gaul

To the undying memory of Blandina Martiola, the purest of girls. She lived eighteen years, nine months and five days.

This is dedicated by Pompeius Catussa, a Sequanian and a plasterer, to his wife. There was no one like her, and she treated him with kindness, she who shared his life for five years, six months, eighteen days and conducted herself blamelessly through that time.

This memorial for his wife was constructed while her husband was alive, and consecrated during construction for himself also.

You who read this, go and bathe in the Baths of Apollo, as I used to do with my wife, and wish that I could do again.

This modest marker (a small stone called a *cippus*) was found in Lyons, France, by the ruins of the Baths of Apollo. Blandina was a common name in the region, and indeed at about the same time as Pompeius was raising this memorial to his wife another Blandina of Lyons was achieving sainthood for bravely withstanding torture to make her renounce her Christian faith.

Pompeius was from a Celtic tribe from the west of Gaul which occupied the territory between the Saône, Rhône and Rhine rivers, and archaeological evidence indicates that their chief city was modern Besançon. As an artisan, he probably worked with the stucco plastering which was a common feature of most Roman homes. The cause of his wife's death is not mentioned, but the major killers of young women in those times were illness and childbirth.

It is interesting that the couple seem to have been married when she was just 13. Marriages at so early an age were common among the aristocracy of the 1st century AD, but most working class girls tended to marry later. It is a touching theme of Roman tombstones that the ideal most praised in a spouse was not fertility or hard work, as might be expected from a sometimes brutally utilitarian and unrelentingly patriarchal people, but rather the ability to sustain a bond of affection which lasted the lifetime of one of the partners.

71 | CLAUDIA SEVERA
Lady in the British garrison at Vindolanda

In 1973 a writing tablet was discovered during excavations at the Roman fort of Vindolanda, located on Hadrian's Wall a few miles from Newcastle. Since then, over 1,000 fragments of such tablets have been found. They are mostly letters exchanged between officers and soldiers in Britain, reports and petitions sent to the Roman governor in London, and accounts, inventories and lists of objects relating to the fort itself. Once a unique archaeological find, similar tablets have now been found at Carlisle and Caerleon. All shed new light on the organization of a Roman fort, its manpower and provisioning, and its relationship with other forts – along the wall and elsewhere. There are over 200 named individuals in the Vindolanda tablets: the writers and their recipients, and the people they refer to. The most famous today is Claudia Severa, author of two surviving letters (and possibly the fragments of two others).

Claudia Severa was the wife of Aelius Brocchus, a prefect stationed in Britain *c.* AD 100, who later served as commander of a cavalry unit in Pannonia. The tablets reveal that he was a friend of Flavius Cerialis, a fellow prefect of the Ninth Cohort of Batavians stationed at Vindolanda. Brocchus and Cerialis were wealthy equestrian officers, and both had brought their wives and children with them to their postings, a common practice by this period despite suggestion in the literary sources that it was frowned upon by some. The remains of women and children's shoes have been found around the *praetorium* (commander's residence) of the fort, an evocative reminder of their presence there. The most northern frontier of the empire may have been cold and wild, but it was home to a mixed community of soldiers, their families, their slaves and civilians.

Claudia Severa's correspondent was Sulpicia Lepidina, Cerialis' wife. It is the personal tone of her letters that makes them so remarkable, along with the fact that these are possibly the earliest known examples of writing in Latin by a woman. In both cases a scribe has written the main text, but Severa has appended lengthy messages to Lepidina in her own hand.

The first, most famous, letter is an invitation to a birthday party:

Claudia Severa to her Lepidina, greetings.
On 11 September, sister, for the day of the celebration of my birthday, I give you a warm invitation to make sure that you come to us, to make the day more enjoyable for me by your arrival, if you are present (?). Give my greetings to your Cerialis. My Aelius and my little son send him (?) their greetings. (2nd hand) I shall expect you, sister. Farewell, sister, my dearest soul, as I hope to prosper, and hail. (1st hand) To Sulpicia Lepidina, wife of Cerialis, from Severa.

In the second letter Severa informs Lepidina that she wants to discuss certain matters in person, and has asked her husband for permission to visit her.

Greetings. Just as I had spoken with you, sister, and promised that I would ask Brocchus and would come to you, I asked him and he gave me the following reply, that it was always readily (?) permitted to me, together with… to come to you in whatever way I can. For there are certain essential things which… you will receive my letters by which you will know what I am going to do… I was… and will remain at Briga. Greet your Cerialis from me. (Back, 2nd hand) Farewell my sister, my dearest and most longed-for soul. (1st hand) To Sulpicia Lepidina, wife of Cerialis, from Severa, wife of Brocchus (?).

The letters suggest that Severa and Lepidina were intimate friends who regularly wrote to each other and exchanged visits, and the appended greetings to Cerialis from Severa and her husband show that the families were close (other tablets reveal that Brocchus and Cerialis sometimes dined together without the presence of their wives). A further tablet seems to refer to a visit to Briga (Celtic for 'hill') by Cerialis and Lepidina. The exact location of this fort is unknown, although presumably it was close to Vindolanda. It is possible that Aelius Brocchus was stationed there.

Although nothing else is known about Claudia Severa beyond what is revealed in her letters, she has provided evidence not only for the presence of literate women in Roman forts, but for the existence of social networks between the wives and families of high-ranking officers. Life in a Roman camp was not lived in isolation.

72 | APOLLODORUS
Trajan's architect

Few people influenced the physical structure of Rome in the early 2nd century AD as much as Apollodorus. He appears to have had just the one name, and is therefore called Apollodorus of Damascus to distinguish him from others of the same name who found fame in literature, rhetoric and philosophy.

We assume that Apollodorus was from Damascus, but beyond this nothing is known of his origins or how he came to the retinue of the emperor Trajan. He was certainly with him when Trajan began his Dacian wars in 101. Apollodorus designed for the emperor a massive bridge over the Danube which served not only as a bridgehead for Trajan's invading force, but as propaganda to demonstrate to the awed natives the extent of Roman technical prowess. The bridge was over a kilometre in length, and so well constructed that some of the pillars had to be destroyed in the early 20th century as a hazard to navigation. Apollodorus himself was so proud of his project that he wrote a (lost) treatise on the construction.

Some of the prisoners from Trajan's Dacian war may well have become familiar with another of Apollodorus' projects. On his return to Rome, Trajan began embellishing his capital with the proceeds of his war booty. Dacian slaves laboured on the enlargement of the Circus Maximus, venue of Rome's chariot races and occasional displays of gladiators and entertainers (from whence comes the modern circus).

Perhaps Apollodorus' masterpiece was the huge basilica and market which he constructed as part of Trajan's forum, much of which can still be seen today. This construction required the excavation of one side of the Quirinal hill to the depth of over 60 metres, and converting the hillside into brick-fronted terraces which march upwards in five gigantic steps.

Another of Apollodorus' constructions were the massive baths of Trajan. The emperor took advantage of both an inadvertent urban clearance by a fire on the Esquiline and the spare water supply which had originally supplied one of Nero's follies, and combined the two into baths, which Apollodorus made into the definitive version of this very Roman form of relaxation.

Apollodorus had firm opinions of how buildings should be constructed, opinions that were to get in the way of his position and career. He once dismissed a design offered by one of Trajan's subordinates with the words: 'You don't understand these things. Push off and draw some pumpkins.' The pumpkins were a reference to the domes which that subordinate, a keen amateur architect, was fond of incorporating into his designs. These pumpkins, however, can still be seen today, liberally scattered among the buildings at Hadrian's villa at Tivoli. Their designer turned out to be none other than Hadrian himself, which suggests that though perceptive architecturally, Apollodorus chose his enemies unwisely.

Hadrian succeeded Trajan in 117, and the career of Apollodorus received a predictable setback. It is possible that he tried to make amends by dedicating to Hadrian a book on siege craft (in which he apparently recommended using pickled cows' intestines as fire hoses on siege towers). However, the emperor to whom the book is dedicated is unspecified, and extant copies have been corrupted by later interpolations as other authors have incorporated their own bright ideas. Consequently Apollodorus' own ideas and motivation have become unclear.

If the treatise was indeed sent at this time, Hadrian's response was to send Apollodorus his plans for the Temple of Venus and Rome, which he was constructing beside the Colosseum. Apollodorus sent back a list of things the emperor had done wrong, demonstrating that his diplomatic skills had not improved with age. Among his criticisms was that the statues of the gods were totally disproportionate for the rooms in which they were placed. Although he was well aware that the statues were mere representations of the deities involved, he could not refrain from commenting sarcastically that the gods 'could not leave their sanctuaries even if they were of a mind to do so'. Since construction was too advanced to remove most of the errors, Hadrian did the next best thing by removing the man who had pointed them out.

Apollodorus was banished, and died in exile. Hadrian's enemies alleged, possibly justly, that Hadrian in fact ordered the execution of his presumptuous critic. However, no emperor could remove the stamp which Apollodorus had made on Rome, and much of his work survives to this day.

73 | ANTINOUS
Boy lover of Hadrian

So this is the new God, Antinous, he who was the emperor Hadrian's servant and the slave to his illicit pleasure; a creature worshipped in obedience to imperial orders and from fear of retribution, someone everyone knew and admitted as human, and not a good or deserving

human either. Rather he was a sordid and despicable
instrument of his master's lust. This shameless and
scandalous boy died ... and how entirely the emperor's
perverted passion survived its loathsome recipient; and
how much his master was devoted to his memory ...
has made immortal his infamy and shame.

The emperor Hadrian (AD 117–38) is perhaps the most complex
character who ever held the purple. Highly intelligent (he is said to
have held the imperial accounts in his head as easily as the average
man balanced his household books), he was capable of swapping
badinage with the top scholars of the day, an architect, and a devotee
of dangerous hunts. Hadrian's memory for people and faces was
so good that he had no need of the *nomenclators* whom most of
the Roman elite used to identify petitioners and minions. He kept
nomenclators for appearance's sake, but regularly used to correct
their mistakes. He passed legislation protecting slaves, and forbade
castration except for medical reasons, and showed great generosity to his friends. Yet he spied on these same friends, and would
unhesitatingly order their execution at the first hint of suspicion.
It is perhaps unsurprising that such a man would struggle to find
a soul-mate, and certainly his wife Sabina was not – he claimed
that he would have divorced her if he had had the same latitude in
such matters as ordinary men. Yet Hadrian fell in love, heart and
soul, with a boy from Asia Minor.

As the opening quote above indicates, Hadrian's love life has
ever aroused shock and scandal. Since late antiquity, moralists such
as St Athanasius have been exercised by Antinous' gender, while
modern readers are appalled that Antinous was in his early teens
when Hadrian fell for him. Yet in Hadrian's day the Romans mut-
tered scandalized rumours of their emperor's proclivity for males of
mature years. It is partly because he found the hothouse atmosphere
of intrigue and scandal in Rome so intolerable that Hadrian spent
much of his reign travelling the far borders of Rome's far-flung

empire. 'I wouldn't want to be Caesar, wandering among the Britons and the frosts of Scythia', remarked a contemporary poet, to whom Hadrian replied that for his part, the poet was welcome to Rome.

In the year 123 Hadrian travelled through Bithynia, in northwest Asia Minor. There his retinue was joined by Antinous, a boy from the town of Claudiopolis. (In Greek mythology Antinous is the first of Penelope's suitors slain by the returning Odysseus.) Antinous was not some casual catamite picked up en route by the emperor's fancy, but more probably a boy of good family who joined the entourage with the aim of becoming an imperial page boy. These, all in their early teens, served the imperial court in Rome. The striking beauty of Antinous (still evident in surviving statues) would undoubtedly have caught Hadrian's attention, but what roused his deeper emotions were the lad's character and quick wit. Furthermore, the boy was superb at athletics and hunting, and Hadrian enjoyed watching the former and partaking in the latter.

Hadrian was a philhellene, never happier than when immersed in Greek culture. After Rome itself, Athens was the city on which he lavished most attention, money and new public buildings. It was customary for Greek men of this and earlier periods to become emotionally attached to young men entering puberty (*ephebes*). Even mighty Jupiter, according to myth, had become entranced with young Ganymede, and had him taken to the heavens by an eagle to serve as his cup-bearer and paramour. It was the job of the older man (the *erastes*) to become his lover's mentor, and to guide the young man's moral, spiritual and physical development. (So 'normal' was this arrangement that some Greek poets are suspected of penning lines to non-existent *ephebes* in order to hide their embarrassing taste for heterosexuality.) Consequently the pro-Greek Hadrian may well have been minded to adopt an *ephebe* of his own.

Romance blossomed between his return to Rome in 125 and his departure for Greece in 128, by when Antinous was prominent in the imperial retinue. He appears to have been something of a diplomat, for there are no indications he was at all resented, and nor did he overtly attempt to influence affairs of state. As far as can be discerned, he reciprocated Hadrian's genuine and deep feelings for him.

In 130 the imperial party arrived in Egypt. Hadrian combined tourism with business, not only running the empire through messengers, envoys and diplomats but also seeing, and either organizing or embellishing the places he visited. During the journey along the Nile, however, Antinous died. Although the sources are frustratingly tight-lipped about what actually happened, this may not have been a natural death. One of the few biographies of Hadrian from antiquity remarks simply: 'he lost his favourite Antinous on the Nile, and wept for him like a woman.' Another report, allegedly from Hadrian himself, is that 'he fell'; with a choice of verb indicating either 'fell' or 'was pushed'.

These simple statements have caused an orgy of speculation. Was Antinous killed by his imperial lover during an argument, or drowned by enemies at court? Did he commit suicide, or even, according to some more outré speculation, die after mutilation in some strange heathen rite? It is probable that Antinous drowned, in part because the Egyptians endorsed his cult so enthusiastically. They believed that death in the waters of the Nile was a very sacred way to die. Given the roughness of the waters, Antinous would have had to be suicidal or extremely foolhardy to have voluntarily entered the Nile.

Possibly Antinous, who was near 18, knew he was getting too old for his role. Or perhaps Hadrian already showed symptoms of the illness that would eventually kill him, and Antinous believed that sacrificing himself in Egypt's sacred river would cause the gods to accept his life in exchange for that of his beloved – who had, incidentally, saved Antinous from a lion in a hunting incident a few days previously. Hadrian's grief was extreme – Antinous was deified, memorials to his cult (identified with Hermes) sprang up around the empire, and the city of Antinopolis was founded at the site of his death.

74 | METILA ACTE
Priestess of the Great Mother

The cult of the Magna Mater, the Great Mother, was one of the few eastern religions granted official status by the Roman authorities. Unlike most Roman religion, men had a secondary role in the cult almost from its foundation in Rome in the late 3rd century BC, when patrician women played the major role in embedding the new religion into their society. Women such as Metila Acte continued this tradition, acting as matriarchal figures in the communities that they served.

The Great Mother was known also as Cymbele, and often took on attributes of other goddesses such as Demeter. She had shrines throughout the empire and her priestess was an important and influential figure in the local community. This was reflected, for example, by her specially reserved place in many theatres.

Metila Acte was priestess of the cult at Ostia, the port city of Rome. This port had a large eastern population, and as the Great Mother was particularly revered in the east, Metila's social standing was correspondingly high. This is also shown by the quality of the marble sarcophagus in which she was buried. The sarcophagus carried the inscription:

To the spirits of the dead.

C. Junius Euhodus of the tribe Palatina, magistrate for five years of the twenty-first lustrum of the guild of carpenters in Ostia, had this made for himself and for his wife, Metila Acte, [who was] priestess of the Great Mother of the gods at the colony of Ostia, a most godly woman.

This inscription shows that Junius Euhodus was also a person of note in the community. Metila's husband was in charge of the

XI *The Death of Caesar* by Jean-Léon Gérôme (1867) depicts the immediate aftermath of Caesar's assassination on the Ides of March, 44 BC. Caesar's bloodied body lies abandoned as the senators rush from the building to celebrate their act. They seem to have naively believed that political life would return to normal after Caesar's death.

XII Julius Caesar in ceremonial armour, now in the Capitoline Museum, Rome. The ribbon tied just below the griffins on the cuirass is a sign of officer rank, and in battle Caesar would have sported his red general's cloak (*palladum*).

XIII Head of the young Octavian as he was
before he took the name Augustus. Born Octavius,
Caesar's heir changed his name to that of his
adoptive father and became Gaius Julius Caesar.
In 27 BC the Senate gave him the title 'Augustus'.

XIV Fresco from Herculaneum of a young man holding a scroll, a pose intended to highlight his social aspirations. Elite members of Roman society were often fluent in Greek as well as Latin. Among the lower classes the degree of literacy would have varied considerably.

XV Roman girl composing. This famous wall-painting from Pompeii shows a young woman of the 1st century AD thoughtfully holding her stylus to her lips while she holds the wood-backed wax tablets on which she is writing. It is uncertain whether this is a genuine portrait, or a whim on the theme of literacy.

XVI This 2nd-century AD relief depicts soldiers of the Praetorian
Guard, the imperial guard stationed by Sejanus in a single camp just
outside Rome during the reign of Tiberius.

XVII Agrippina Minor. Note the elegant coiffure typical of aristocratic Roman ladies of the period. The sculptor did not have to go to any lengths to flatter his subject, as Agrippina was reportedly an attractive young woman.

XVIII Julia Domna with her husband Septimius Severus, and Caracalla. The picture originally featured Caracalla's brother Geta, but his likeness was erased after Caracalla killed him while he took refuge in his mother's lap. Herodian took a particular interest in the family of Julia Domna since she was, like himself, a Syrian.

XIX This relief from the ancient city of Palmyra depicts Queen Zenobia, wife of Odaenathus. Zenobia claimed to be descended from Cleopatra, and ruled Palmyra in her son's name after Odaenathus was assassinated. After her capture by the emperor Aurelian in 272 she was paraded through the streets of Rome in golden chains.

XX Emperor Marcus Aurelius prepares to sacrifice before the Temple of Jupiter Optimus Maximus Capitolinus. The *mola* (sacred flour) is prepared and incense sprinkled onto a fire. The assistant who will do the actual killing stands with the axe. The god usually accepted the animal's death and some prime cuts: the rest of the sacrifice was eaten by priests and worshippers. This relief is one of II extant panels, probably made to commemorate the emperor's victories over the Sarmatian and German tribes.

finances of his guild, and presided over its major dinners, meetings and sacrifices. His office was for five years, whilst most priestesses of the Great Mother seem to have held their office for only one or two years. However, on standing down the priestesses joined a supervisory board which oversaw the performance of the cult in their region.

From the date on the sarcophagus of the *lustrum* (a regular purification ceremony) we are able to establish the date as around 170. The symbolism on the sarcophagus – lowered, yet burning, torches, winged victory in flight and the portraits of Metila and her husband as a mythological couple who cheated death – shows the strong belief the pair held that their souls would live on and that they would be together in the afterlife.

75 | MARCUS AURELIUS
The imperial philosopher

The end of Rome's Golden Age coincides with the death of Marcus Aurelius, yet the problems that afflicted Rome over the next century had already developed during Aurelius' lifetime. However, his competence and determination prevented the situation from deteriorating into crisis. Unlike the ad hoc selection of emperors of later years, Aurelius was trained for the job since childhood. His father had died a few years after his birth in AD 121, leaving the boy to be raised by his millionaire mother Domitia Lucilla. Aurelius became a favourite of Hadrian, who ordered Aurelius' adoption by his successor Antonius Pius. A strong family connection became even stronger when Aurelius married his cousin Faustina in 146.

Aurelius was interested in philosophy, an interest his elders encouraged by giving him a string of famous teachers. Among them was the orator Fronto, with whom Aurelius corresponded regularly, discussing philosophy and trivia.

Then to lunch. What do you think I had to eat? A titchy bit of bread [Aurelius had a sore throat], while I watched others wolfing down boiled beans, onions, and fish full of roe.… After the sixth hour we went home. I did but a little work, and sub-standard work at that. Then I sat on the bed of my dear mother, and we had a long gossip.

Aurelius was blessed with a tranquil family life. He got on well with his mother, his adoptive family and his wife. The latter bore him 13 children, of whom Commodus was the only surviving male (he had a twin who died). In fact, so close was the family bond that when Aurelius became emperor in March 161, he insisted on his adoptive brother Lucius Verus being made co-emperor with him. Although he had passed through the usual course of offices, Aurelius was totally lacking in military experience (see pl. xx). Therefore, when the Parthians decided to test Rome's new emperor by seizing Armenia and invading Syria, it was Verus who led the Roman military response (though even Verus left the actual commanding to his very experienced staff).

The Parthians were soundly beaten, and their principal cities – Ctesiphon and Seleucia on the Tigris – were taken, partly because Parthia was weakened by plague. Inevitably the Roman army became infected, and by 166 it reached Rome. The timing could not have been worse for Aurelius, who had another major crisis on his hands. The Danube frontier was under pressure from the migrant Germanic tribes who were to trouble the empire over the next century. The plague followed even when Aurelius finally set out in 168, causing the physician Galen to jump the imperial ship at Aquelia in north Italy. In 169 Verus died, possibly from a heart attack, leaving Aurelius sole emperor.

Around this time, Aurelius started writing letters to himself. Not intended for publication, his *Meditations* are rambling, slightly disorganized, and occasionally self-referential and highly compressed. Lofty stoic ideas are sometimes expressed with remarkable coarseness.

('A man can surround himself with so much wealth and possessions that he has nowhere left to crap.') Nevertheless, the text, with its contemplation of the transitory nature of life and fame, inspired many in later generations.

> Reason spreads. What it has in itself, it passes to others, and so grows. So either teach them better if you have the power to do so, or if you cannot, remember that... you should bear with them patiently, since you are the one blessed with mildness and goodness.

So Aurelius expressed himself in his musings, explicitly telling himself not to let power go to his head. But from 169 onward, Aurelius, despite his personal inclination, was essentially a military ruler. He led the army in Germany and on the Danube. His legions had to fight in Spain against ravaging Moors, and the east was still restless. Faustina died in 175, but Aurelian struggled on. A brief respite allowed him to return to Rome for a triumph in 176, but fresh barbarian incursions sent him hurrying north to the frontier again, where he remained until his death in 180. Aurelius had decided that stability and continuity were essential, and so did the greatest disservice to his empire by inflicting it with Commodus as his successor. He believed that his son's deficiencies might be remedied by the best education and advisors possible, but Commodus ignored these advantages to become Rome's worst ruler since Nero. Later generations remembered Aurelius' reign as a beacon of good rule and stability, and he himself is considered as one of the few emperors who actually improved while in power.

76 | AULUS GELLIUS
Grammarian and writer

What we know of Aulus Gellius is as much as he wished to tell us, for there is almost no mention of the man outside his own works. Fortunately much of Gellius' character comes through clearly in his writing – he is charming, self-deprecating, and a somewhat madcap mixture of the obsessive and easily distracted. He will chase down every trivial reference to a grammatical point right up to the moment when this brings him to an interesting quotation, which diverts him into a legal or biographical observation. Much of his charm comes from the mystery of what the next page will be about. The same chapter might contain wrangling over the minutiae of stoic philosophy, or a report of a Roman magistrate who took a prostitute to court for hitting him over the head because he tried drunkenly to break into her house.

Gellius, a product of Rome's now cosmopolitan empire, seems, from the few hints in this writing, to have been born in a Roman colony in Africa, around AD 127. Clearly wealthy, he used his resources to travel and to spend time with some of the greatest minds of his day. He certainly knew Fronto, teacher of Marcus Aurelius (no. 75), and was a pupil of the learned Sulpicius Apollinaris, a grammarian from North Africa who also taught the future emperor Pertinax.

In about 145 Gellius travelled to Greece, where he intended to complete his education. As a student and tourist he visited the great men of Greece and attended some of the great festivals such as the Pythian games of Apollo. During the winter evenings he wrote up some of the miscellaneous items he had come across in his studies or in dinner parties and discussions. In the introduction of the published work he offers this explanation:

> I have arranged my material in the same haphazard way
> that I collected it together in the first place. Furthermore

(being well aware of my limitations), I named my work casually, without premeditation, and indeed almost like some country bumpkin.... The title of *Attic Nights* simply comes from where and when I was up late at night [writing this]. So in the dignity with which my work is named I fall as far short of all other writers as I do in care and elegant style.

The lack of 'elegant style' has earned the eternal gratitude of those readers familiar with the florid and tortuously baroque efforts of some of Gellius' contemporaries. Even when delving into issues such as whether a Latin dative can ever end with a 'u', Gellius carries his readers at least some of the way with his own freshness and evident enthusiasm for his topic. Gellius also includes numerous quotations, and as such is one of the greatest repositories of extracts from extinct works ranging from treatises on the Vestal Virgins, a lost Egyptian history and dowries in archaic Rome. From Gellius we know that Pythagorian philosophers abstained from meat for moral reasons, but from beans because the flatulence they induce is unconducive to the serene contemplation of higher things.

Perhaps due to his interest in the law, when Gellius returned to Rome – where he appears to have spent most of his life – he became a judge adjudicating civil lawsuits, though he continued to collect trivia and assemble it into books as often as other duties allowed. As he specifically adds that these duties included 'the care of my children', we can assume that Gellius was married and an indulgent father. In fact, it would appear that the books he began in Athens were concluded some 30 years later, and one reason why Gellius continued his hobby was the diversion it afforded his children.

Not only his offspring but later ages appreciated his efforts, and Gellius was read assiduously through late antiquity and in the Middle Ages. If in these days enthusiasm has waned for his interest in exotic Latin grammar, the remaining trivia in his works makes Gellius a varied and fascinating read.

77 | HERODIAN
Civil servant and historian in Asia Minor

Early in the 3rd century AD, Herodian, a minor functionary in the Roman civil service, had a flash of insight. This was that the death of Marcus Aurelius in 180 marked the end of the most stable and prosperous era in Roman history, and Herodian himself was fated to live in the interesting, if somewhat unedifying, times that followed. Aurelius was succeeded by his son Commodus, who precipitated civil war, the Severan dynasty and the accession of the highly unusual emperor Elagabalus (no. 83). Early in Herodian's history he relates the Year of Five Emperors (193) and he finishes with the Year of Six Emperors (238). During this turbulent period, which changed the empire for ever, only one of the 17 emperors in Herodian's history died of natural causes.

Herodian joined the civil service at around the time when Septimius Severus became emperor in 193. Herodian's native language was Aramaic, and yet he wrote in Greek using several Latin sources, so he was probably trilingual – a useful attribute in the civil service of a multi-national empire. Functionaries such as he were particularly useful to Julia Domna, the Syrian empress of Septimius Severus who continued to play a major part in the running of the empire under Caracalla (see pl. XVIII). Herodian was therefore part of the imperial machinery as Rome began the downward spiral into chaos which is known today as the 3rd-century crisis. Caracalla murdered his brother to become sole emperor, before he too was killed in 217 (while relieving himself in the course of a stomach upset). Caracalla's successors lasted a year before being ousted by Elagabalus, who was replaced by Alexander Severus, and after him came Maximinus Thrax and Gordian I in rapid succession. Through it all, men like Herodian struggled to keep the empire's administration running.

The definitive history of these times had already been written by Herodian's contemporary, Cassius Dio. Nevertheless, Herodian felt that his position in the civil service gave him an insider's perspective. This inspired him to write his *History of the Roman Empire since Marcus Aurelius* – essentially a memoir of his personal views on the progressive collapse of Roman society. As a historian, Herodian is emphatically an amateur. A fan of the great historian Thucydides, like him Herodian interspaces his text with long speeches in which his protagonists say what the historian feels they ought to have said. Sadly, in Herodian, they say it in so wordy and pompous a fashion that the reader is left feeling that as a civil servant he probably exemplified the worst of that breed. Nevertheless, content which includes earthquakes, deranged emperors, city-engulfing conflagrations and wars both civil and foreign makes Herodian a lively read, whatever his failings as an author.

Although feeling little empathy with the Syrians, Herodian is much more sympathetic towards his imperial countrymen in Rome. Elagabalus receives relatively impartial treatment, possibly because Herodian's career flourished during his reign, when the actual administration of Rome was largely done by Elagabalus' saner relative, Julia Maesa. It may also be that the moral principles which Herodian reveals in his writing make it difficult for him to report on paper some of the more spectacular sexual excesses of the imperial court.

Less understandable is Herodian's omission of Caracalla's bestowing of citizenship on every free person in the empire. Even if this was not seen at the time as having the huge significance which later historians attribute to it, it was not an event that a contemporary writer should have passed over in silence. Despite Herodian's lack of insight, his chronological and geographical vagueness and his inaccuracy, he is the only contemporary historian of the period apart from Cassius Dio. Herodian's history stops with the accession of Gordian in 238, and it is generally believed that he himself did not last much longer. For all his flaws, even a historian like Herodian is sorely missed in the chronicling of the next 60 years, when times would become even more volatile.

78 | DIDIUS JULIANUS
The man who bought an empire

The ensuing scramble for power that came after the murder of the emperor Commodus between senators and generals resulted in civil war and the killing of his successor, Publius Helvius Pertinax. What followed was one of the most shocking events in Roman history. On 28 March 193, Marcus Severus Didius Julianus, a 60-year-old senator with a distinguished public career, bought the Roman empire at auction.

Julianus was not the first to buy his way to power and he would not be the last. Even Commodus' successor had offered each Praetorian Guard a bounty (or 'donative') of 12,000 sesterces if he was made emperor. But the events of this year show the role of the Praetorian Guard in the making of an emperor, and how their power was eclipsed by the might of provincial armies.

Like Claudius, Pertinax had become emperor thanks to the support of the Praetorian Guard, but he had a reputation as a fierce disciplinarian and, fearing that he would abolish the privileges they had enjoyed under Commodus, a group of Praetorians murdered him less than three months after he came to power. This disgraceful murder of the man they were charged to protect further debased the reputation of the Praetorians, but what was to follow was yet more outrageous. Pertinax's father-in-law, Flavius Sulpicianus, was city prefect, responsible for internal policing and security. After Pertinax's murder, he held a meeting of the Praetorian Guard in their camp with the intention of asking them to support him as emperor. But Julianus and his supporters shouted over the wall at the Praetorians, with placards for them to read, promising to restore the memory of Commodus and to pay each guard a donative if Julianus became emperor instead. The Praetorians were sufficiently impressed to allow Julianus into the camp. Julianus and Sulpicianus then vied to win their support. Eventually Julianus offered a massive donative of 25,000 sesterces for each soldier, and this bribe swayed them to his side. They proclaimed him emperor, and the Senate ratified his position later that day.

For Julianus, this was the shocking culmination of a successful career. He had been groomed for office, having been brought up by Domitia Lucilla, Marcus Aurelius' mother, and supported by her and her son in his political career. He became quaestor before the legal age, and held the offices of aedile and praetor. Under Marcus Aurelius he had served as governor of Gallia Belgica (northern France and Belgium), Dalmatia (Croatia) and Germania Inferior (Holland), and had proved himself a successful general in all three posts. While in Germania Inferior, he was accused of conspiring against Commodus; fortunately for him, Commodus pardoned him and had his accusor executed instead. He later governed Bithynia-Pontus (in Turkey) and Africa.

Cassius Dio described Didius Julianus as 'an insatiate money-getter and a wanton spendthrift, who was always eager for revolution', but Julianus' career reveals that he must have been more than this. There is even some suggestion that Pertinax had selected Julianus as his successor. They had worked closely together in the past and had shared the consulship, probably in 175. Be this as it may, the people of Rome were outraged by the manner of Julianus' accession by bribery. They rioted on his first full day as emperor, occupying the Circus Maximus and throwing stones at him. While he attempted to govern, they called for Pescennius Niger, the governor of Syria, to be made emperor instead. Furthermore, when Septimius Severus, the general of the army in Pannonia, received news of the murder of Pertinax, he declared himself Pertinax's legal successor. He rose in revolt and marched on Rome with two legions. As Severus' army approached Rome at the end of May, Julianus asked the Senate to name Severus as his co-emperor, but his action came too late. The Praetorian Guard had received letters from Severus promising that they would not be punished if they surrendered the murderers of Pertinax. They promptly abandoned

Julianus, possibly because he had not yet paid them their promised donative. The Senate sentenced him to death, and after a reign of a mere 66 days, he was killed in the palace by a soldier on 2 June 193. According to Dio, his last words were 'But what evil have I done? Whom have I killed?'

The writer of the *Historia Augusta* (a later Roman collection of biographies of emperors) sums up his life thus: 'These charges were brought against Julianus: that he had been a glutton and a gambler; that he had exercised with gladiatorial arms; and that he had done all these things, moreover, when advanced in years, and after escaping the stain of these vices in his youth. The charge of pride was also brought against him, though he had really been very unassuming as emperor. He was, moreover, very affable at banquets, very courteous in the matter of petitions, and very reasonable in the matter of granting liberty.' Severus was made emperor. One of his first acts was to disband the existing Praetorian Guard, recruiting a new one. Never again would the Praetorians wield the power to create an emperor; from now on it would be the armies which played the decisive role. Indeed, Severus left Rome within a month to march against the armies of the governors of Syria and Britain, who both sought to make themselves emperor in his place.

Part 6

Decline and Fall

AD 200–476

The Didius Julianus debacle (no. 78) was merely a taste of what Rome would endure from the 3rd century AD onwards. This was a time of transformation that encompassed political, military, economic and religious change, as institutions which had become corrupt and ossified under the empire gave way to a new era in which lay the seeds of the medieval Europe to come. This period of Roman history is commonly characterized in the popular imagination as one of inevitable decay and fragmentation of empire. However, while 'decline' was both widespread and evident, some scholars argue that this may be too simplistic a term to describe the changes – and new developments – which took place in this period of dramatic events and far-reaching transitions.

For centuries one of the greatest strengths of the empire had been its ability to absorb new people, yet from the 3rd century the northern frontiers of the empire began first to buckle, then to collapse, under pressure from migrating German-speaking tribes – the Alemanni, Vandals and Goths to name but a few. At the same time the emergent Sassanian empire threatened Roman hegemony in the east, overrunning parts of Roman Mesopotamia and Asia Minor. Frequent campaigns, with the associated problems of supplying and paying the soldiers – an enormous economic strain on the empire – were fought at both ends of the Roman world, although, in time-honoured fashion, the Romans also attempted to negotiate with their troublesome neighbours. It was at one such meeting in 375 that the emperor Valentinian I (no. 91) died of apoplexy in the face of barbarian insolence; in the following century embassies to Attila the Hun would include Pope Leo the Great (no. 97) and the historian Priscus (no. 98), but even the inclusion of such notable figures had mixed success in reining in the barbarians.

Distracted by external threat, the empire was vulnerable from within. For nine years (260–69) Postumus (no. 81) governed a breakaway 'empire' of the Gauls, and the emperor Gallienus was powerless to do anything about it. Less successful was the attempt a few years later by Zenobia (see pl. xix), wife of Odaenathus (no. 82), to establish an independent state in Syria (which her husband had already dominated), Roman Egypt, Arabia, and parts of Asia Minor. At the same time the emperor himself was threatened with usurpation. From the reign of Maximinus Thrax (235–38), it became common for emperors to rise from fairly obscure origins through the ranks of the military to the purple. The role of the army in defending Rome from its many external and internal threats meant that more than ever it played a key role in deciding who should be emperor – and it could be swift to change its mind.

Many Romans believed that the troubles of the 3rd century and beyond were caused by neglect of Rome's traditional gods, and this led to persecution of deviant religious groups such as the Christians. But Christianity grew in influence and power during this period until finally, in 313, Constantine (no. 88) granted tolerance to the Christians. Even then the relationship between Christianity and the traditional Roman religion was strained. Although championed by the foremost intellectuals of the day like Vettius Agorius Praetextatus (no. 94), pagan martyrs such as Hypatia (no. 93), and even the emperor Julian (no. 90), paganism was doomed. By the end of the 4th century, Christianity was the dominant religion of the Roman empire. However, Christianity was by no means a single creed, and the fathers of the early church such as Augustine (no. 96) struggled to impose their particular viewpoint against the forces of 'heresy'. On the other side of the empire Isaac of Armenia (no. 95) helped to invent the Armenian alphabet as a means of passing the gospel to the people.

Surprisingly, the empire proved remarkably resilient in the face of these external threats and its internal turmoil, in no small part due to administrative and structural changes that took place from the reign of Diocletian (284–305) (no. 87) onwards. Thanks to Diocletian, the rapid turnover of emperors had been halted and the empire effectively divided into two parts, east and west. Changes had been made to provincial administration and taxation, so that the number of provinces and the weight of taxation were both hugely increased. The emperors became distant figures, distinguished from their subjects by outward appearance and pageantry, and their portraits depicted them as stern soldiers, embodying military might. Rome, far from the frontiers of the empire, became marginalized and obsolete. Instead the emperors travelled the empire, residing in new imperial residences such as Nicomedia and Trier. And although the west would eventually succumb to barbarian pressure in 476, the eastern empire, based in Constantinople, continued, albeit as an ever-shrinking state. It was eventually destroyed in the 15th century, due in large part to invaders from the now resurgent west in medieval Europe.

79 | CLODIA LAETA
Vestal Virgin buried alive

Information about Clodia Laeta is plentiful. She was of a senatorial family, she had no physical disability or impairment of speech or hearing, and both her parents were alive when she was six years old. We know these things because Clodia became a Vestal Virgin, and had she failed any of these criteria she would not have been selected.

The Vestals were Rome's foremost female priesthood. It was their duty to maintain Rome's good relations with Vesta, goddess of the hearth, and preserver of the entire 'family' of Roman citizens. Unlike other gods which were represented by statues in temples, Vesta was represented by a sacred fire in a shrine. If the sacred fire was to go out this signified disaster for Rome, so one of the most important duties of the Vestals was to tend the fire and so ensure the constant presence of the goddess. Although the Vestals were virgins, this was compulsory only for the duration of their priesthood. When released from their duties after 30 years, they could marry. However, it was believed that marrying a Vestal was very unlucky, and many of them chose to remain in their quarters at the shrine even when they had served their term.

Clodia was discharged from the custody of her parents into the tutelage of the emperor, who was also Rome's chief priest, the *pontifex maximus*. For the first ten years of her service Clodia learned her duties, which included collecting water from the sacred spring on the Palatine, and preparing the special flour (*mola*) which was sprinkled on the animals before sacrifice.

Among the many privileges that the Vestals enjoyed was the right to sit in the front row during the games. It may have been there that Clodia captured the attention of Caracalla, who had become emperor in 211. He was a pug-faced, violent individual who had become sole ruler of Rome by killing his younger brother as he cowered in his mother's lap. He followed this with a purge of 20,000 individuals who he considered potential enemies or sympathizers of his brother's cause, including the daughter of Marcus Aurelius.

Four Vestal Virgins, including Clodia Laeta, were among the victims of his barbaric acts. Since the Vestals came from senatorial families politics may have been involved, but Caracalla chose the charge of lewdness against Clodia. This was, according to Caracalla's host of enemies, because he had failed to seduce her. Either she rejected his advances, or Caracalla had failed due to the impotence which the historian Cassius Dio claims blighted the emperor's sex life.

Two Vestals, perhaps because they were aware of what had taken place between Caracalla and Clodia, were executed. Another threw herself to her death from the roof of her home. Clodia was entombed alive, following the gruesome ritual described by Dio of Halicarnassus.

> While still alive they are carried in their bier in a funeral procession, followed by their friends and relatives who mourn as though for someone already dead. They are taken as far as the Colline Gate, and sealed into a tomb which has been constructed underground within the wall.

It was rare that this barbaric practice was actually implemented. A previous episode had been recorded under Domitian, but it is difficult to know how valid the charges were. Certainly the Romans did not take lewdness by the Vestals lightly (the male lover was also killed); not least because they believed that unchastity by a Vestal meant that Vesta would abandon the city and her sacred fire would die.

Clodia did not go quietly. As she was dragged to her tomb she shrieked for all to hear that the charges were false. 'Antoninus [Caracalla] himself knows that I am a virgin', a claim which was interpreted by Dio to mean that 'though claiming to be the purest of all men, he killed four Vestal Virgins, one of whom he had sexually molested – in as far as he was able to do so'.

If the charges against Clodia were unjust, as was almost univer-sally believed, the priestess and her goddess obtained vengeance when Caracalla was assassinated a few years later in 217.

80 | ELAGABALUS
Priest of the sun god and emperor of Rome

The Roman empire faced massive challenges at the start of the 3rd century AD. There were economic and social problems within its borders, and an urgent external threat from both barbarians and the Sassanian Persian empire, against which Rome could muster only a demoralized and sullenly mutinous army. It was not the best moment for the legions to choose for their leader a 14-year-old boy with a fondness for orgiastic rites to his Syrian sun god and a penchant for wearing woman's underwear. Perhaps someone with the political guile of Augustus might have carried this off as a colourful facet of his character, but an emperor who spent most of his four-year reign struggling to escape his dominant mother and grandmother stood little chance of imposing his personality on the world.

The boy known today as Elagabalus was born Varius Avitus Bassianus in 203. The two most important people in his life were both women – his mother Julia Soaemias Bassiana, and his grandmother, Julia Maesa. It was originally expected that the child would spend his life as high priest of the god El-Gabul, the patron god of his native city of Emesa (modern Homs) in Syria. Elagabalus was soon joined in Emesa by his mother and grandmother. The Julias had been exiled by the current emperor, Macrinus, who distrusted them as they were close relatives of the previous emperor, Caracalla. Julia Maesa was powerful, wealthy and well-connected, and she did not take her exclusion passively. With money and promises she suborned the local legion to declare for her grandson, whom she promoted as a son of Caracalla born outside marriage. At first Macrinus failed to realize the extent of the threat, and allowed the revolt to gather pace until he was forced to intervene in person. Elagabalus defeated Macrinus on 8 June 218 at the Battle of Antioch, and he and his son were killed soon thereafter.

The new emperor, who came to be called after the god he worshipped, took his time coming to Rome. Although not formally confirmed as emperor by the Senate, he dated his accession from the date of his victory, and immediately assumed the full array of imperial titles. These suggestions that Elagabalus was not going to be a conventional emperor were confirmed by the news that he was bringing his god to Rome. The sun god of Emesa, a huge black stone, was transported to the city where a temple had been prepared for it on the Palatine. For his entire reign, Elagabalus tried to enforce the primacy of his god under the Romanized name of Sol Invictus, the Unconquered Sun.

With the wanton disregard of Roman sensibilities which was to characterize the rest of his reign, Elagabalus abandoned his first marriage – a hasty political affair – and decided that he would wed Aquilia Severa, a Vestal Virgin. Their children, he announced, 'would be gods'. But these children were not forthcoming. This may have been because Elagabalus preferred male company – his most stable relationship was not with any of the female partners in his marriages, but with a charioteer called Hierocles. Roman scandal alleged that Hierocles would haul Elagabalus out of brothels where he had been soliciting custom dressed as a female prostitute, and thrash him for being a naughty girl.

Exactly what Elagabalus got up to is now impossible to determine. The Romans generally tolerated homosexuality, and Trajan and Hadrian were widely respected despite their sexual orientation. However, Elagabalus' preference for a female role outraged contemporaries and later Christian writers to the extent that the historical tradition has become irreparably corrupted. The *Historia Augusta* is generally more interested in scandal than fact, so much so that the life of Elagabalus is dismissed by many historians as little more than imaginative pornography. For example Lampridius' claim that: 'He chose noble and good-looking boys from all over Italy and sacrificed these human victims… he tortured them according to the Syrian rite, and inspected their innards for signs of favour from his god', is discredited because the more accurate Herodian (no. 77) makes no such claim. As a Syrian, Herodian probably knew that no such rites were practised in his native land.

While Elagabalus outraged the aristocracy, the plebs initially found their oddball emperor highly diverting. They were less impressed, however, by him giving high office to his mother's Syrian cronies, and they resented his insistence on 'marrying' El-Gabul to Juno Caelestis as a way of combining his own and conventional Roman religion. It also became evident that Elagabalus intended to remain a fully practising priest of his god. Most of the executive decisions of the empire were made by the Julias, who turned out to be highly competent administrators. Fortunately for Rome, the peace which Macrinus had made with the Sassanians stayed more or less firm for the duration of Elagabalus' reign, and the northern barbarians were unwontedly quiet.

As long as mother and daughter were in harmony the situation remained basically dysfunctional but stable. However, Julia Maesa could see clearly that the Roman people were becoming disaffected, and the legions had lost faith in their former favourite to the point where there had already been two mutinies. In an effort to boost his public image, Elagabalus adopted a cousin in 221, who took the name of Alexander. While Julia Maesa backed Alexander to replace Elagabalus, Julia Soaemias uncompromisingly supported her son, and the conflict between Rome's two most powerful women brought the administration to a halt. Elagabalus attempted to dispose of Alexander, but found he was helpless against Julia Maesa's political manoeuvering and Praetorian disgust at their current emperor. He and his mother were killed by the soldiery and their bodies thrown into the Tiber. No further attempt was made to give the Roman empire a unified religion until Constantine, almost a century later.

81 | POSTUMUS
Leader of a breakaway empire

M. Cassianus Latinius Postumus was born in about AD 230, at a time when the Roman world was in chaos. Barbarian tribes raided across the Danube and Rhine borders, and the Sassanian Empire represented a resurgent threat in the east. So dangerous had the Sassanians become in the 250s that the emperor Valerian gathered Rome's forces and marched against them. Stripped of front-line units, the Rhineland provinces were devastated by invading Teutonic tribesman. Worse followed with the news that Valerian had been defeated and captured by the Persian emperor Shapur.

The defence of Rome fell to Valerian's son, Gallienus, and the defence of Germania Inferior to Postumus, who had risen from lowly origins to become governor. The best literary source for this period is the *Historia Augusta*, an error-strewn and idiosyncratic text which describes Postumus thus:

> This man, heroic in war and steadfast in peace, was highly respected in all aspects of his life. Gallienus even trusted him with the care of his son Saloninus, as his protector and instructor in the conduct and duties of a prince.

Postumus was indeed a capable warrior and administrator. In the summer of 260 he inflicted a series of defeats on the Germans so severe that they left his province alone for another decade. Sadly, the return of peace led to Saloninus deciding that he was more qualified to govern than Postumus. In the subsequent falling out between the two men, the army took Postumus' side and killed Saloninus, possibly in Cologne where he had taken refuge.

Predictably, Gallienus was less than impressed, and rather than face his emperor's wrath, Postumus and his province seceded from the Roman empire. They were rapidly joined by the rest of Gaul and Britain, who vastly preferred a commander on the spot to one whose duties might take him and a defending army to other parts of the empire. Postumus did not seek to extend his rule, and was very happy to leave the remainder of the empire to Gallienus. When the emperor came storming over the Alps seeking vengeance, Postumus would not engage him in battle, and also politely declined an invitation to single combat. Eventually it dawned on Gallienus that the two last armies in the Roman world had better things to do than fight each other. The de facto partition of the empire was recognized to the extent that its two halves agreed to fight back-to-back against the waves of external invaders.

Postumus celebrated by taking the war to the Franks and Alemanni in 262–63, while Gallienus also succeeded in quelling his foes. Part of the success of Gallienus and Postumus against the barbarians was because the pair had developed the new concept of defence in depth, by which a highly mobile army, concentrated behind the frontiers, was able to reinforce the border where it came under attack. Gallienus used his breathing-space to have another attempt at conquering Postumus, but again Postumus avoided battle.

The 'Empire of the Gauls', as the breakaway state was named, was a properly organized and highly functional unit which represented how the northwest of Europe was growing in economic strength relative to the rest of the empire. Provinces of Postumus' empire received governors, the courts were functional, and the coinage of Postumus was of better quality than that of the 'official' mint in Rome. These coins were produced 'with the authority of the Senate'. As it is very unlikely that the Senate in Rome gave this permission, Postumus' empire probably had its own senate as well.

Coin finds suggest that Postumus used diplomacy as well as military power to keep the barbarians in check. He probably paid off some tribes, and allowed barbarian peasants to bring abandoned farmland back into cultivation. Sadly, it appears that the policy of buying off attackers caused financial instability, and this in turn created unrest. When Postumus marched against Mainz to defeat a pretender called Laelianus, he refused to allow his soldiers to sack the city. The soldiers took exception so strongly that Postumus was killed in the disturbances which followed.

Postumus' death in 269 did not bring about the collapse of his empire. This survived until conquered by Aurelian in 274. Thereafter the prosperous west suffered crushing taxes which paid for defence elsewhere. In the bad times which followed Postumus was fondly remembered, and his story may have formed the kernel of the legend of King Arthur.

82 | ODAENATHUS
Husband of Queen Zenobia

The establishment of the breakaway Gallic empire in the west (see no. 81) was only one of the shocking events of AD 260. Affairs were coming to a head in the east. The defeat and capture of the Roman emperor Valerian meant that the aggressive new Sassanian rulers of the Persian empire were overrunning Rome's eastern provinces and had captured Antioch, the traditional centre of Roman government in the east. It was left to a local, Septimus Odaenathus, to defeat them on Rome's behalf.

Odaenathus was from Palmyra, an oasis city located on the frontiers of Roman Syria and the Persian empire, and an important stop on the caravan routes that crossed the Syrian desert. The Palmyrenes were ethnically Semitic, although they had long been exposed to the Mediterranean as well as eastern cultural influences. 'Palmyra' was in fact the Greco-Roman name for the city, known locally as Tadmor. Odaenathus' family probably received Roman citizenship from Septimius Severus in the 2nd century, and bilingual Greek and Palmyrene inscriptions call him 'Ruler of Tadmor' as early as 251. By 258 he had acquired high Roman rank, being referred to in inscriptions as 'most famous senator' and 'most famous consular'.

The Romans rallied their forces in the east after the capture of Valerian, and were joined by Odaenathus. One source claims that Odaenathus had previously sent gifts to the Persian king. These had been contemptuously rejected, as had any possible alliance, and Odaenathus had decided instead to turn to the Romans, seeking the best deal for Palmyra in an unsettled political climate. Together Romans and Odaenathus drove back the Persians, but – Valerian having died after being forced to swallow molten gold – one of the Roman generals proclaimed his two sons as emperors. Odaenathus again joined loyal Roman troops to defeat the usurpers at Emesa in Syria (modern Homs). In return Gallienus, Valerian's son and co-emperor, awarded Odaenathus the position of *corrector totius orientis* ('Corrector of the Whole East'), a remarkable title that officially recognized his role as ruler of Rome's provinces on the eastern frontier and granted him the power to give orders to all the Roman governors of the region.

Over the next few years Odaenathus campaigned with great success in Persian territories, leading Roman troops as well as Syrian levies according to Zosimus (a pagan historian writing in the 5th century). He took back Antioch, conquered Ctesiphon (the Persian capital), and restored Roman rule in the east. At the same time, his military might was used to re-establish Palmyrene trading interests in Babylonia.

Odaenathus chose to use Roman titles and remained loyal to Rome, but he behaved as a Near Eastern dynast. He began to style himself 'King of Kings', and even awarded this title to his son and heir, Herodian, in a ceremony outside Antioch. A lead token discovered there depicts Herodian wearing a crown shaped like that of an Arsacid (Parthian) king – presumably Odaenathus wore one too. This was a powerful image in the east, one that proclaimed the legitimacy of his kingship to those living there. The upper echelons of the Palmyrene court were entirely staffed with easterners, as Odaenathus was concerned to maintain the support of local aristocracies, recognizing that ultimately his power rested upon their support, and not on Rome. He may even have sought to enhance his image by fostering high culture in his court, one prominent member of which was the rhetor Cassius Longinus. But Odaenathus' passion was for hunting, as the *Historia Augusta* relates: 'from his earliest years he expended his sweat, as is the duty of a man, in taking lions and panthers and bears and other beasts of the forest, and always lived in the woods and the mountains, enduring heat and rain and all other hardships that pleasures of hunting entail.'

Odaenathus married twice; the name of his first wife is unknown, his second was Zenobia, enemy of Rome. Both bore him two sons, and this may have been a source of conflict. One source claims that Zenobia conspired to place her son, Valballathus, on the throne and arranged for the successful assassination of Odaenathus and Herodian at Emesa in 266. Valballathus assumed his father's titles, but Zenobia was now the real power behind the throne.

Odaenathus had considered his Roman titles to be hereditary, but some of the Roman governors in the region failed to recognize the authority of his heir. Ultimately Zenobia would lead Palmyra to an ill-fated war against Rome in an attempt to establish full independence, temporarily taking over Roman Egypt, Arabia and parts of Asia Minor. Unlike Odaenathus, she was unable to reconcile Palmyrene and Roman interests.

83 | SYMMACHIUS
Victorious gladiator

In the 17th century two mosaics were found together in a property on the Via Appia outside Rome. Today they can be seen in the Museo Arqueológico Nacional in Madrid. The paired mosaics depict named gladiators in combat, and appear to have been made to commemorate specific gladiatorial bouts between fighters of different types. Each mosaic consists of two panels, with the fight represented below and the victory above. In both mosaics referees supervise the bout. One image depicts the triumph of the *retiarius* ('net-fighter') Astyanax over the heavy *secutor* ('chaser') Kalendio; the second illustrates the victory of a light gladiator of unknown type Symmachius over a gladiator of similar type, Maternus, and is accompanied by inscriptions that can be translated thus:

> **UPPER REGISTER:** (Symmachius) 'I kill my opponent.'
> (Crowd) 'So we see, Symmachius, you who were born
> successful. Yet Maternus was skilful.'

> **LOWER REGISTER:** 'In the fight between these two
> gladiators it was Symmachius who dealt the death-blow.
> Yet Maternus was skilful.'

The implication is that Maternus was the more technically proficient of the two, but Symmachius crucially knew how to win. Nothing else is known of these gladiators, although the mosaics can be dated to the mid-3rd century AD or later.

They illustrate, however, the popularity of gladiatorial games, first attested at Rome in the 3rd century BC in the context of an aristocratic funeral. Games became an important means for magistrates to fulfil their civic obligation to spend money for the public good (receiving support and prestige in return), and professional gladiators came to be identified with Roman martial values. Initially the gladiators were slaves, prisoners of war and condemned prisoners, but as the popularity of games grew more and more the gladiatorial ranks were swelled by free men, who were attracted by the potential rewards of victory. Suetonius reports that Tiberius once paid 100,000 sesterces for the appearance of famous free gladiators, an enormous sum in those times. Skilful gladiators stood to win large cash prizes, and despite their low social status, like Symmachius they could become heroes.

84 | AURELIA AMIMMA
Divorced a Roman soldier

The city of Dura-Europos in eastern Syria was excavated in the 1930s. The archaeologists uncovered a wealth of material – papyrus documents, inscriptions and archaeological remains – revealing much about the lives of the city's inhabitants, including their cultural diversity and their relationship with the soldiers of the Roman garrison who were stationed there. Aurelia Amimma lived in Dura in the 3rd century AD. She is glimpsed in a single Greek papyrus that records her divorce from a Roman soldier, Julius Antiochus:

> In the consulship of our Lords the emperors Valerian and Gallienus, Augusti, on the day before the Kalends of May, year 565, in the Colony of the People of Europos... Julius Antiochus, soldier of the local detachment of the Fourth Scythian Legion, and Aurelia Amimma of Dura, his wife, state that they have ended their mutual common life.

Aurelia Amimma is described as a native of Dura. The name 'Amimma' is apparently Aramaic, the native language of the region, but 'Aurelia' is Roman, which shows she or her family had received Roman citizenship, most likely obtained in 211, when the emperor Caracalla granted citizenship to all non-slaves who were inhabitants of the empire. The emperor Caracalla's full name was Marcus Aurelius Severus Antoninus Augustus, and since new Roman citizens took on a name of the person who had granted them citizenship, all new citizens of 211 came to be called either Aurelius or Aurelia.

Her ex-husband, on the other hand, combines a Roman name (Julius) and a Greek one (Antiochus). Antiochus was a recurring name among the Macedonian Seleucid kings who ruled Syria after its conquest by Alexander the Great. Julius Antiochus probably came from the Hellenized western part of Syria, perhaps from one of the cities founded by the Seleucid kings. Syria became a Roman province in 64 BC and one of Julius Antiochus' ancestors appears to have been awarded Roman citizenship not long afterwards, probably by Augustus.

Thus this papyrus apparently shows a man of Greco-Macedonian origin from western Syria, from a family long exposed to Roman authority and culture, moving to Dura with a detachment of his legion. There he married Aurelia Amimma, a local Aramaic woman, whose family were relatively recent Roman citizens. When they divorced, they gave each other permission to remarry and agreed not to make any further claims against each other.

85 | JULIUS TERENTIUS
A soldier killed by the Persians

In AD 239, the walled town of Dura-Europos was an eastern outpost of the Roman empire, a bulwark against the new and extremely aggressive Sassanian dynasty of Persia. The garrison of Dura was crucial in preventing the Persians from advancing along the Euphrates valley into the heart of Roman Syria.

The core of this garrison was an auxiliary unit of around 1,000 men, named the Twentieth Cohort of Palmyrenes, which was raised not only from Dura itself, but also from nearby Palmyra and the nomads of the desert steppe between the two cities. Papyrus documents, paintings and inscriptions preserved at Dura have made this one of the best-documented units in the whole of the Roman army.

A vivid wall-painting that comes from one of Dura's temples shows the soldiers of the cohort drawn up, performing a ritual sacrifice in front of a group of three statues that represent either Palmyrene gods or members of the imperial family. The mural also depicts the tribune (commander) of the unit, presiding over the sacrifice, and he is named in a label as Julius Terentius.

Terentius is also commemorated in a stone inscription set up after his death by his wife. Excavators discovered this, broken into fragments, in what must have been their home.

In memory of Julius Terentius,
Tribune of the Twentieth Cohort of Palmyrenes,
brave on campaign, mighty in war, now deceased.
Aurelia Arria buried her beloved husband.
May the gods of the underworld receive him,
may the earth cover him lightly.

The inscription emphasizes, in epic hexameter verse, Terentius' warlike virtues, and suggests that he may have died in action. The question is, when, and where? By sheer chance, the American excavators of Dura also found and recorded a graffito on the walls of a house that reads as follows: '30 April 239 – the Persians descended upon you.' This Persian attack on Dura is not recorded anywhere else, but it fits well with other evidence that shows Persian attacks in 238, further north, in the area known to the Romans as Mesopotamia. There is no evidence that Dura fell at this time. Did Terentius die heroically defending the city against the Persian attack? If so, he may also have prevented a Persian pincer attack threatening the security of the whole Roman east, as other Persian victories were to do a few decades later.

86 | ST ALBAN
Christian martyr

The 3rd-century crisis rocked the faith of many Romans in the established religion, and a large number turned to Christianity as an alternative. The fierce exclusion of the old gods by Christians was seen as highly antisocial by the authorities, who believed that the gods accepted sacrifice and ritual from the community as a whole. Those members of the community who refused to sacrifice to the ancient gods were therefore denying divine protection to everyone. From there it became easy to blame Christians for the misfortunes affecting the state, and a number of persecutions followed.

In Britain there were three major bouts of persecutions, under Severus in 209, under Decius in 254 and under Diocletian in 304. On one of these occasions in the town of Verulamium (modern-day St Albans), a Christian cleric was taken in by a pagan soldier called Albanus. Albanus was so struck by the man's evident goodness that he himself became a Christian, and when the governor's men came looking for the cleric, Albanus stepped forward with his face hidden by a hooded cloak, and announced that he was the man they were seeking.

When he was brought before the governor, Albanus' pretence was exposed. But the soldier stubbornly refused to sacrifice to the old gods of Rome, though he was whipped for his disobedience. Tradition says he was sentenced to die on 20 June, although which year is unknown. Christian sympathizers blocked the bridge leading to the place of execution, but not to be denied his martyrdom, Albanus crossed the stream on foot (we are told it dried up for him to cross). A further setback followed, in that the executioner refused to do the deed, confessing himself also a Christian. Eventually executed, Albanus found the martyrdom he sought, and his burial place in a nearby cemetery became a place of pilgrimage.

The first mention of the story of Albanus is in 480, by which time he had become St Alban. In 793 King Offa of Mercia established a church to the martyr's memory at the place of his execution, and the church stands today in Hertfordshire, in the town that bears the saint's name.

87 | DIOCLETIAN
The emperor who abdicated

A man named Diocles was born *c.* 240 on the Dalmatian coast, possibly near Salona. He was of humble birth – many thought he was the son of a scribe, others that he was a freedman. It is hard to imagine a more unlikely emperor of Rome, yet Diocles was one of a series of emperors who rose from obscure origins to rule the empire. Unlike his forerunners, however, he succeeded in bringing to an end a long period of military anarchy, and thus laid the foundations for what we now call 'Late Antiquity'. The empire was starting to show some signs of recovery from all the economic and political crises of the 3rd century. The emperor Aurelian had repelled an Alemannic invasion of Italy and recovered the Palmyrene kingdom and the 'Gallic empire' for Rome. The following two emperors, Probus (276–82) and Carus (282), had campaigned successfully against the Germans and Persians respectively.

Little is known of Diocles before 284, when he appears in the ancient sources as the commander of Numerian's personal bodyguard. We can assume that, having joined the army, he had worked his way up the ranks. There is some suggestion that he came to prominence under Carus and he may have commanded the border defence of an area of the Lower Danube river.

One source, written many years after the events, claimed that Diocles' accession had been prophesized. He had been in Gaul, in a junior post, and was in a tavern making up his accounts. A druidess said to him, 'you are far too greedy and far too stingy,' to which Diocles replied in jest, 'I shall be generous enough when I become emperor'. The druidess responded, 'you will become emperor when you have slain a Boar'. Years later, the emperor Numerian (Carus' son) died in suspicious circumstances, supposedly at the hands of the prefect of the guard, a man named Aper. Diocles, by now commander of the emperor's bodyguard, summoned a meeting of the army and killed Aper in front of the soldiers, declaring 'at last I have killed my fated boar' – the latin for boar being *aper*. The veracity of this story cannot be proved, but Diocles was certainly ambitious, capable and popular with the troops, who acclaimed him emperor. His first act was to change his name to Gaius Aurelius Valerius Diocletianus, known to us as Diocletian.

Diocletian's first priority was to halt the rapid turnover of emperors that had contributed so significantly to the empire's problems in the 3rd century. Aiming to consolidate his position, he marched against Carinus (Carus' other son), and then against the Teutons and Sarmatians on the Danube. Realizing that a single emperor would struggle to defend the empire against so many external threats, he adopted an innovative approach. In December 285 he appointed a friend, Maximian, as a junior 'Caesar' to share the burden. Maximian, described by Aurelius Victor as 'rather uncivilized' but 'nevertheless a good soldier of sound character', was sent to Gaul to deal with the Bagaudae rebellions while Diocletian moved to fortify the eastern frontier. The following year Maximian was elevated to the rank of 'Augustus', senior emperor. Diocletian and Maximian adopted the epithets Iovius (Jupiter) and Herculius (Hercules) respectively, which may have served to emphasize that Diocletian was the dominant partner. Then together, in 293, they adopted two other junior 'Caesars' – Constantius and Galerius – as their designated successors. Thus the Tetrarchy, or 'rule of four', was established. Although there was no formal division of the empire, Diocletian and Galerius ruled in the east, Maximian and Constantius in the west. Ultimately this system would fail, but for 20 years at least there was a period of stability within the empire that allowed Diocletian to turn his attention to reform. This included a stringent overhaul of the tax system, reorganization of provincial administration, and a controversial (and unsuccessful) 'Edict of Maximum Prices' that attempted to fix the prices of basic commodities on an empire-wide basis.

Although they praise the new emperor for his good sense and ability, the ancient sources stress his autocratic disposition. He wore silk, purple and gems, using his extravagant dress to set himself apart from his subjects. That was not all: 'He was the first of all after Caligula and Domitian to permit himself to be called "Lord" in public and to be worshipped and addressed as a god.' Ammianus Marcellinus (no. 89) reports that on one occasion in Syria Galerius was made to march on foot in front of Diocletian's carriage for nearly a mile. Often interpreted as a deliberate humiliation of Galerius, it could also be seen as a traditional means of demonstrating respect. A more distant, autocratic style of rulership by Rome's emperors had begun to develop from the later 2nd century; under Diocletian this trend was formalized. The emperor was distinguished from his subjects by his clothes, his titles and his residences. Enormous imperial palaces were constructed in places like Antioch and Milan, and became the backdrop for strict new ceremonies, imperial pageantry and public receptions. At the same time a new style of imperial portraiture was developed, and the four tetrarchs were depicted as being stern and vigilant, with the cropped hair and stubbled beards of campaigning soldiers.

Christian sources claim that Diocletian's heretofore worthy reign came to an abrupt end in 303, when his persecution of Christians began. One such source, Lactantius, claimed that on one occasion Diocletian was sacrificing to the pagan gods, and was distraught when the augurs returned with negative omens. Christian attendants had been present at the sacrifice, and they provided a perfect scapegoat for the pagan priests, who laid the blame of the bad omens on them. 'Diocletian raged, not only against his own domestics, but indiscriminately against all; and he began by forcing his daughter Valeria and his wife Prisca to be polluted by sacrificing.' Widespread persecutions followed (though Lactantius also claimed that Galerius was their most enthusiastic proponent; Diocletian just went along with them), continuing until 311, six years longer than Diocletian's reign.

On 1 May 305 Diocletian and Maximian abdicated, and it appears that Diocletian had planned this surprising move for many years.

He retired to a newly constructed palace in Salonae and resumed the name Diocles. Almost immediately the tetrarchy began to break up, yet Diocles resisted calls to return to power, as Lactantius reports: 'when solicited by Herculius and Galerius for the purpose of resuming control, he responded in this way, as though avoiding some kind of plague: "If you could see at Salonae the cabbages raised by our hands, you would surely never judge that a temptation."' His successors were unable to tolerate his continued existence, however, not believing that he would remain in retirement, and in the summer of 313 he committed suicide. An old man in poor health, he is said to have drunk poison rather than suffer the dishonour of assassination. The most successful emperor that Rome had seen for generations, and the only one to voluntarily lay down his power, Diocletian was deified and buried in Salonae.

88 | CONSTANTINE

Christian emperor

To some Constantine was a saint who began the transformation of the Roman empire into a Christian one. To others he was, in Gibbon's words, 'a cruel and dissolute monarch' who was indifferent to religion, his conversion to Christianity being an act of politics rather than faith. The problem arises from the contradictory ancient accounts of Christian and pagan writers; there is no neutral account of Constantine's rise to power.

Constantine was the son of Constantius, who had been Caesar under Diocletian's tetrarchy (no. 87) and had become Augustus, as Constantius I Chlorus, on Diocletian's retirement in 305. Constantine was in his early thirties and serving in the eastern empire with Galerius, but he made a timely return to his father's side for, in July 306, Constantius died. Constantine was illegally declared Augustus by the army in Eboracum, modern-day York (the position of emperor was not hereditary). In October 306, Maxentius, son of the retired Maximian, was declared Augustus in Rome itself, with the support of the Senate and the Praetorian Guard. Over the next six years the emperors battled it out, as Constantine, Maxentius, Maximian (who came out of retirement), Galerius, Maximinius Daia and Licinius (who declared himself Augustus in the east in 308) vied for control of the Roman empire. Constantine married Maximian's daughter, Fausta, in 307; Maximian perished in 310; Galerius died of illness in 311; and in 312 Constantine marched his armies on Rome.

If Maxentius had been sensible, he would have fought Constantine from behind the Aurelianic Walls (the fortifications built by the emperor Aurelian between 270 and 273 to ward off barbarian attack). But apparently Maxentius had received an omen – on that day an enemy of Rome would die. So confident was he that Constantine was this enemy that he led his army out and across the Tiber, a mistake that would have devastating consequences. According to Christian sources Constantine had also received a sign. Lactantius recounts how Constantine had a dream advising him to put a chi-rho symbol (for 'Christos') on the shields of his troops; Eusebius relates that Constantine called on God in heaven and Jesus Christ to come to his aid, and (in a later version) claimed that Constantine had had a vision of a cross in the sky. Whatever the truth, Constantine proved superior; Maxentius tried to retreat back into the city but the only escape route was across the Milvian Bridge. An effective bottle-neck, Maxentius' troops were cut down. Eventually the bridge collapsed, and large numbers of soldiers – including Maxentius himself – were driven into the river where they drowned.

Constantine was now sole emperor in the west, but Licinius, who defeated Maximinius Daia in 313, reigned in the east. At a meeting at Milan in 313, Licinius married Constantine's half-sister Constantia, and relations remained relatively good between the two emperors – with the exception of the occasional battle – until 324 when Constantine finally crushed Licinius at the Battle of Chrysopolis. The meeting at Milan had another important outcome. Together

Constantine and Licinius published an imperial letter generally known as the 'Edict of Milan'. This provided for freedom of worship for both Christians and pagans, and for the restoration of property confiscated from Christians during the recent persecutions in the eastern empire. Often presented as Constantine's initiative, there is actually no evidence that Constantine was seriously involved in drafting it.

It is not clear when Constantine became a Christian or to what degree his Christianity has been exaggerated. One of Constantine's first acts as emperor in 306 had been to end the persecutions in his western territories, yet an anonymous panegyric of 310 suggests that Constantine was publicly advertising Apollo as a patron deity at this time. Similarly, coins struck between 310 and 320 represent him with Sol Invictus (the Unconquered Sun). There are no Christian symbols on the Arch of Constantine, set up in 315 to celebrate the victory of the Milvian Bridge, and its inscription is rather vague, claiming that he was victorious 'by the inspiration of the deity'. Yet a medallion of the same year shows him with a chi-rho Christian symbol on his helmet. It has been suggested that Constantine was reluctant to advertise his Christianity in a strongly pagan Rome, though it is also possible that he was showing caution by claiming the support of several different gods. This need not have been cynical, since at the time it was perfectly normal and acceptable to worship more than one god.

Constantine was clearly sympathetic to the Christian Church. In 313 he received a petition asking him to intervene in a dispute between the established church in North Africa and a sect that would later be known as the Donatists (which took a very hard line against clergy who had not resisted the persecutions strongly enough). Constantine set up two conferences of bishops to investigate the dispute, in Italy and in Arles (Gaul) in 314. Eusebius quotes a letter in which Constantine emphasized his desire to avoid division in the Church, and the councils found against the Donatists. A second dispute, the 'Arian controversy', arose in 324/5 between followers of Arius, who believed that Christ was a distinct entity separate from and subordinate to God the Father, and orthodox Christians who believed that they were one and the same in the form of the Holy Trinity. The matter was settled (temporarily) at the Council of Nicaea, attended by Constantine, where the Holy Trinity was proclaimed. Christ and God the Father were 'of the same substance'. Some accounts suggest Constantine was personally involved in formulating this, and there was a precedent – the pagan emperor Aurelian had arbitrated in a church dispute back in the mid-3rd century, and Roman emperors, as *pontifex maximus* (high priest), had always been important in the pagan state religion. However, the extent of Constantine's involvement was different, attesting to his interest in Christianity and setting an important precedent for state–church relations.

Christianity also had an impact on Constantine's domestic policies. The clergy were freed from the obligation to hold public office, and they received financial subsidies. Penalties against those who chose to be celibate and childless (in place since the time of Augustus) were relaxed. Churches were built in Rome and elsewhere (including the original Vatican in Rome, and the Church of the Holy Sepulchre in Jerusalem). But there is little evidence of active suppression of pagans, and a law of 319 explicitly permitted worship at pagan shrines and altars.

In almost all other respects, Constantine continued the policies of Diocletian. Diocletian had set up imperial courts in places like Trier and Milan, and Constantine took this further by refounding the Greek city of Byzantium as 'Constantine's City'. According to Zosimus: 'Unable to endure the curses of almost everyone, he sought out a city as a counterbalance to Rome', though those sympathetic to Constantine suggest he was simply uncomfortable among Rome's pagans. Rome was no longer the focus of empire.

Constantine died in 337, after 13 years of sole rule. He was baptized shortly before his death, a practice quite common among Christians to avoid mortal sin between baptism and death. Pagan sources, however, suggest that Constantine became a Christian because Christianity was the only religion to offer him forgiveness. Constantine had been no saint in life. He was probably responsible for the murder of Maximian, and he had had Licinius and his young son put to death in 325/6, and even more shockingly killed his own son, Crispus, in 326. Shortly afterwards he murdered his wife, Fausta, apparently in an overheated bath. The reason for their murders is unknown.

By consolidating many of Diocletian's reforms Constantine created 'Late Antiquity' as we know it, and he ordered toleration of Christianity, taking an active role in the government of the church. But it was left to another to make Christianity the official state religion.

89 | AMMIANUS MARCELLINUS
The soldier historian

The crushing weight of taxation, the demoralization of the army and the religious conflicts of the dying empire in the west have been preserved for us by Ammianus Marcellinus, who not only recorded events, but actively participated in them and often wrote from a first-person perspective. Ammianus was, as he tells us, a soldier, a Greek and a gentleman. By the last, he probably means a member of the curial class, the leading men in the cities.

Ammianus loved the city of Antioch and lived there at several times in his life; though the evidence he was born there is limited. As Ammianus was the same age as the emperor Julian (no. 90), whom he knew and admired, his birth date is *c.* 330. As befitted his high social standing, Ammianus started his military career as a cavalryman in his late teens under 'Ursicinus, who was the governor of Nisibis, an officer to whom the command of the emperor had particularly attached me as a household guard.'

Ammianus was with Ursicinus when he helped to put down the rebellion of Silvanus the Frank in Gaul, and campaigned against the Germanic Alemanni. Soon afterwards the army was back east facing the threat of the Persian king Shapur II. In 359 Ammianus was probably present at the siege of Amida, which he describes at length. When Ursicinus fell from favour, Ammianus shared his eclipse, but when the pagan emperor Julian came to power after Constantius' death in 361, his fortunes were revived. Like Julian, Ammianus was a pagan and no admirer of Christianity. Ammianus often drew contrasts – invariably in Julian's favour – with the emperor's Christian predecessor, Constantius. However, Ammianus was no uncritical admirer of Julian in general, and sometimes implicitly condemns his policies.

Ammianus was with Julian on the ill-fated Persian expedition of 363. When Julian died on campaign, Ammianus took part in the retreat to Antioch, but thereafter gave up the military life. In the void left by his military career, he filled in his time by travelling. One of the most interesting and valuable aspects of his writings are his prolonged digressions into economic and social conditions in the east of the empire and beyond, as Ammianus did not just fight against the Persians, but also studied them, and found much to admire in their culture. From what he recounts as personal observation, it appears that Ammianus saw Egypt, the lands around the Black Sea and Greece before he arrived in Rome in 378 and settled down to write history.

This was evidently the realization of a long-held ambition, for Ammianus began his history with the accession of the emperor Nerva in 96, at precisely the point where Tacitus left off. He wrote in Latin, and like the work of Tacitus, Ammianus' *Res Gestae* was both of a high literary standard and generally accurate. Had the first 13 books of Ammianus' history survived, posterity would have been able to enjoy a relatively solid, reliable and continuous narrative for most of the history of Rome under the emperors. As it is the 18 surviving books cover times which Ammianus experienced personally, between 353 and 378, the latter date being that of the Battle of Adrianople, when Rome's last field army was destroyed by the Goths.

Ammianus was highly impressed with Rome: 'Rome, fated to last as long as mankind shall endure, and to be increased with a sublime progress and growth.' But the city did not return the compliment, and the historian seems to have been ejected in 383, probably because a famine made it imperative to reduce numbers in the city (although Ammianus notes indignantly that many entertainers – including hundreds of dancing girls – were allowed to stay). Ammianus retired to Antioch, there to put the final polish on his history. We know that he was still at work in 390, but it would appear that he finished soon after, for although he describes the splendid Serapeum in Egypt, he does not describe its destruction by Christian fanatics in 391, as he almost certainly would otherwise have done. With the closing of his work, our knowledge of Ammianus ends too. If he died before 400, he was spared the sack of Rome by the Goths, and the dismemberment of the empire he had served so well.

90 | JULIAN THE APOSTATE
The last pagan emperor

By the year 330, Christianity was the dominant religion in the empire. The Christians in previous generations had appealed for religious tolerance from the civic authorities, but many changed their minds once they gained the ascendancy. Temples of the old religions were burned, their gods renamed 'devils'. Those who practised the old ways came to be contemptuously known as 'pagans' – unsophisticated rustics.

Julian was born in 331 in Constantinople, into an atmosphere charged with religious tension. This was not just tension between Christianity and the other religions of the empire, but also within

Christianity itself, where issues such as the nature of the Holy Trinity were being (sometimes literally and violently) thrashed out. As the son of the half-brother of Constantine (no. 88), Julian seemed unlikely to succeed to the imperial purple, as Constantine's successor, Julian's cousin Constantius II, was deeply suspicious of his relatives. While still a child Julian saw many of his closest family, including his father, killed by imperial command. He himself was exiled to Cappadocia, where the zealously Christian Constantius ensured that Julian was given a strict religious upbringing.

Much as Julian loathed his mentors, seclusion in exile kept him out of the unusually lethal infighting among the heirs of Constantine. While executions, barbarian invasion and civil wars thinned out his relatives at an alarming rate, Julian grew to the age of 18 as a thoughtful youth, who, by virtue of remaining alive, had risen steadily through the imperial hierarchy. He had rarely been in the company of children his own age, and even his contemporaries considered him slightly odd. In 354 Constantius executed Gallus, Julian's half-brother. As Constantius needed to go east to fight the Sassanian Persians, he turned to Julian as the only remaining available member of his family. In November 355, Julian was summoned to Milan where he was married to Helena, the emperor's sister, and given command in the west.

For a young man brought up on a diet of Neoplatonist philosophy and Arian Christianity, Julian showed a remarkable aptitude for warfare. During the years up to 360 he fought a series of successful campaigns against Germanic tribes, retaking Cologne in 356 and defeating the Alemanni in the Battle of Strasbourg the following year. The soldiery took to their idiosyncratic young leader, who insisted on defying contemporary fashion and wearing a beard in the manner of philosophers or the heroes of the early Republic. When Constantius ran into difficulties in his own campaign, he ordered Julian to send troops east. This provoked great unrest in the western army, and civil war was only averted by the death of Constantius in 361, who made Julian his heir.

Emperor Julian had his agenda prepared. Cities were encouraged to re-assume powers abrogated by central government, and the court at Constantinople had the number of its members sharply reduced. Those killers of Julian's family who were still alive soon came to regret their actions. They were arrested, tortured and executed. As a further reaction to his lonely and miserable childhood, Julian rejected Christianity (hence his common appellation 'the Apostate'). He did not take up the ancestral religion of Rome, but a form of monotheism called theurgy, based on sun-worship and Neoplatonism.

In an edict of 362, he gave the Christian cause a huge setback by offering the same choice to his subjects, declaring all religions equal before the law. He ordered 'pagan' temples to be reopened, and the wealth removed from them by churches to be restored. He also ordered bishops declared heretics by the church to be allowed to return to teaching. This latter measure was less about religious tolerance than about exploiting the tendency of the Christian church to divide through schism. Julian himself wrote a text entitled 'Against the Galileans' (he called Christians 'Galileans' to emphasize the foreignness of their religion). This opens with the lines: 'It is, I think, expedient to set forth to all mankind the reasons by which I was convinced that the fabrication of the Galileans is a fiction of men composed by wickedness.'

Several other texts of Julian's have survived for posterity. Julian was intensely interested in the arts, both visual and literary. When the people of Antioch mocked his beliefs and composed satirical verses about his beard he replied in kind with the *Misopogon* ('Beard hater').

Please don't let anyone think your satires offend me. I have
myself supplied the ammunition with my goatish chin.
I could, I suppose, make it as smooth and bare as those
of your pretty young men, and of all women, though they
are naturally beautiful. However, even when old you try

to emulate your sons (and your daughters) by your soft
and prissy lifestyles, and your mincing manners, so you
carefully smooth your cheeks, and ever so delicately hint
at being male.

In 363 Julian led his army against the Sassanians, and achieved
his usual success. He defeated the Persians under the walls of their
capital Ctesiphon, but was unable to take the city, partly because
expected reinforcements did not arrive. As he was withdrawing
to the Roman frontier he encountered and defeated the Persians
again at Maranga on 26 June 363. While engaged in follow-up
operations a few days after this battle he was stabbed through the
side by a spear, a wound which ultimately proved fatal. Although
those close to him do not suggest this, later reports alleged that
the fatal spear was wielded not by a Persian but by a Christian in
Julian's own army.

It is interesting to speculate what sort of empire Rome might
have become had Julian lived as long as his hero Augustus. As it was,
his efforts to create social institutions equal to Christian charities
died with him, and these charities continued to funnel new converts
into the church. Julian's own take on religion was too philosophical
and abstract to attract many adherents, and many felt that the old
civic religions of Rome were both spiritually bankrupt and ill-suited
to the changed times.

Nevertheless, Julian had many admirers, including the historian
Ammianus Marcellinus, a friend and contemporary (no. 89), while
the rhetorician Libanius said of the emperor: 'His reputation spread
across the world, every soldier loved the man who so loved action;
men of letters loved him also... he so awed the barbarians that
they begged permission to become a part of the Roman dominion,
considering it better to live under him than in their own country.'

91 | VALENTINIAN
Bulwark against the barbarians

When Flavius Valentinianus was elevated to the imperial purple on 26 February 364, the Alemanni were ravaging Gaul and Raetia (parts of modern Switzerland, Austria and Bavaria), the Sarmatians and Quadi were rampaging through Pannonia (modern Hungary), the Goths were devastating Thrace and Moesia (in the area of modern Serbia, Romania and Bulgaria), the Picts, Saxons, Scots and Attacotti were causing chaos in Britain, and the Austoriani were attacking Africa. Valentinian spent the next 11 years defending Rome's frontiers, and his anger at the barbarians ultimately caused his death.

Valentinian was born in 321, the son of a peasant who had risen through the ranks of the army to become military commander of Britain. Ammianus Marcellinus (no. 89) suggests that Valentinian owed his early advancement to the reputation of Gratian, his father, who was a successful and popular military commander. Valentinian was military tribune in Gaul in 357, an officer in Mesopotamia in 360/1 and military commander and tribune of Carnuntum in 362. His career was temporarily stalled, however, by his faith. Valentinian was a Christian, and Julian (no. 90) exiled him to Egyptian Thebes in 362. The sources give different reasons for his banishment: Theodoret claims that he struck a pagan priest; Orosius that he refused to sacrifice and left voluntarily. His exile was brief, however, and he was recalled by Jovian, Julian's successor. When Jovian died soon afterwards, Valentinian was chosen as emperor at a meeting of the empire's chief generals and ministers. A month later – and against advice – he chose his younger brother, Valens, as his co-emperor.

Almost immediately both emperors suffered a violent illness, which they attributed to black magic. An investigation took place, but no evidence to support their belief could be found. Once fully recovered, the emperors focused on dividing the empire between them. Valentinian took the west, Valens the east. They then parted, never to see each other again and never to interfere in each other's affairs. Indeed, when Valens was threatened by the usurper Procopius, Valentinian declined to send extra troops to his brother's aid. Fortunately Valens was able to defeat his enemy on his own.

Valentinian is presented by Ammianus as an uncouth and uncultured military man: 'He had two savage man-eating she-bears called Gold-dust and Innocence, to which he was so devoted that he had their cages placed near his bedroom.' This can probably be explained by Valentinian's background. His family were natives of Cibalae in Pannonia (the region of Lake Balaton in modern Hungary), the proverbial backwater of the empire, peopled by unsophisticated country dwellers. The contrast with the educated Ammianus could not be more pronounced. Ammianus does not shy from describing Valentinian's 'savage impulses', 'passionate outbursts of anger' (which he attributes to intellectual weakness) and 'ruthless behaviour'. 'His very voice and expression, his gait and his complexion changed when he was in a rage.' He stands accused of being prone to hasty decisions, influenced by bad ministers and at the mercy of his generals and courtiers who controlled access to his person. (Ammianus' friendship with Julian might have influenced his judgment.)

Ammianus does, however, praise Valentinian's military and administrative skills, and his religious tolerance. He took the field against the Alemanni and other tribes many times during his reign, but he also took a long-term view of the problem of barbarian invasion by constructing or refurbishing an entire chain of forts and watch-posts across the Rhine and Danube frontiers, and by consolidating strategic bridgeheads. The success of these measures later resulted in a treaty with the Alemannic King, Macrianus, in 374. In addition to this he restored order in Britain and suppressed a rebellion in Africa. Administrative reforms included changes to the structure of the Senate and to army conscription, and attempts to protect the urban poor from the extortion of Roman officials and to make the collection of taxes more reliable and efficient. Although a Christian, he tolerated paganism, even granting the request by Agorius Praetextatus (no. 94) that nocturnal sacrifices be allowed to take place in Achaea, where they traditionally formed part of ancient mystery cults. Valentinian was also the only emperor who declined to intervene in doctrinal controversy, going so far as to refuse to summon a council on the faith. According to the Church historian Sozomen, he declared that 'it is not right that I, a layman, should meddle in such matters. The bishops, whose business it is, may meet of their own accord if they wish.'

In 372, Valentinian had ordered the construction of a fort in the territory of the Quadi, in the Upper Danube region. The Quadi were further outraged when their king was murdered by the Roman general in charge of the work. They promptly invaded Pannonia, killing local peasants and carrying off large quantities of livestock. Consequently in 375 Valentinian and his armies crossed into Quadi territory to exact revenge. Their arrival was met by a series of bad omens, such as comets blazing in the sky and lightning strikes, and his mood was already despondent when envoys arrived from the Quadi to sue for peace. But their manner was unrepentant and they blamed the Romans, claiming that their invasion had been provoked. Ammianus describes how these words 'brought on a paroxysm of anger in Valentinian, and he began his answer boiling with fury... He gradually grew calmer and was adopting a milder tone when he was struck as if by lightning. His breathing and speech were obstructed, and a fiery flush overspread his face. Then his pulse failed and he was drenched in a deadly sweat.' He was carried to a bed, but died shortly afterwards.

Valentinian is best known for his temper; but he was the last great emperor in the west, the bulwark against the barbarians. He died on 17 November 375 at Brigetio in Pannonia at the age of 54, succeeded by his two sons. The elder, Gratian, by his first wife Marina Severa, had already been pronounced co-Augustus in 367 at a time when Valentinian had been ill; the younger, Valentinian II, by his second wife Iustina, was only a toddler.

92 | STILICHO
Rome's last great general

By the end of the 4th century, the 1,000-year-old Roman empire was sinking under waves of barbarian invasions. However, Rome did not go down without a fight, and showed that under capable leadership the empire could still hold its own. But capable leadership was not always forthcoming, and when it was, jealousy and political infighting often rendered it useless. Flavius Stilicho, Roman general and virtual ruler of the west at the start of the 5th century, illustrates in his life much of what was good and bad in the Roman empire of his day.

Stilicho was himself a product of the barbarian invasions, in that his father was alleged to have been a Vandal auxiliary leader in the army of the emperor Valens. Stilicho was born in about 358. His mother was a Roman, and Stilicho never seems to have thought of himself as anything else. He joined the army in the late 370s and rose rapidly through the ranks due to his skill and ability. In 384 he went on a mission to Persia as the emperor Valentinian II's representative, and secured a peace on very favourable terms to Rome which guaranteed that whatever other troubles afflicted the empire during Stilicho's lifetime, trouble with Persia was not among them.

Valentinian II was assassinated in 392. However, Stilicho's career continued to prosper under his replacement, Theodosius. The new emperor's first item of business was Eugenius, a puppet of the Frankish warlord Argobast, who had ambitions of ruling the western empire. Stilicho was one of the leaders who helped to secure victory against the usurper at the decisive Battle of the Frigidus in 394. Another was the young leader of the Goths, Alaric, the man who was later to become the first barbarian to sack Rome for 800 years.

Owing to both his earlier services under Valentinian and his help in reunifying the empire, Stilicho became a close ally of Theodosius, and married his niece Serena. However, a collapsing empire left little time for domestic bliss, and Stilicho spent the next two years campaigning against invading barbarians, and gaining the respect of the army with victory after victory. He never lost a battle or campaign in his entire life. He was less adept on the political front, partly as his absence on campaign allowed jealous politicians to undermine him at the imperial court. One such courtier, Rufinus, had Stilicho's armies pulled out of Illyria in the middle of a campaign, causing a contingent of indignant soldiery to lynch Rufinus when they returned to Constantinople.

In 395, Theodosius died. His son Arcadius became emperor in the east, and another son, young Honorius, in the west. Rome's empire was never again to be reunited. Since Honorius was too young to rule in his own right, Stilicho, as Honorius' guardian, became the de facto ruler of the western empire. Both he and his wife were devout Christians, and he quickly topped up the imperial coffers by forced exactions from non-Christian temples in Rome. To further show his contempt for the 'pagans' he ordered the burning of Rome's ancient Sybilline books, a collection of prophecies that had been regularly consulted for guidance over the centuries.

Stilicho claimed that his daughter Maria had been betrothed to Honorius by Theodosius, and they were married in Milan in 398. By then Stilicho had led Roman armies into Gaul, defeating the German invaders there and clearing the pirates from the Saxon shore. However, he had to travel quickly to Greece, where his former ally Alaric had invaded. Stilicho quickly penned Alaric in Corinth, but he and his Goths escaped under circumstances which strongly suggested complicity on Stilicho's part. If so, this was not the last time Stilicho was to co-operate with his favourite enemy. Alaric was temporarily bribed from aggression by Constantinople, while Stilicho returned to Rome to enjoy a consulship in the year 400.

In 403, possibly egged on by a faction in the eastern court, Alaric descended on the western empire with his army. Stilicho engaged the Goths in north Italy. Probably like Stilicho himself, the Goths were Arian Christians, and assumed that fighting would stop for

Easter Sunday. To their outrage, the Romans descended upon them, took them by surprise and captured a massive amount of booty, as well as Alaric's wife. A further defeat at Verona forced Alaric into a hurried retreat.

Stilicho celebrated a triumph (the last ever held in Rome) in 404 and then turned his attention to a yet more massive invasion of Ostrogoths, Vandals, Sueves, Alans, and Burgundians, some 120,000 in all who came swarming over the Alps in 406 under a leader called Radagaisus. The invaders got as far as Florence before Stilicho could use their vast numbers against them, throttling their supply chains, and finally falling on and totally destroying their army.

This was the pinnacle of Stilicho's career. In 407 another wave of barbarians hit Gaul, and the British, fed up with Rome's inability to defend them, declared for a local usurper called Constantine. At this time Stilicho was attempting to annex Illyricum for the western empire, claiming that he needed the troops which the region supplied so abundantly. Stilicho also made peace with Alaric, forcing the outraged Senate of Rome to recognize him as one of their number. Maria, Stilicho's daughter, died at this time, and Honorius, eager to escape the confinement of his overbearing relative, was not pleased when he discovered he was to be re-wed to yet another of Stilicho's daughters, Thermantia.

Honorius was influenced by a courtier called Olympius, and he suspected (as have some modern historians) that Stilicho had ambitions to see his son, Eucharius as emperor. Consequently Honorius countermanded the annexation of Illyricum, and addressed the troops gathering for the campaign to re-take Gaul, inciting them against Stilicho. What seems suspiciously like a well-organized political coup followed, with close allies of Stilicho being killed or imprisoned. Stilicho dismayed his supporters by refusing to use his loyal troops to defend himself – an action that would have destroyed Rome's last armies in civil war. Instead he took shelter in a church in Pavia, only coming out when he was promised a chance to defend himself before the emperor.

This promise turned out to be a lie, and Stilicho was executed on 22 August 408 without a fair trial. He went to his death with unflinching bravery, a fate that was soon shared by his son. A purge of his friends turned into a general pogrom of barbarians living in Italy. As subsequent events quickly proved, Honorius had, by killing Stilicho and alienating Rome's barbarian allies, succeeded more brilliantly than any foreign invader in leaving Rome exposed and defenceless.

93 | HYPATIA
Scholar and martyr to religious fanaticism

Two of the ancient world's greatest wonders were to be found in the city of Alexandria, namely the lighthouse at Pharos and the Great Library, which served as much as a beacon for scholars as the lighthouse did for sailors. Even in late antiquity scholarship flourished in the city, and one of the last products of that tradition was Hypatia, daughter of Theon.

Hypatia was born around 360. Her father was a distinguished scholar at the Museum of Alexandria, and the young Hypatia assisted in his work. She almost certainly contributed to his commentary on Ptolemy's *Almagest* (a pioneering work on mathematics and astronomy). She also probably helped to produce a version of Euclid's *Elements* which has remained the canonical edition ever since.

Alexandria was no ivory tower, but a city constantly wracked by strife between Greeks and Jews, and lately with Christianity added to an already volatile mixture. Hypatia herself followed Neoplatonism, a set of beliefs which tied in well with her scientific view of the universe. However, her 'pagan' beliefs did not stop many Christians from studying with her, including Synesius of Cyrene, who remained a lifelong friend. Some letters of his survive, including one in which he asks for advice on the construction of an astrolabe, the development of which was of great importance to the science of astronomy and navigation. All the sources agree that Hypatia was a charismatic teacher, though not all approved.

John, bishop of Nikiu, wrote that 'the female philosopher, a pagan named Hypatia, was constantly devoted to magic, astrolabes and instruments of music. She ensnared many people through Satanic guile'. John was writing well after the period, but he drew his sources from the tradition of militant Christianity which was making life unpleasant for both pagans and Jews in Alexandria.

These Christians strongly disliked Hypatia. Her charisma and evident ability made her an advertisement for the non-Christian beliefs she espoused, and this in turn made her their enemy. Among those they believed to be entrapped in her satanic web was Orestes, the Roman prefect of Alexandria. While unbiased sources for Hypatia's life are not easy to come by, it seems reasonable to interpret the evidence we have as indicating that Orestes attempted to take a moderate line in the religious debate raging in the city, and that his approach was, rightly or wrongly, seen as having been encouraged by Hypatia.

Hypatia herself had never married (which encouraged those who felt that someone of her scientific ability had to be a witch), and according to one early biography, she took extreme steps to discourage those who admired her for her body rather than her mind.

Matters took a turn for the worse with the promotion of Cyril to the patriarchate of Alexandria. Cyril was a zealous Christian of unbending beliefs who took a dim view of the compromises Orestes was making with those of other faiths. Church and state rapidly clashed on this issue, and Hypatia came to embody in her person the key issues about which the debate revolved. The fanatical element among the Christians saw Hypatia as a major obstacle to the Christianization of their city, while the pagans revered her as a symbol of Alexandria's contribution to learning and Mediterranean culture.

Hypatia continued with considerable bravery to go about her daily life, and this would prove to be her undoing. 'A multitude of believers in God arose under the guidance of Peter and they sought out the pagan woman who had ensnared and enchanted the people of the city and their prefect.' (This Peter was a lector, rather than a Christian cleric, though John, bishop of Nikiu who is again quoted here, assures us 'this Peter was in every way a perfect believer in Christ'.)

They found her, apparently while she was travelling in a carriage, and dragged her to a church called Caesarion. There, the mob stripped her naked, and proceeded to rip the living flesh from her bones using, according to different reports, potsherds or oyster shells for the purpose. This treatment is close to a contemporary punishment for witchcraft, which may have inspired the mob's actions. Thereafter Hypatia's body was dragged through the streets and burned.

The murder caused a scandal, not least because Hypatia's killers went unpunished. Her death unsurprisingly proved exemplary to other scholars, who abandoned Alexandria thereafter. Or in the triumphant words of her chronicler: 'The patriarch Cyril was acclaimed "the new Theophilus"; for he had destroyed the last remains of idolatry in the city.'

94 | VETTIUS AGORIUS PRAETEXTATUS
Pagan leader in the Senate

Despite the pre-eminence of Christianity in late imperial Rome, a few influential pagans remained in the city, led by Vettius Agorius Praetextatus. He and his friends, who included the statesman and writer Symmachus, were celebrated as men of culture by Macrobius, who made Praetextatus a principal character in his *Saturnalia*. Conversely St Jerome called Praetextatus an idolator, who went straight to hell on his death.

Praetextatus' career is known to us in detail from an inscription on his tomb, which intentionally separates his secular and religious offices into two lists. The religious offices come first, demonstrating their importance to Praetextatus. He was augur, priest of Vesta, priest of the Sun, *quindecemvir* (one of 15 priests assigned to look over the Sibylline Books), curial of Hercules, initiate of Liber and the Eleusinian mysteries, *pontifex maximus*, temple overseer, initiate of the cult of Mithras, and father of fathers.

In his equally illustrious political career he used his rank to defend classical Roman religion and ideals. Made proconsul of Achaia in 362 by the pagan emperor Julian (no. 90), shortly before the latter's death he persuaded the next emperor (Valentinian I) not to enforce in Greece his law against nocturnal sacrifices, a pagan practice. As prefect of Rome in 367 he stopped private buildings from encroaching on temple grounds, and restored an important shrine in the Forum. As Praetorian Prefect of Italy and Illyricum he investigated the demolition of temples by Christians. Despite his efforts, in 382 the emperor Gratian ended official toleration of traditional Roman religious practices, ordering the removal of the Altar of Victory from the Senate House. Praetextatus' response is unknown, but Symmachus' unsuccessful appeal survives and there was a general outcry at Rome. Renowned for his fairness and integrity, Praetextatus was elected consul for 384. How he planned to make use of this highest of public offices is unknown, for he died shortly after the election.

Praetextatus' monument also commemorates his wife, Fabia Aconia Paulina, to whom he was happily married for 40 years. She is described as 'modest, faithful, pure in mind and body, kind to all, a blessing to her household'. Together they had a son, whose name is unknown, and they owned houses on the Esquiline and Aventine hills. Praetextatus mixed his learning with humour. He once joked to Pope Damascus: 'Make me bishop of Rome, and I will become a Christian straight away.'

95 | ISAAC OF ARMENIA
Keeping the faith

At the far eastern extreme of the empire, around the shores of Lake Van, the mountainous country of Armenia was in fact older than Rome itself. In the 1st century BC, under its most powerful monarch, Tigranes the Great, Armenia became a regional power that briefly challenged Rome for suzerainty of Asia Minor and north Syria. However, in the intervening years Armenia impinged on Roman consciousness, mainly in the context of the rivalry between Rome with the Parthian and Sassanid (Persian) empires. Possession of Armenia was frequently disputed between the two, and little heed paid to the stubborn belief of the Armenians that they actually belonged to themselves.

In AD 301, a generation before Isaac's birth, Armenia became the first nation to adopt Christianity as its official religion, over a decade before Constantine issued his Edict of Tolerance which permitted the existence of the church in Rome. Isaac's family were at the forefront of the spread of the new religion. The first patriarch (called the *Catholicus*) of the Armenian church was St Gregory the Illuminator, a direct ancestor of Isaac, who was reputed to be a descendant of the ancient kings of Persia. Isaac himself was born in 338, the son of the previous patriarch, St Narses (by some accounts, his mother was a princess of the royal house). However, both parents died while Isaac was young, an odd contrast to the extraordinary age which Isaac himself achieved.

Isaac studied in Constantinople, at that time the fledgling new capital of Rome's eastern empire (it officially became so in 359). His speciality was Eastern languages, something which was soon to become urgently required by his people. The rivalry between Rome and Persia flared anew, and when the dust settled once more in 387 Armenia was partitioned, with about three quarters of the country held by the Persians (who won that particular round convincingly), and the rest held by the Romans. The church became the centre of a culture war. Christianity was now one of the forces keeping together the identity of the sundered nation, but the Persians adamantly refused to permit the use of Greek by the church, while the Romans were equally opposed to the use of Persian.

With their ancient kingdom in danger of permanent cultural division, a triumvirate formed to save Armenia's national identity. It consisted of an ascetic monk, Mesrob, Isaac, now Patriarch, and the king Vramshapuh, who had succeeded his brother Khosrov IV in 389 and ruled the larger part of Armenia as a Parthian vassal (in fact he may not even have been allowed to call himself 'king'). The plan was, despite its simplicity, a stroke of genius. If Armenians could use neither Greek nor Persian, why not write in their own tongue, which did not lend itself well to being written in either of the other two languages in any case? The fact that Armenian did not exist as a written language meant that Mesrob had to create one, probably from an ancient tongue called Zend. Created in 406, the new written language was promoted enthusiastically by church and state. Isaac initiated the change with a rough but useable translation of biblical material in about 411, and thereafter a flood of other material, mainly religious texts, ushered in the 'Golden Age' of Armenian literature.

Isaac also dispatched scholars to the great centres of Christian learning of the eastern empire; Miletus, Edessa and Constantinople itself. On their return these men were sent to set up religious centres within Armenia itself, both within the Roman portion and to the east, where the king had persuaded the Persians to allow the rebuilding of the churches and monasteries they had destroyed during the persecution by Shapur II. When, alarmed by the spread of Armenian letters in his jurisdiction, the Roman governor banned the use of the new alphabet, Isaac appealed directly to the emperor, Theodosius II, who wrote a letter (the content of which survives) reinstating and reinforcing the status of Armenian as a written language.

In later life Isaac became more reclusive. He played little part in politics when relations with the Persian part of the kingdom broke down once more. He probably died before the Council of Ephesus in 431, though his life and his followers were so influential that many generations believed he had attended. Certainly he was there in spirit, for his long service provided the continuity to establish the eastern church and preserve the identity of the Armenian people.

96 | AUGUSTINE
Father of the church

As Rome's failing empire reeled from crisis to crisis, the thoughts of many leading men turned from the material to the spiritual. Intellectual debate was less about the impending disaster facing the Roman empire and how to overcome this, and more of higher matters – the nature of God and man's relationship with the divine.

The ideas propounded at this time, in which Augustine became a major intellectual force, profoundly shaped the later development of Europe, though Augustine himself was from Africa. He was born on 13 November 354 in Tagaste, a small town in today's Algeria. His father, Patricus, was a town councillor and a pagan, but his mother Monica was a Christian, and a lady of very strong character.

Perhaps as a reaction to his strict and provincial upbringing, when he went to study in Carthage in 370 Augustine threw himself into student life with joyful abandon. His work went well, he indulged in the theatres, the taverns, and, as he later recounts mournfully in his *Confessions,* 'every kind of licentiousness'. These included the acquisition of a concubine who, probably in 372, gave Augustine a son. Little is known of this unfortunate woman whom Augustine seems to have regarded as little more than a reproach in human form, chiding him by her existence for his weakness and lust. Nevertheless, she was to share his life for over a decade.

During this time Augustine went through a succession of spiritual and intellectual enlightenments. First, on reading the *Hortensius* of Cicero, Augustine became captivated by philosophy. Next, he was enraptured by the ideas of Manichaeism and for a while became a fervent proselytizer of that creed. Falling out of love with Manichaeism, he embraced Neoplatonism, despite the fact that he never fully mastered Greek, the language in which most of that philosophy's key works were written.

While on these journeys of the spirit, Augustine taught rhetoric in Carthage, where he won the crown during a poetic tournament. Then, in 383 he moved to Rome, despite the protests of his mother, who followed him to Italy on the death of her husband. Augustine opened a school of philosophy, but this proved unsuccessful, so he took up a professorship in Milan. Here he came under the influence of St Ambrose, and was converted to the Catholic version of Christianity.

So ardently did Augustine promote his new Catholic faith that when the See of Hippo near Carthage became vacant in 396, Augustine was invited to become bishop, a post he would hold for the next 34 years. During these decades Augustine threw himself into the debates which were to shape the Catholic church, firmly arguing the viewpoint of his faith against the alternative tenets of his day, which he roundly condemned as heresies. Augustine was well aware that there were many different varieties of Christianity circulating at this time, from Arianism, which denied the Holy Trinity and taught that Jesus was created by God, to Monophysitism, which believed that Jesus was altogether a separate being from the father. The Catholic church, with Augustine at the intellectual spear-point, uncompromisingly took the middle ground, insisting that God was a trinity of father, son and holy ghost, different but indivisible.

However, Augustine's first influential work was inspired not by theological debate, but by the sacking of Rome by the Goths in 410. *The City of God* was partly written to refute claims that the

Romans, by abandoning their ancestral gods, had caused these gods to withdraw their protection from the city and so create its downfall.

Another major intellectual struggle was with another schism of Christianity called Donatism. This conflict rapidly descended to the physical level, and after an extensive violence on both sides, Augustine accepted that force should be used to suppress what he saw as heresy – thus starting perhaps the first religious persecution of Christians by the church.

The struggle with the teachings of the British (or Irish) monk Pelagius remained on an intellectual level. Pelagius argued that children were born innocent, in contrast to Augustine who believed that the corruption of Adam and Eve was born into their successors, and all men were guilty of 'original sin' until their redemption through Christ. Here too, Augustine prevailed, but many were unconvinced and Pelagian beliefs lingered in the west for centuries.

For Augustine, however, the major threat to what he saw as the only true faith was Arianism. And in Augustine's day, it was Arianism rather than Augustine's Catholicism that had the major support. Arianism was the creed of Rome's Gothic conquerors, and of several of the generals who defended the empire. Augustine supported Boniface, a Catholic general, in his struggles against the Arian Visigoths. He was appalled by a political compromise by which Boniface's daughter was baptized an Arian. To Augustine it must have seemed that he was fighting a losing battle. In 428 the war came to Africa, and Augustine's See too came under the rule of a Gothic and Arian commander. By now Augustine was in his seventies, and had handed day-to-day control of affairs to his nominated successor.

Eventually Boniface managed to regain control of the area, and was reconciled with Augustine. Yet even as Augustine lay dying in 430, Hippo was again under siege by barbarian troops. Rome's western empire was doomed, eventually Arianism would be overcome and Augustine's work would live on.

97 | LEO THE GREAT
The pope who stopped Attila the Hun

During his 21-year papacy Leo the Great combatted heresy in the west, doctrinal controversy in the east, and interceded with invading barbarians in Italy. He corresponded with all parts of the empire, and his many surviving letters and sermons depict a man of great energy and passion who took his pastoral duties as leader of the Holy See very seriously.

Although the exact date and place of Leo's birth are unknown, he was of Tuscan descent and his father's name was Quintianus. Leo first appears in history in 430 opposing heresy as a deacon of the Roman church under Pope Celestine I (422–32). Although based in Rome, Leo appears to have had contact with Christians in Gaul. During his pontificate, Sixtus III was sent to Gaul by the emperor Valentinian III to settle a dispute between the military commander and the chief magistrate there. While in Gaul, Sixtus died. Leo was elected his successor and consecrated in Rome on 29 September 440.

In a time of general disorder, Leo's aim as pope was to secure a strong and united church, and he made it his mission to combat heresies. Adherents of Pelagianism (which denied original sin) were required to confess their faith before communion; Manichaeism (a fusion of different religions based on reason, not faith) was denounced in 443, and Leo encouraged the people to inform on its practioners, who were exiled if they refused to repent. Priscillianism (a belief in the existence of two kingdoms of light and darkness) was repressed. Bishops thought to be tainted by heresies were excommunicated.

Leo was a strict disciplinarian. Believing in the primacy of his papacy he secured a rescript from Valentinian III that recognized his jurisdiction over all the western provinces of the empire, and with it reined in bishops such as St Hilary of Arles, who had usurped papal authority by deposing and consecrating new bishops in nearby provinces. Others, such as Anastasius of Thessalonica, were reproved for using authority in a despotic manner: 'although as a rule there exist among careless or slothful brethren things which demand a strong hand in rectifying them.'

Although papal jurisdiction was not recognized in the east, eastern bishops had approached various popes for support in their infighting. Leo was no exception, although his inability to read Greek meant that he had a limited grasp of the subtleties involved in the Greek doctrinal disputes on which he was asked to offer opinions. In particular Leo was drawn into the Eutychian controversy about the nature of Christ. Eutyches was a revered archimandrite (senior abbot) of a large monastery at Constantinople who believed that after the Incarnation Christ had only one nature, that is, that Christ's humanity had been absorbed into his divinity. He was accused of heresy and deposed by Flavian, the patriarch of Constantinople.

Eutyches, however, had powerful friends. The emperor Theodosius II reinstated Eutyches and declared his teachings orthodox. The outraged Flavian wrote to Leo for guidance. Leo's reply of 449 was addressed to Flavian, and two years later this letter was read aloud to the Council of Chalcedon: 'For he that is true God is true man; nor in this unity is there any unreality, while the lowliness of the manhood and the loftiness of deity were their separate spheres. For just as God is not changed by the compassion exhibited, so the manhood is not absorbed by the dignity bestowed. Each form, in communion with the other, performs the function that is proper to it.' The council of over 600 bishops approved Leo's dogma, that Christ was one person with two perfect natures. 'This is the faith of the fathers, this is the faith of the Apostles. So we all believe, thus the orthodox believe. Anathema to him who does not thus believe. Peter has spoken through Leo.'

Leo's status as a statesman and protector of his flock are further emphasized by an unlikely story. According to Christian sources, Leo was asked by the emperor to intercede when Attila the Hun crossed into Italy in 451. Their meeting supposedly took place in 452 on the banks of the river Minicius, near Mantua in northern Italy. Leo secured Attila's promise to leave Italy and negotiate a peace. In truth Attila's decision to withdraw to the Danube was probably more influenced by the condition of his forces, recently defeated in Gaul and weakened by plague. Leo did, however, persuade the Vandals not to destroy Rome or slaughter its inhabitants when they captured and plundered the city for two weeks in 455. Both incidents served to increase papal authority.

Leo the Great died on 10 November 461 and was buried in the vestibule of St Peter's on the Vatican (which he had been responsible for restoring, along with many other churches). In 688 his remains were transferred to the Basilica of St Peter and an altar erected over them, which can be visited today.

In 1754 Pope Benedict XIV made Leo a 'Doctor of the Church' in recognition of his profound influence on the development of the Roman Catholic Church. Leo had been a tireless correspondent. Believing that his own primacy derived from St Peter, he had sought to instruct his flock on issues such as dogma, ecclesiastical discipline and church organization. His surviving 143 genuine letters and 97 sermons are remarkable for their clarity of thought and forcefulness. He advocated prayer, fasting and charity and encouraged his bishops to consult him in person. Under his close pastoral supervision the influence of the Roman Church was consolidated throughout the empire.

98 | PRISCUS
Ambassador to Attila the Hun

The waves of barbarian invasions which broke over the Roman empire were partly caused by what one writer has called the 'billiard-ball theory of history'. Huns attacking from the steppes of central Asia put pressure on the eastern Germanic tribes, especially the Ostrogoths. These in turn leaned on the Visigoths, and these, caught between their Germanic cousins and the borders of the empire, turned on Rome.

In the 5th century matters got worse as the Huns, the original cause of many of Rome's problems, turned up on the Roman frontiers, and showed no signs of stopping there. In military terms the Romans could do nothing, given the state of their enfeebled army, but they could and did use bribes and diplomacy in an attempt to contain this new threat.

Of the many embassies that were sent to Attila one in particular stands out. This is the embassy of Maximinus, who took in his entourage the Sophist philosopher Priscus, who wrote a first-person eyewitness account of the trip.

Priscus was a subject of Rome's eastern empire, born in Panium in Thrace in the opening decades of the 5th century. He became a bureaucrat, as bureaucracy was almost the only growth industry of the Rome of his day, and found a position on the staff of Maximinus, ambassador of the emperor Theodosius II. From his account of the embassy to Attila, which he undertook in 448, it is evident that he kept a diary of his peregrinations, for it contains entries such as:

> We set out with the barbarians, and arrived at Sardica, which is 13 days for a fast traveller from Constantinople. Halting there, we considered it advisable to invite Edecon and the barbarians with him to dinner.

Or later:

> When we arrived at Naissus we found the city deserted, as though it had been sacked; only a few sick persons lay in the churches. We halted at a short distance from the river, in an open space, for all the ground adjacent to the bank was full of the bones of those who had been slain.

He makes comments on the customs of those whose lands he passed through:

> The lady who governed the village – she had been one of Bleda's wives – sent us provisions and good-looking girls to console us (this is a Scythian compliment). We treated the young women to a share in the eatables, but declined to take any further advantage of their presence.

Priscus recounts a debate that he had with a former Roman citizen he met at the court of Attila. This man was free, and stayed with the Huns voluntarily, preferring life with Attila to that in the empire. He explained that he could not tolerate the continual wars, corruption, merciless taxation or the slowness, favouritism and injustice of the courts. The indignant Priscus responded by reeling off a list of the ancient institutions by which the Roman constitution protected men against such abuses.

> My interlocutor shed tears, and confessed that the laws and constitution of the Romans were fair, but deplored that the governors, not possessing the spirit of former generations, were ruining the State.

The high point of the embassy was a dinner in the presence of Attila himself, whom Priscus describes as a grave, imposing figure of spartan tastes. The entertainment was a display of the insensitivity of earlier ages, in which the guests were entertained by the behaviour of a 'Moorish dwarf' and a mentally disturbed man, though Attila himself was unamused.

The embassy, concerning the return of deserters, giving of gifts and other administrative affairs, was not a great success, though Priscus recounts meeting some 'western Romans' who were also paying court to Attila. Since Attila was to invade Italy soon afterwards, it may be assumed that their embassy was even less successful.

This journey was not the end of Priscus' travels. He visited Rome at least once, and thereafter accompanied Maximinus on further diplomatic missions to Egypt and Arabia. He became a trusted member of the senior staff of the high imperial official Euphemius during the reign of the emperor Marcian. Eventually he retired to write a history of his times. He wrote eight books, of which only fragments such as his embassy to Attila have survived. The last events he chronicled occurred in 472, and he probably died soon after.

99 | CONSENTIUS
Amateur chariot racer

A Roman racing chariot was engineered with speed as the primary objective. Stability came a distant second, and the safety of the driver received little more than passing consideration. Reconstructions of Roman racing chariots suggest that they were made of dried rawhide (which under the right conditions sets like wood, but is much lighter). They were essentially tiny platforms with large wheels and a basic handrail (see pl. IV). With about 20 highly excited horses jostling for places at speed on a narrow track with tight corners, pile-ups were frequent, and often lethal. Although amateurs such as Consentius might occcasionally risk their necks, chariot racing was on the whole a sport left to professionals.

While the dangers involved in chariot racing were extreme, so were the rewards. Juvenal remarks that profits of 100 lawyers would be outweighed by those of a single charioteer. We know of some star charioteers who minimized their risks by appearing only for races which offered top prizes, and the few who retired with their winnings did so as millionaires. But although racing was highly profitable, this should not have concerned young Consentius. Probably born in 425, he was from the leading family in the Gallo-Roman nobility – a social group which, it has been argued, had perhaps more money than necessary. While Rome had already lost much of Gaul to the conquering Visigoths, relations between Gauls, Visigoths and Romans were generally equable, and all three groups fought side-by-side to defend Gaul when the need arose. Consequently young Consentius lived a life of relative luxury, and in his day Gaul seemed richer and stronger than the failing power of Italy.

Given the importance of Consentius' family (which included a prefect of Gaul amongst its members), it comes as no surprise that young Consentius attended the emperor (probably Valentinian III) at his court in Ravenna. At this time Ravenna was the imperial capital, being both more defensible then Rome and nearer to the empire's crumbling frontiers. Despite the ongoing military emergency that was the late empire, the emperor still took the time to celebrate the new year, and one event in the celebrations was a chariot race, with young men at the court standing in for the professional charioteers.

Consentius received his chariot by lot, and was partnered for the new year race with a member of one of the other colours. (Roman charioteers raced as members of the green, red, blue or white factions – support for the different colours among race enthusiasts was fanatical.) The start line was staggered on one of the bends on the track, to prevent any runner having an advantage. However, once the runners had passed a white line painted on the track, they were free to cut in to take the line closest to the *spina*, a low wall dividing the middle of the circuit. If this manoeuvre propelled your chariot wheels into the legs of another team's horses, so much the better.

Consentius got off to a slow start, and ended up running last. 'The contestants, horses and men, are warmed by the race, yet chilled by fear.' Consentius' partner held the lead for five laps, but then, his horses blown, he lost the lead. As they cantered toward the finish line, Consentius suddenly whipped his team forward, moving into the inside track. One of his opponents tried to cut him off, yet Consentius proved the better charioteer. 'His [opponent's] horses were brought down... the spokes were jammed by legs entering

the wheels, and the spinning rim shattered the entangled feet…
He was flung from the chariot, prostrate forehead running with
blood', while Consentius crossed the winning line.

We know so much about the race as it was written as a poem,
Carmina 23, by Consentius' friend Sidonius Apollinarus. Sidonius
was of another noble family and deeply embroiled in politics at the
highest level. We know from his letters that Consentius' family had
an extensive estate, the Octaviana, with vineyards, olive groves and
a substantial library. Apart from some tantalizing hints, Consentius
vanishes from history after his epic win, but it is probable that he
lived to see Romulus Augustulus deposed by his barbarian overlords, and this moment was to come to mark the fall of the Roman
empire in the west.

100 | ROMULUS AUGUSTULUS
The last emperor

No one can accuse the Romans of not being precise. According to
their records, Rome was founded by Romulus on 21 April 753 BC.
Rome became a de facto empire with the victory of Augustus at
Actium on 2 September 31 BC. The western Roman empire ended
506 years after that on 4 September AD 476, after being a going
concern for 1,229 years, 4 months and 13 days. By coincidence, the
last 'emperor' of the west carried the names of both Rome's founder
and its first emperor – Romulus Augustus.

As an emperor, Romulus Augustus was seen even by his contemporaries as something of a joke. The Greeks of the eastern
empire called him Momyllus Augustulus (Momyllus meaning
'small disgrace' and 'Augustulus' with its '-ulus' suffix meant something like 'pathetic little Augustus'). Compared to the majesty of
Trajan's empire, Romulus' dominions were something of a joke. They
consisted of Italy, a small part of Gaul, and parts of north Africa

when they felt like belonging. The rest was under the rule of the eastern (soon to be Byzantine) empire and independent kingdoms set up by Rome's barbarian conquerors.

Nor did Romulus actually rule any of this. The ruling was done by his father, Orestes, who was born as a Roman in the Danube province of Pannonia. Orestes had a barbarian mother, and when the province was conquered by Attila the Hun, he gladly took service with the invader, rising to a high position in Attila's court. On Attila's death Orestes, now very wealthy, returned to live among the Italians, who seem to have had no hard feelings about Orestes' previous employment. He married a daughter of an aristocrat called Romulus, and it was from this uncle that young Romulus received his name. Augustus was also a common name at the time, and his christening, probably in 461, did not necessarily signal any imperial ambitions by his parents.

In 475 the reigning emperor Julius Nepos ordered Orestes to gather an army to repel Euric, a Gothic king threatening to invade from Gaul. Having assembled the army as ordered, Orestes decided on a better use for it, and marched on Ravenna, then the imperial capital, and seized power. Given his non-Roman mother, Orestes decided that a better figurehead for the empire would be his son, Romulus Augustulus, who accordingly became Roman emperor on 29 August 475, when he was 14 or 15 years old.

There was no eastern emperor at this time. However, the two generals fighting it out for that title unanimously refused to accept Romulus' usurpation, and continued to recognize Nepos as emperor. Nepos had briefly taken shelter with his predecessor, who was now bishop of Salona, and continued unavailingly with attempts to assert his imperial authority over part of Dalmatia, across the Adriatic from Italy.

Meanwhile Romulus obediently sat on the throne while his father set up a government. A chief minister was appointed, and Orestes entered into negotiations with the eastern empire, the Vandals of Africa and his own troops. It was the latter negotiations that were to prove fatally difficult. The Italians were incapable of defending themselves, so the army which had put Romulus on the imperial throne was composed almost entirely of Germans. In other parts of what had once been the western empire, the German soldiery supported itself by being allocated one third of the lands of the people they were defending. This had not happened in Italy, and one of the reasons the soldiers had supported the enthronement of Romulus was that his father had strongly implied that such land grants would be forthcoming.

A year later, the soldiers were still denied 'their' land, and impatience boiled over. The army rose in revolt under a commander called Odoacer. While Romulus remained nervously in Ravenna, his father went to deal with the mutineers. Feelings ran higher than Orestes had anticipated, and he had to seek shelter from his men in Pavia. This city was overrun, and Orestes was killed.

This left the question of what would become of Romulus and his empire. Odoacer took Ravenna, and on 4 September 476 removed Romulus from his throne. (Romulus didn't abdicate, as his reign had never been recognized by any but his own soldiers, and that recognition proved to be temporary.) Odoacer took over the rule of Italy, though he did so nominally as a subordinate of Nepos, a situation which lasted until Nepos died in 480. (This gives Julius Nepos a strong claim to have been the last 'real' western emperor.) After Nepos, rule of the west reverted in name to the eastern emperor, but in reality the west was now a shifting mosaic of Germanic kingdoms.

Fortunately for Romulus, ex-emperors of the west were no longer worth killing. He was sent off to live in Campania, and may even have received a pension. At least one letter from an imperial official called Cassiodorus in 507 discusses the pension arrangements of a 'Romulus'. There is no reason to believe that Romulus Augustulus did not peacefully end his days in the early years of the 6th century, having outlived the Roman empire of the west by several decades.

List of Emperors

Julio-Claudian Dynasty

Augustus 31 BC–AD 14
Tiberius 14–37
Caligula 37–41
Claudius 41–54
Nero 54–68

Civil War of 69

Galba 68–69
Otho 69
Vitellius 69

Flavian Dynasty

Vespasian 69–79
Titus 79–81
Domitian 81–96

The Adoptive Emperors and the Antonine Dynasty

Nerva 96–98
Trajan 98–117
Hadrian 117–38
Antoninus Pius 138–61
Marcus Aurelius 161–80
  and Lucius Verus 161–69
Commodus 180–92

Civil War of 193

Pertinax 193
Didius Julianus 193

Severan Dynasty

Septimius Severus 193–211
Geta 211
Caracalla 211–17
Macrinus 217–18
Elagabalus 218–22
Alexander Severus 222–35

Third-century Crisis

Maximinus Thrax 235–38
Gordian I 238
Gordian II 238
Pupienus and Balbinus 238
Gordian III 238–44
Philip the Arab 244–49
Decius 249–51
Trebonianus Gallus 251–53
Aemilius Aemilianus 253
Valerian 253–60
Gallienus 253–68
Claudius II 268–70
Quintillus 270
Aurelian 270–75
Tacitus 275–76
Florianus 276
Probus 276–82
Carus 282–83
Numerian 283–84
Carinus 283–85
Postumus 260–69
Laelianus 269
Marius 269
Victorinus 268–71
Tetricus 271–74

Later Roman Empire

Diocletian 284–305
(Maximian 286–305)
Constantius I 305–6
Galerius 305–11
Severus II 306–7
Maxentius 306–12
Maximinus Daia 310–13
Constantine 306–37
(Licinius 308–24)
Constantine II 337–40
Constans I 337–50
Constantius II 337–61
Julian 360–63
Jovian 363–64

House of Valentinian

Valens 364–78 /
  Valentinian I 364–75
Gratian 367–83
Valentinian II 375–92
Eugenius 392–94

Theodosian Dynasty

Theodosius I 379–95
Arcadius 395–408 /
  Honorius 395–423
Theodosius II 408–50 /
  Johannes 423–25 /
  Valentinian III 425–55

The Final Emperors

Petronius Maximus 455
Avitus 455–56
Majorian 456–61
Severus III 461–65
Anthemius 467–72
Olybrius 472
Glycerius 473–74
Julius Nepos 474–75
Romulus Augustulus 475–76

Sources of Quotations

Quotations have been translated
from the original texts by the
authors, except where an asterisk
precedes the sources in this list:
in those cases quotations are taken
from the published editions cited
in the bibliography.

1 Faustulus
Livy, *History of Rome*, 1,
    Introduction
Aulus Gellius, *Attic Nights*, 7.7
Dionysius of Halicarnassus, *Roman
    Antiquities*, 1.84
2 Titus Tatius
Livy, *History of Rome*, 1.11, 1.13–14
3 Tanaquil
Livy, *History of Rome*, 1.34, 1.39, 1.41
Plutarch, *Roman Questions*, 36
4 Servius Tullius
Livy, *History of Rome*, 1.48–49
5 Brutus
Livy, *History of Rome*, 1.59, 2.5
6 Lucretia
Livy, *History of Rome*, 1.57, 1.59
7 Cloelia
Livy, *History of Rome*, 2.13
Juvenal, *Satires*, 8.264
8 Vindicius
Livy, *History of Rome*, 1.4
9 Cincinnatus
Dionysius of Halicarnassus, *Roman
    Antiquities*, 10.24–25
10 Verginius
Livy, *History of Rome*, 3.48
12 Titus Manlius
Livy, *History of Rome*, 8.7, 8.8
Valerius Maximus, *Memorable
    Doings and Sayings*, 2.6

14 Regulus
Polybius, *Histories*, 1.35
Horace, *Odes*, 3.5
*Florus, *Epitome of Roman History*,
    1.18.25
*Valerius Maximus, *Memorable
    Doings and Sayings*, 9.2
15 Fabius Pictor
Dionysius of Halicarnassus, *Roman
    Antiquities*, 1.74
16 Plautus
Aulus Gellius, *Attic Nights*, 3.3.11,
    3.3.14
Horace, *Epistles*, 2.1.175–76
Plautus, *Miles Gloriosus*, 234–37
Plautus, *Pseudolus*, 117–22
17 Cato the Elder
Livy, *History of Rome*, 34.2,
    39.44
Plutarch, *Life of Cato*, 22
Cato, *On Agriculture*, 2.3.7
18 Fabius Maximus
*Plutarch, *Makers of Rome (Life of
    Fabius Maximus)*, 1, 17, 27.
Virgil, *Aeneid*, 6.847
21 Laelius
Livy, *History of Rome*, 21.46
22 Spurius Ligustinus
Livy, *History of Rome*, 42.34
26 Staberius Eros
Pliny, *Natural History*, 35.199
Syrus, *Sententiae*
29 Cicero
Cicero, *Letters to Atticus*, 3.7
30 Verres
*Cicero, *The Verrine Orations*, 2.4.18,
    2.4.49, 1.18.56
Pliny the Elder, *Natural History*,
    34.3.6
31 Catiline
*Sallust, *The War with Catiline*, 61

32 Sallust
Sallust, *The War with Catiline*, 5
*Cassius Dio, *Roman History*, 43.9.2,
  43.47.4
33 Tiro
Cicero, *To the family*, 35
Cicero, *To his friends*, 16
34 Clodia
Cicero, *For Marcus Caelius*, 47, 64
Catullus, 58
37 Julius Caesar
Suetonius, *Life of Caesar*, 1
38 Horace
*Horace, *Odes*, 2.7
Horace, *Epistles*, 19
40 Agrippa
Suetonius, *Life of Augustus*, 94
Cassius Dio, *Roman History*,
  54.39.1–3
44 Eumachia
CIL X, 810, 811, 813
45 Hilarion of Oxyrhynchus
Oxyrhynchus pap. (4) 744
46 Virgil
Virgil, *Aeneid*, 6.851–53
47 Sulpicia
Sulpicia, *Six Poems*, 2, 1, 4
48 Antonia Augusta
Valerius Maximus, *Memorable
  Doings and Sayings*, 4.3.3
Tacitus, *Annals*, 3.3
Suetonius, *Life of Caligula*, 23, 24
Cassius Dio, *Roman History*, 58.11.7
Josephus, *Jewish Antiquities*, 18.181
49 Sejanus
Tacitus, *Annals*, 4.1, 4.9, 4.58.
Cassius Dio, *Roman History*, 58.4
50 Pontius Pilate
Josephus, *Jewish Antiquities*, 18.4
Josephus, *The Wars of the Jews*, 9.4
Tacitus, *Annals*, 15.44

54 Locusta
Suetonius, *Life of Caligula*, 49
Tacitus, *Annals*, 66
57 Antonia Caenis
Ovid, *Metamorphoses*, 12.261
58 Petilius Cerealis
Tacitus, *Histories*, 5.20–25
59 Frontinus
Frontinus, *De Aquis*, 1.2
Martial, *Epigrams*, 10.58
Pliny the Younger, *Letters*, 9.19
61 Amazonia
Juvenal, *Satires*, 6
62 Epictetus
Spartianus, *Hadrian*, 16
Epictetus, *Discourses*, 1.2, 1.24
63 Martial
Martial, *Epigrams*, 11.62, 11.16, 12.21,
  10.47
64 Pliny the Elder
Pliny the Elder, *Natural History*,
  9.117
Pliny the Younger, *Letters*,
  3.5.8–9
65 Larcius Macedo
Pliny the Younger, *Letters*, 3.14
66 Minicius Acilianus
Pliny the Younger, *Letters*, 1.10
67 Domitian
Suetonius, *Life of Domitian*, 12
68 Agricola
*Tacitus, *The Agricola and the
  Germania*, 4, 12
70 Blandina Martiola
Epigram CIL XIII
71 Claudia Severa
Vindolanda Tablets, 2.291–92
73 Antinous
St Athanasius, *Against the Heathen*,
  9.5
Florus, *Historia Augusta*, 13, 16

75 Marcus Aurelius
Marcus Aurelius, *Letters to Fronto*, 3.6.5
Marcus Aurelius, *Meditations*, 9.8.9
76 Aulus Gellius
Aulus Gellius, *Attic Nights, Preface*
78 Didius Julianus
*Cassius Dio, *Roman History*, 74.16
Historia Augusta, *Life of Didius Julianus*, 9.2
79 Clodia Laeta
Dionysius of Halicarnassus, *Roman Antiquities*, 2.67, 78.16
80 Elagabalus
Lampridius, *Elagabalus,* 7
81 Postumus
Historia Augusta, *The Lives of the Thirty Pretenders*, 3
82 Odaenathus
Historia Augusta, *The Lives of the Thirty Pretenders*, 15
83 Symmachius
Epigram CIL VI 10205
84 Aurelia Amimma
P. Dura 32
87 Diocletian
Eutropius, *Abridgement of Roman History*, 9.19.2
Historia Augusta, *Lives of Carus Carinus and Numerian*, 14.1–15.6
Aurelius Victor, *Of the Caesars*, 39
Ammianus Marcellinus, *Roman History*, 14.11.10
Lactantius, *Of the manner in which the persecutors died*, 10, 15.1
88 Constantine
Zosimus, *New History,* 2.30
89 Ammianus Marcellinus
Ammianus Marcellinus, *Roman History*, 14.9.1, 14.6.3,

90 Julian the Apostate
Julian the Apostate, *Misogen*, 1.2
91 Valentinian
Sozomen, *Ecclesiastical History*, 6.7
Ammianus Marcellinus, *Roman History*, 30.6
93 Hypatia
John of Nikiu, *Chronicle*, 84.87
94 Vettius Agorius Praetextatus
Macrobius, *Saturnalia*, 1.17–24,
St Jerome, *To Pammachius against John of Jerusalem*
97 Leo the Great
Anastasius of Thessalonica, *Letter,* 14
Leo the Great, *Letter,* 28
99 Consentius
Sidonius Apollinarus, *Carmina*, 23

Further Reading

General Reading

Bradley, P. *Ancient Rome. Using evidence* (Melbourne: Edward Arnold, 1990).

Dixon, S. *Reading Roman Women. Sources, genres, and real life* (London: Duckworth, 2001).

Matyszak, P. *Chronicle of the Roman Republic* (London and New York: Thames & Hudson, 2003).

Potter, D. and Mattingly, D. (eds) *Life, Death and Entertainment in the Roman Empire* (Ann Arbor: Univ. of Michigan Press, 1999).

Potter, D. (ed) *A Companion to the Roman Empire* (Oxford: Blackwell, 2006).

Scarre, C. *Chronicle of the Roman Emperors* (London and New York: Thames & Hudson, 2000).

Syme, R. *Tacitus* (Oxford: Clarendon Press, 1958).

Wiedemann, T. *Emperors and Gladiators* (London: Routledge, 1992).

Part 1
From Royal Subjects to Republican Citizens 753–300 BC

Alfoldi, A. *Early Rome and the Latins* (Ann Arbor: University of Michigan Press, 1963).

Braund, D. and Gill, C. (eds) *Myth, history and culture in Republican Rome: Studies in honour of T.P. Wiseman* (Exeter: Exeter University Press, 2003).

Cornell, T.J. *The Beginnings of Rome. Italy and Rome from the Bronze Age to the Punic Wars (c. 1000–264 BC)* (London: Routledge, 1995).

Cristofani, M. *La grande Roma dei Tarquini* (Rome: 'L'Erma' di Bretschneider, 1990).

Drummond, A., Walbank, F.W., Astin, A.E. and Frederiksen, M.W. *The Cambridge Ancient History Volume 7, Part 2: The Rise of Rome to 220 BC* (Cambridge: Cambridge University Press, 2nd ed. 1990).

Fraschetti, A. *The Foundation of Rome* (Edinburgh: Edinburgh University Press, 2005; trans. M.J. Hill and K. Windle).

Forsythe, G. *A Critical History of Early Rome: From Prehistory to the First Punic War* (Berkeley: University of Calif. Press, 2005).

Holloway, R. R. *The Archaeology of Early Rome and Latium* (London: Routledge, 1996).

Miles, G. *Livy: Reconstructing early Rome* (Ithaca: Cornell University Press, 1995).

Oakley, S. P. *A Commentary on Livy Books VI–X* (Oxford: Clarendon Press, 1997; 2 vols).

Ogilvie, R. M. *A Commentary on Livy Books 1–5* (Oxford: Clarendon Press, 1965; 2nd ed. 1970).

1 Faustulus

Plutarch, *Parallel Lives, I* (Cambridge, Mass.: Loeb Classical Library, 1914; trans. B. Perrin).

2 Titus Tatius

Livy, *The Early History of Rome* (London: Penguin Books, 1988; trans. A. De Selincourt).

Propertius, *Elegies* (Cambridge, Mass.: Loeb Classical Library, 1913; trans. H.E. Butler).

3 Tanaquil

Livy, *The Early History of Rome* (London: Penguin Books, 1988; trans. A. De Selincourt).

McDougall, I. 'Livy and Etruscan women', *Ancient History Bulletin* 4.2 (1990), 24–30.

Plutarch, *Roman Questions* (Cambridge, Mass.: Loeb Classical Library, Moralia IV, 1936; trans, F.C. Babbit).

4 Servius

Ridley, R.T. 'The enigma of Servius Tullius', *Clio* 57 (1975), 147–77.

Thomsen, R. *King Servius Tullius. A historical synthesis* (Copenhagen: Gyldendal, 1980).

5 Brutus

Ridgeway, W. 'The value of the traditions respecting the early kings of Rome', *Classical Journal* 14.6 (1919), 371–82.

6 Lucretia

Donaldson, I. *The Rapes of Lucretia. A myth and its transformations* (Oxford: Clarendon Press, 1982).

Lee, A.G. 'Ovid's Lucretia', *Greece and Rome* 22 (1953), 107–18.

Pomeroy, S. *Goddesses, Whores, Wives and Slaves: Women in Classical Antiquity* (New York: Schocken, 1995).

7 Cloelia

Roller, M.B. 'Exemplarity in Roman Culture: The case of Horatius Cocles and Cloelia', *Classical Philology* 99.1 (2004), 1–56.

Wiseman, T.P. 'Roman Republic, Year One', *Greece and Rome* 45.1 (1998), 19–26.

8 Vindicius

Boren, H. *Roman Society: A social, economic and cultural history* (Lexington, Mass.: D.C. Heath, 1977).

Finley, M.I. *Classical Slavery* (London: F. Cass, 1987).

Livy, *The Early History of Rome* (London: Penguin Books, 1988; trans. A. De Selincourt).

9 Cincinnatus

Livy, *The Early History of Rome* (London: Penguin Books, 1988; trans. A. De Selincourt).

10 Verginius

Livy, *The Early History of Rome* (London: Penguin Books, 1988; trans. A. De Selincourt).

Wiseman, P. *Clio's Cosmetics: Three studies in Greco-Roman literature* (Leicester: Leicester University Press Totowa, N.J, 1979).

11 Marcus Manlius

Horsfall, N. 'From history to legend: M. Manlius and the geese', *Classical Journal* 76.4 (1981), 298–311.

Raaflaub, K.A. (ed) *Social Struggles in Archaic Rome: New perspectives on the conflict of the orders* (Oxford: Blackwell, 2005).

Skutsch, O. 'The fall of the Capitol', *Journal of Roman Studies* 43 (1953), 77–78.

12 Titus Manlius

Livy, *History of Rome, Books VI–X* (London: Penguin Books, 1982; trans. Betty Radice).

Valerius Maximus, *Memorable Doings and Sayings* (Cambridge, Mass.: Loeb Classical Library, 2000; trans. D.R. Shackleton Bailey).

13 Decius Mus

Broughton, T. *The Magistrates of the Roman Republic* (New York: Scholars Press, 1984).

Sekunda, N. and Hook, R. *Early Roman Armies* (London: Osprey, 1995).

Part 2
From Italians to Romans 300–88 BC

Bagnall, R. *The Punic Wars: Rome, Carthage and the Struggle for the Mediterranean* (London: Pimlico, 1999).

Boatwright, M.T., Gargola, D.J. and Talbert, J.A. *The Romans: From Village to Empire* (New York: Oxford University Press, 2004).

Dillon, M. and Garland, L. *Ancient Rome: From the early Republic to the assassination of Julius Caesar* (London: Routledge, 2005).

Walbank, F.W., Astin, A.E., Frederiksen, M.W. and Ogilvie, R.M. (eds) *The Cambridge Ancient History. Vol. VII, Part 2, The Rise of Rome to 220 BC* (Cambridge: Cambridge University Press, 2nd ed., 1990).

Walbank, F.W., Astin, A.E., Frederiksen, M.W. and Ogilvie, R.M. (eds) *The Cambridge Ancient History. Vol VIII, Rome and the Mediterranean to 133 BC* (Cambridge: Cambridge University Press, 2nd ed., 1989).

14 Regulus

Appian, *The Punic Wars* (Cambridge, Mass.: Loeb Classical Library, 1912; trans. H. White).

Florus, *Epitome of Roman History* (Cambridge, Mass.: Loeb Classical Library, 1929; trans. E. Seymour Forster).

Silius Italicus, *Punica* (Cambridge, Mass.: Loeb Classical Library, 1934; trans. J.D. Duff).

Valerius *Maximus, Memorable Doings and Sayings* (Cambridge, Mass.: Loeb Classical Library, 2000; trans. D.R. Shackleton Bailey).

15 Quintus Fabius Pictor

Frank, T. 'Roman historiography before Caesar', *American Historical Review* 32.2 (1927), 232–40.

Forsythe, G. *The historian L. Calpurnius Piso Frugi and the Roman Annalistic tradition* (London: Lanham, MD., 1994).

Mellor, R. *The Roman Historians* (London: Routledge, 1999).

16 Plautus

Moore, T.J. *The Theater of Plautus* (Austin: University of Texas Press, 1998).

Segal, E. *Roman Laughter. The comedy of Plautus* (Cambridge, Mass.: Harvard University Press, 1968).

Stace, C. 'The slaves of Plautus', *Greece and Rome* 15.1 (1968), 64–77.

17 Cato the Elder

Astin, A.E. *Cato the Censor* (Oxford: Clarendon Press, 1978).

18 Fabius Maximus

Plutarch, *Makers of Rome* (London: Penguin Books, 1978; trans. I. Scott-Kilvert).

19 Claudius Marcellus

Patterson, M. 'Rome's choice of magistrates during the Hannibalic War', *Transactions and Proceedings of the American Philological Association* 73 (1942), 319–40.

Plutarch, *Makers of Rome* (London: Penguin Books, 1978; trans. I. Scott-Kilvert).

20 Quinctius Crispinus

Konstan, D. *Friendship in the Classical World* (Cambridge: Cambridge University Press, 1997).

Sidnell, P. *Warhorse: Cavalry in Ancient Warfare* (London: Hambledon Continuum, 2006).

21 Laelius

Momigliano, A. *Alien Wisdom: The Limits of Hellenization* (Cambridge: Cambridge University Press, 1990).

Taylor, L.R. 'Forerunners of the Gracchi', *Journal of Roman Studies* 52 (1962), 19–27.

Scullard, H.H. *Scipio Africanus: Soldier and Politician* (London: Thames & Hudson, 1970).

22 Spurius Ligustinus

Livy, *History of Rome, Vol. XII, Books 40–42* (Cambridge, Mass.: Loeb Classical Library, 1938; trans. E.T. Sage and A.C. Schlesinger).

23 Cornelia

Dixon, S. *Cornelia, Mother of the Gracchi* (London, Routledge, 2007).

Stockton, D.S. *The Gracchi* (Oxford: Clarendon Press, 1979).

Plutarch, *Parallel Lives, X* (Cambridge, Mass.: Loeb Classical Library, 1921).

24 Rutilius Rufus

Hendrickson, G.L. 'The memoirs of Rutilius Rufus', *Classical Philology* 28.3 (1933), 153–75.

Kallet-Marx, R. 'The trial of Rutilius Rufus', *Phoenix* 44.2 (1990), 122–39.

Keppie, L. *The Making of the Roman Army; From Republic to Empire* (London: Routledge, 1998).

25 Cornelius Sulla

Baker, G.P. *Sulla the Fortunate: Roman general and dictator* (New York: Cooper Square Press, 2001).

Keaveney, A. *Sulla: The Last Republican* (London: Routledge, 2005).

26 Staberius Eros

Hopkins, K. 'Everyday life for the Roman schoolboy', *History Today* 43 (1993), 25–30.

Suetonius, *The Lives of Illustrious Men (The Lives of the Caesars, II)* (Cambridge, Mass.: Loeb Classical Library, 1914; trans. J.C. Rolfe).

Too, Y.L. (ed) *Education in Greek and Roman Antiquity* (Boston: Brill, 2001).

27 Pasiteles

Kleiner, D. *Roman Sculpture* (New Haven: Yale University Press, 1992).

Waldstein, C. 'Pasiteles and Arkesilaos, the Venus Genetrix and the Venus of the Esquiline',

*American Journal of Archaeology
and of the History of the Fine Arts*
3.1/2 (1887), 1–13.

Part 3
Life in Troubled Times 88 BC–AD 14
Beard, M. and Crawford, M. *Rome
in the Late Republic: Problems
and Interpretations* (London:
Duckworth, 1999).

Brunt, P.A. *The Fall of the Roman
Republic* (Oxford: Clarendon
Press, 1988).

Crook, J.A., Lintott, A. and
Rawson, E. (eds) *The Cambridge
Ancient History. Vol 9: The last age
of the Roman Republic, 146–43
BC* (Cambridge: Cambridge
University Press, 1993).

Goodman, M. *The Roman World,
44 BC–AD 180* (London: Routledge,
1997).

28 Hortensius
Bauman, R. A. *Lawyers in Roman
Transitional Politics: A study of
the Roman jurists in their political
setting in the late Republic and
Triumvirate* (Munich: C.H. Beck,
1985).

Geiger, J. 'M. Hortensius M. f. Q.
n. Hortalus', *The Classical Review*
20.2 (1970), 132–34.

29 Cicero
Everitt, A. *Cicero. The life and times
of Rome's greatest politician* (New
York: Random House, 2003).

Griffin, M.T. and Atkins, E.M.
*Cambridge Texts in the History
of Political Thought: Cicero, On
Duties* (Cambridge: Cambridge
University Press, 1991).

Plutarch, *Fall of the Roman Republic*
(London: Penguin Books, 1972;
trans. R. Warner).

30 Verres
Brunt, P. A. 'Patronage and politics
in the "Verrines"', *Chiron* 10
(1980), 273–90.

Cicero, *The Verrine Orations*
(Cambridge, Mass.: Loeb
Classical Library, 1928; trans.
L. H. G. Greenwood).

31 Catiline
Cicero, *Orations, X* (Cambridge,
Mass.: Loeb Classical Library,
1976; trans. C. MacDonald).

Hutchinson, L. *The Conspiracy of
Catiline* (New York: Barnes and
Noble, 1967).

Sallust, *The War with Catiline*
(Cambridge, Mass.: Loeb
Classical Library, 1921; trans.
J.C. Rolfe).

32 Sallust
Cassius Dio, *Roman History,
IV* (Cambridge, Mass.: Loeb
Classical Library, 1916; trans. E.
Cary and H.B. Foster).

Syme, R. *Sallust* (Berkeley and Los
Angeles; London: University of
California Press, 1964).

33 Tiro
Treggiari, S. 'The freedmen of
Cicero', *Greece and Rome* 16.2
(1969), 195–204.

Smith, W. (ed) 'Tiro', *Dictionary
of Greek and Roman Antiquities*
(Boston: C. Little and J. Brown,
1870).

34 Clodia
Skinner, M.B. 'Clodia Metelli',
Transactions of the American

Philological Association 113 (1983), 273–87.

35 Atticus

Cicero, *Letters to Atticus* (Cambridge: Cambridge University Press, 2004; trans. D. R. Shackleton-Bailey).

Cornelius Nepos: *Three Lives – Alcibiades, Dion, Atticus* (Oak Park: R. Roebuck Bolchazy-Carducci Publishers; New Edition 1987).

36 Servilia

Means, T. and Dickinson, S.K. 'Plutarch and the family of Cato Minor', *Classical Journal* 69.3 (1974), 210–15.

Potter, F.H. 'Political alliance by marriage', *The Classical Journal* 29.9 (1934), 663–74.

37 Julius Caesar

Canfora, L. *Julius Caesar: The People's Dictator* (Edinburgh: Edinburgh University Press, 2006).

Goldsworthy, A. *Caesar: Life of a Colossus* (London: Yale University Press, 2006).

Meier, C. *Caesar. A biography* (New York: Basic Books, 1996).

Weinstock, S. *Divus Julius* (Oxford: Clarendon Press, 1971).

38 Horace

Anderson, W.S. 'Horace, the unwilling warrior: Satire I.9', *The American Journal of Philology* 77.2 (1956), 148–66.

Horace, *The Complete Odes and Epodes: with the Centennial Hymn* (London: Penguin, 1983; trans. W.G. Shepherd).

39 Augustus

Everitt, A. *Augustus. The life of Rome's first emperor* (London: Random House, 2007).

Shotter, D.C.A. *Augustus Caesar* (London: Routledge, 1991).

Wallace-Hadrill, A. *Augustan Rome* (Bristol: Bristol Classical Press, 1993).

40 Agrippa

Roddaz, J-M. *Marcus Agrippa* (Rome: L'Ecole Francaise de Rome, 1984).

Reinhold, M. *Marcus Agrippa: A Biography* (Geneva, NewYork: The W.F. Humphrey Press, 1933).

41 Julius Zoilus

Smith, R.R.R. *The Monument of C. Julius Zoilos* (Mainz am Rhein: Verlag Philipp von Zabern, 1993).

42 Nonius Balbus

Baldwin-Bowsky, M. 'Roman arbitration in central Crete: an Augustan Proconsul and a Neronian Procurator', *The Classical Journal* 82.3 (1987), 218–29.

43 Livy

Livy, *The History of Rome from its Foundation: Rome and Italy* (London: Penguin Classics, 1982; trans. B. Radice).

Syme, R. 'Livy and Augustus', *Harvard Studies in Classical Philology* 64 (1959), 27–87.

Machiavelli, N. *Discourses on Livy* (Oxford: Oxford University Press, 2003; trans. J. Conaway Bondanella and P. Bondanella).

44 Eumachia

Berry, J. *The Complete Pompeii* (London: Thames & Hudson, 2007), 114–15.

Moeller, W.O. 'The date and dedication of the building of Eumachia', *Cronache Pompeiane* 1 (1975), 232–36.

45 Hilarion of Oxyrhynchus

Corbier, M. 'Child-exposure and abandonment', in S. Dixon (ed), *Childhood, class and kin in the Roman World* (London: Routledge, 2001), 52–73.

Harris, W.V. 'Child-exposure in the Roman Empire', *Journal of Roman Studies* 84 (1994), 1–22.

46 Virgil

Martindale, C. (ed) *The Cambridge Companion to Virgil* (Cambridge: Cambridge University Press, 1997).

Frank, T. 'What Do We Know about Vergil?' *The Classical Journal* 26.1 (1930), 3–11.

Part 4

Romans and Caesars AD 14–75

Alston, R. *Aspects of Roman History, AD 14–117* (London: Routledge, 1998).

Goodman, M. *The Roman World, 44 BC–AD 180* (London: Routledge, 1997).

47 Sulpicia

Richlin, A. 'Sulpicia the satirist', *Classical World* 86.2 (1992), 125–40.

Skoie, M. *Reading Sulpicia. Commentaries 1475–1990* (Oxford: Oxford University Press, 2002).

Santirocco, M.S. 'Sulpicia Reconsidered', *The Classical Journal* 74.3 (1979), 229–39.

48 Antonia Augusta

Kokkinos, N. *Antonia Augusta. Portrait of a great Roman lady*
(London and New York: Routledge, 1992).

49 Sejanus

Boddington, A. 'Sejanus. Whose conspiracy?' *The American Journal of Philology* 84.1 (1963), 1–16.

50 Pontius Pilate

Bond, H.K. *Pontius Pilate in History and Interpretation* (Cambridge: Cambridge University Press, 1998).

Johns, A. *Pontius Pilate, 20 BC–AD 36* (Ilfracombe: Stockwell, 1986).

Lemonon, J-P. *Pilate et le Gouvernement de la Judée: Textes et Monuments* (Paris: Gabalda, 1981).

51 Caligula

Barrett, A. *Caligula: The corruption of power* (London: Batsford, 1989).

Wilkinson, S. *Caligula* (London: Routledge, 2005).

52 Pallas

Braund, D. *The Administration of the Roman Empire 241 BC–AD 193* (Exeter: University of Exeter Press, 1988).

53 Agrippina

Barrett, A.A. *Agrippina: Sex, power and politics in the early empire* (London: Routledge, 1999).

54 Locusta

Grimm-Samuel, V. 'On the mushroom that deified the Emperor Claudius', *The Classical Quarterly* 41.1 (1991), 178–82.

Kaufman, D. 'Poisons and poisoning among the Romans', *Classical Philology* 27.2 (Apr. 1932), 156–67.

55 Cornelius Pulcher

Kajava, M. 'When did the Isthmian Games return to the Isthmus?'

(Rereading 'Corinth' 8.3.153) *Classical Philology* 97.2 (2002), 168–78.

56 Numerius Quinctius

Easterling, P.E. and Hall, E. (eds) *Greek and Roman actors: Aspects of an ancient profession* (Cambridge: Cambridge University Press, 2002).

57 Caenis

Levick, B. *Vespasian* (London: Routledge, 1999).

58 Petilius Cerialis

Birley, A.R. 'Petillius Cerialis and the Conquest of Brigantia', *Britannia* 4 (1973), 179–90.

59 Frontinus

Blackman, D.R. and Hodge, T. *Frontinus' Legacy: Essays on Frontinus' De Aquis Urbis Romae* (Ann Arbor: University of Michigan Press, 2001).

Peachin, M. *Frontinus and the curae of the curator aquarum* (Stuttgart: Steiner, 2004).

60 Josephus

Rajak, T. *Josephus: The historian and his society* (London: Duckworth, 1983).

Rajak, T. *The Jewish Dialogue with Greece and Rome: Studies in cultural and social interaction* (Leiden: Brill, 2002).

61 Amazonia

Coleman, K. 'Missio at Halicarnassus', *Harvard Studies in Classical Philology* 100 (2000), 487–500.

62 Epictetus

Long, A.A. *From Epicurus to Epictetus: Studies in Hellenistic and Roman Philosophy* (Oxford: Clarendon Press, 2006).

Long, A.A. *Epictetus: A Stoic and Socratic guide to life* (Oxford: Clarendon Press, 2002).

63 Martial

Braund, S. *The Roman Satirists and their Masks* (Bristol: Bristol Classical Press, 1996).

Sullivan, J.P. *Martial: The unexpected classic. A literary and historical study* (Cambridge: Cambridge University Press, 1991).

Part 5
Citizens of the Empire AD 75–200

Prosopographia Imperii Romani saec I. II. III (Berolini; Lipsiae: Walter de Gruyter, 1933).

Wells, C.M. *The Roman Empire, 30 BC–AD 284* (London: Fontana, 1984).

64 Pliny the Elder

Beagon, M. *Roman Nature: the Thought of Pliny the Elder* (Oxford: Clarendon Press, 1992).

Healy, J.F. *Pliny the Elder on Science and Technology* (Oxford: Oxford University Press, 1999).

65 Larcius Macedo

Bradley, K.R. *Slavery and Society at Rome* (Cambridge: Cambridge University Press, 1994).

66 Minicius Acilianus

Saller, R. P. 'Familia, Domus, and the Roman Conception of the Family', *Phoenix* 38.4 (1984), 336–55.

Sherwin-White A.N. *The letters of Pliny: A Historical and Social Commentary* (Oxford: Clarendon Press, 1966).

67 Domitian

Southern, P. *Domitian: Tragic Tyrant* (London: Routledge, 1997).

68 Agricola

Birley, A.R. 'Agricola, the Flavian Dynasty and Tacitus', in B. Levick (ed) *The Ancient Historian and his Materials* (Farnborough: Gregg International, 1975), 139–54.

Hanson, W.S. *Agricola and the Conquest of the North* (London: Batsford, 1987).

Tacitus, *The Agricola and the Germania* (London: Penguin Books, 1970).

69 Tiberius Claudius Maximus

Connolly, P. *Tiberius Claudius Maximus: The Cavalryman* (Oxford: Oxford University Press, 1997).

70 Blandina Martiola

Joshel, S. *Work, Identity and Legal Status at Rome. A Study of the Occupational Inscriptions* (Norman and London: University of Oklahoma Press, 1990).

Kampen, N, Pomeroy, S. and Shapiro, A. (eds), *Women in the Classical World: Image and Text* (New York and Oxford: Oxford University Press, 1994).

Brogan, O. *Roman Gaul* (Cambridge, Mass.: Harvard University Press, 1953).

71 Claudia Severa

Vindolanda Tablets online http://vindolanda.csad.ox.ac.uk/

Bowman, A. *Life and Letters on the Roman Frontier* (London: British Museum Press, 1994).

Bowman, A. and Thomas, J.D. *The Vindolanda Writing Tablets.* Vol 2. (London: Society for the Promotion of Roman Studies, 1994).

Salway, P. *Roman Britain* (Oxford: Oxford University Press, 1984).

72 Apollodorus

Birley, A.R. Hadrian. *The Restless Emperor* (London: Routledge, 1997).

Boatwright, M.T. *Hadrian and the City of Rome* (Princeton: Princeton University Press, 1987).

Calcani, G. (ed) *Apollodorus of Damascus and Trajan's Column: From tradition to project* (Rome: L'Erma di Bretschneider, 2003).

73 Antinous

Curtis, P. (ed) *Antinous: The Face of the Antique* (Leeds: Henry Moore Institute, 2006).

Royston, L. *Beloved and God: The Story of Hadrian and Antinous* (London: Phoenix, 1997).

74 Metila Acte

Wood, S. 'Alcestis on Roman Sarcophagi', *American Journal of Archaeology* 82.4 (1978), 499–510.

von Domaszewski, A. 'Magna Mater in Latin Inscriptions', *The Journal of Roman Studies* 1 (1911), 50–56.

Nelson Robinson, D. 'A Study of the Social Position of the Devotees of the Oriental Cults in the Western World, based on the Inscriptions', *Transactions and Proceedings of the American Philological Association* 44 (1913), 151–61.

75 Marcus Aurelius

Birley, A. *Marcus Aurelius: A Biography* (London: Batsford, 1987).

76 Aulus Gellius

Holford-Strevens, L. *Aulus Gellius: An Antonine Scholar and his Achievement* (Oxford: Oxford University Press, 2005).

77 Herodian

Echols, E.C. *Herodian of Antioch's History of the Roman Empire* (Berkeley: University of California Press, 1961). Roos, A.G. 'Herodian's Method of Composition', *Journal of Roman Studies* 5 (1915), 191–202.

78 Didius Julianus

Cassius Dio, *Roman History*, IX (Books 71– 80) (Cambridge, Mass.: Loeb Classical Library, 1927; trans. E. Cary and H.B. Foster).

Herodian, *History of the Empire*, I (Books 1–4) (Cambridge, Mass., Loeb Classical Library, 1969; trans. C.R. Whittaker).

Historia Augusta, I (Cambridge, Mass.: Loeb Classical Library, 1921; trans. D. Magie).

Part 6
Decline and Fall AD 200–476

Ammianus Marcellinus, *The Later Roman Empire (AD 354–378)* (London: Penguin Books, 1986).

Jones, A.H.M. *The Later Roman Empire 284–602: A Social, Economic, and Administrative Survey. 3 Volumes.* (Oxford: Blackwell, 1964).

Jones, A.H.M. 'The Social Background of the Struggle Between Paganism and Christianity', in A. Momigliano (ed) *The Conflict Between Paganism and Christianity in the Fourth Century* (Oxford: Clarendon Press, 1963), 17–37.

Jones, A.H.M., Martindale, J.R. and Morris, J. (eds) *The Prosopography of the Later Roman Empire, Volume I AD 260–395* (3 vols, Cambridge, Cambridge University Press, 1971–92).

Mitchell, S. *A History of the Later Roman Empire* (Oxford: Blackwell, 2007).

Momigliano, A. (ed) *The Conflict Between Paganism and Christianity in the Fourth Century* (Oxford: Clarendon Press, 1963).

Potter, D. *Prophecy and History in the Crisis of the Roman Empire. A historical commentary on the Thirteenth Sibylline Oracle* (Oxford: Clarendon Press, 1990).

Potter, D. *The Roman Empire at Bay, AD 180–395* (London: Routledge, 2004).

79 Clodia Laeta

Wildfang, R.L. *Rome's Vestal Virgins: A study of Rome's Vestal priestesses in the late Republic and early Empire* (London: Routledge, 2006).

80 Elagabalus

Ray Thompson, G. *Elagabalus, Priest-emperor of Rome* (Lawrence: Univ. of Kansas (dissertation), 1972).

Syme, R. *Emperors and Biography: Studies in the Historia Augusta* (Oxford: Clarendon Press, 1971).

81 Postumus

Drinkwater, J.F. *The Gallic Empire: Separatism and community in the north-western provinces of the Roman Empire, AD 260–274* (Stuttgart: Historia Einzelschriften 52, 1987).

82 Odaenathus

Potter, D. 'Palmyra and Rome: Odaenathus' titulature and the use of the Imperium Maius', *Zeitschrift fur Papyrologie und Epigraphik* 113 (1996), 271–85.

83 Symmachius

Oliver, J.H. 'Symmachi, homo felix', in *Memoirs of the American Academy in Rome* XXV (Rome: American Academy, 1957), 2–15.

Potter, D. 'Spectacle', in D. Potter (ed) *A Companion to the Roman Empire* (Oxford: Blackwell, 2006), 385–408.

Toynbee, J.M.C. 'Review: Memoirs of the American Academy in Rome Vol XXV', in *Classical Review* 9.1 (1959), 70–72.

84 Terentius

Pollard, N.D. *Soldiers, Cities and Civilians in Roman Syria* (Ann Arbour: University of Michigan Press, 2000).

Welles, C.B. 'The Epitaph of Julius Terentius', *Harvard Theological Review* 34.2 (1941), 79–102.

85 Aurelia Amimma

Campbell, J.B. 'The marriage of soldiers under the empire', *Journal of Roman Studies* 68 (1978), 153–66.

Phang, S.E. *The marriage of Roman soldiers (13 BC–AD 235): Law and family in the imperial army* (Boston, Mass.: Brill, 2001).

Welles, C.Bradford, O.Fink, Robert, and Gilliam, J. Frank (eds) *The Excavations at Dura-Europos conducted by Yale University and the French Academy of Inscriptions and Letters Final Report* 5, part 1: The parchments and papyri (New Haven: Yale University Press, 1959).

86 St Alban

Henig, M. and Lindley, P. (eds) *Alban and St Albans: Roman and Medieval Architecture, Art and Archaeology* (Leeds: British Archaeological Association, 2001).

87 Diocletian

Barnes, T.D. *The New Empire of Diocletian and Constantine* (Cambridge, Mass.: Harvard University Press, 1982).

Corcoran, S. *Empire of the Tetrarchs* (Oxford: Clarendon Press, 2nd ed., 2000).

Leadbetter, B. '*Patrimonium Indivisium*'? *The Empire of Diocletian and Maximian, 285–289', Chiron* 28 (1998), 213–28.

Williams, S. *Diocletian and the Roman Recovery* (London: Routledge, 1996).

88 Constantine

Barnes, T.D. *Constantine and Eusebius* (Cambridge, Mass.: Harvard University Press, 1981).

Lieu, S. and Montserrat, D. (eds) *Constantine: History, Historiography and Legend* (London: Routledge, 1998).

Weiss, P. 'The vision of Constantine', *Journal of Roman Archaeology* 16 (2003), 237–59.

89 Ammianus Marcellinus

Matthews, John F. *The Roman Empire of Ammianus* (London: Duckworth, 1989).

Syme, R. *Ammianus and the Historia Augusta* (Oxford: Clarendon Press, 1968).

90 Julian the Apostate

Tougher, S. *Julian the Apostate* (Edinburgh: Edinburgh University Press, 2007).

Murdoch, A. *The Last Pagan: Julian the Apostate and the death of the ancient world* (Stroud: Sutton Pub., 2005).

91 Valentinian

Alföldi, A. *A Conflict of Ideas in the Late Roman Empire: The Clash between the Senate and Valentinian I* (Oxford, Clarendon Press, 1952; trans. Harold Mattingly).

Burns, T.S. *Barbarians within the Gates of Rome: A Study of Roman Military Policy and the Barbarians, ca. 375–425 AD* (Bloomington: Indiana University Press, 1994).

Nagl, A. 'Valentinianus I', *Paulys Real-Encyclopädie der classichen, Altertumswissenschaft* (Stuttgart, 1873), VII, A 2, 2158–204.

92 Stilicho

Cameron, A. 'Theodosius the Great and the regency of Stilicho', *Harvard Studies in Classical Philology* V.73 (1968), 247–280.

93 Hypatia

Musurillo, H. *Acts of the Pagan Martyrs* (Oxford: Clarendon Press, 1954).

94 Vettius Agorius Praetextatus

Momigliano, A. (ed) *The conflict between paganism and Christianity in the fourth century* (Oxford: Clarendon Press, 1963).

95 Isaac of Armenia

The Catholic Encyclopedia, VIII (New York: Robert Appleton Company, 1910).

Meyendorff, J. *Imperial Unity and Christian Divisions: The Church, 450–680 AD* (New York: St Vladimir's Seminary Press, 1989).

96 St Augustine

Brown, P. *Augustine of Hippo* (London: Faber, 1967).

97 Leo the Great

Freeland, J.P., and Conway, A.J. *St Leo the Great: Sermons (Fathers of the Church 93)* (Washington D.C.: Catholic University of America Press, 1996).

Meyendorff, J. *Imperial Unity and Christian Divisions: The Church, 450–680 AD* (New York: St Vladimir's Seminary Press, 1989).

98 Priscus

Rohrbacher, D. *The Historians of Late Antiquity* (London: Routledge, 2002).

Browning, R. 'Where Was Attila's Camp?' *Journal of Hellenic Studies* 73 (1953), 143–45.

99 Consentius

Cameron, A. *Circus Factions: Blues and Greens at Rome and Constantinople* (Oxford: Clarendon Press, 1976).

100 Romulus Augustulus

Murdoch, A. *The Last Roman: Romulus Augustulus and the Decline of the West* (Stroud: Sutton, 2006).

Sources of Illustrations

Index